*England
Especially for Women*

ENGLAND

Especially for Women

Gerie Tully

Abelard-Schuman   New York

Acknowledgments

With sincere appreciation, I want to acknowledge the help of the following people in making this book possible: Andrew Glaze, Peter French-Hodges, Maria Fritz, Debbie Kelly, Ed Finkle, and Hans Rutishauser for the loan of his beautiful villa at Aldea Do Mar in the Algarve, to provide me the time, place, peace, and tranquillity necessary to pull this book together.

Thanks, too, to my assistant, translator, driver, etc., Lucio Arena.

Copyright © 1975 by Gerie Tully

All rights reserved. Except for use in a review, the reproduction or utilization of this work in any form or by any electronic, mechanical, or other means, now known or hereafter invented, including xerography, photocopying, and recording, and in any information storage and retrieval system is forbidden without the written permission of the publisher. Published simultaneously in Canada by Fitzhenry & Whiteside Limited, Toronto.

Manufactured in the United States of America

Library of Congress Cataloging in Publication Data

Tully, Gerie.
  England especially for women.

  Includes index.
  1. London—Description—1951-   Guide-books.
2. England—Description and travel—1971-   Guide-books. I. Title
DA679.T87   1975   914.2'04'857   75–12710
ISBN 0–200–04027–8

Dedication

To my lovely new daughter-in-law
Judy Bello
my official welcome to the family

Contents

Introduction   xvii

Part I
Before You Go

1 Making the Most of Your Trip   3

2 Tips for Travelers   6

Packing Hints 6 / What to Take 9 /
Health Hints 9 / Relax 10 / Beauty Hints 11 /
Extra Tips 13

3 From Here to There   14

4 Useful Information   18

TRAVELING IN BRITAIN 18

Air Travel 18 / Train Travel 18 / All-Line Railrover Ticket 19 / Thrift Rail Coupons 19 / BritRail Pass 19 / Bus and Coach Travel 20 / Green Line Coaches 20 / Taxis 20

ENGLISH GOVERNMENT REGULATIONS 21

Passports and Visas 21 / Vaccinations 21 / Customs 21 / Currency Regulations 22

Contents

CLIMATE 22

SIZE CHARTS 23

WEIGHTS AND MEASURES 26

Time Conversion 26 / Telephone Service 27 / Postage 27 / Currency 27 / Tipping 28 / VAT Tax 29 / Electrical Equipment 29 /

POLICE, FIRE OR AMBULANCE 29

5 A Word About Language — 30

Part II
London

6 Welcome to London — 35

HOW TO GET AROUND 36

Double-Decker Buses 36 / Subway 37 / Taxis 38

USEFUL ADDRESSES 38

CALENDAR OF EVENTS 40

7 Where to Stay — 44

HYDE PARK HOTELS 45

Deluxe 45 / Four Star 46 / Three Star 48 / Bed-and-Breakfast Hotels 49

MARBLE ARCH–OXFORD STREET AREA HOTELS 52

Deluxe 52 / Four Star 53 / Three Star 55 / Bed-and-Breakfast Hotels 57

THE STRAND HOTELS 57

Deluxe 57 / Four Star 57

PARK LANE AREA HOTELS 58

Deluxe 58

PICCADILLY AREA HOTELS 59

Deluxe 59 / Four Star 60 / Three Star 61 / Two Star 62 / Bed-and-Breakfast Hotel 62

SOUTH KENSINGTON HOTELS 62

Four Star 62 / Three Star 62

Contents ix

8 Wining and Dining 64
SOME ENGLISH SPECIALTIES 65
RESTAURANTS 66
Expensive 66 / Moderate 73 / Inexpensive 77
CHAIN RESTAURANTS 84
MEDIEVAL RESTAURANTS 86
RIVERSIDE RESTAURANTS 86

9 Nighttime Entertainment 89
BOOKING OFFICES 90
BALLET 90
OPERA 91
CONCERTS AND RECITALS 91
THEATERS 92
Musicals 94
MUSIC HALLS 95
CINEMAS 96
CABARETS 97
Expensive 97 / Moderate 99
DISCOTHEQUES 100
JAZZ CLUBS 103
FEMALE IMPERSONATORS 104
PUBS 105

10 Sightseeing 108
TOURS 109
Day Tours 110 / Night Tours 111 / Thames River Trips 112 / Canal Trips 113
ON YOUR OWN 113
The Traditional Sights 113 / London's Streets 123 / London on Foot 124
MUSEUMS AND GALLERIES 127
PARKS 131

Contents

11 Excursions Out of London — 133
- TOURS 134
- WINDSOR 136
- HAMPTON COURT 138
- CAMBRIDGE 139
- Lunching in Cambridge 141
- OXFORD 141
- Lunching in Oxford 143
- BLENHEIM PALACE 144
- SULGRAVE MANOR 144
- CANTERBURY 145
- HATFIELD HOUSE 146
- SYON HOUSE 147
- The Gardening Centre 147
- WADDESDON MANOR 148
- WOBURN ABBEY 148

12 Sports — 151
- RIDING 151
- SWIMMING 152

13 Beauty Comes First — 153
- HAIRDRESSERS 153
- HAIRDRESSERS WITH TRICHOLOGISTS 156
- SALONS FOR BEAUTY TREATMENTS 157
- BEAUTY CLINICS FOR SPECIAL PROBLEMS 158
- AROMATHERAPY 160
- CELL THERAPY 160
- COSMETICS 161
- EAR-PIERCING SPECIALISTS 161
- EYE CARE AND CONTACT LENSES 161
- FOOT CARE 162
- HAND- AND NAIL-CARE SPECIALISTS 162
- PERFUMES 162

SAUNAS 163

WIGGERIES 164

BEAUTY FARMS 164

HEALTH HYDROS 165

14 Shopping 167

Sales 168

DEPARTMENT STORES 169

BOUTIQUES 170

LEATHER GOODS 170

FOR HIM 171

TOYS 171

JEWELRY 171

GIFTS 172

ANTIQUES AND BRIC-A-BRAC 172

BOOKS AND PERIODICALS 174

REPAIR SERVICES 174

Handbags 174 / Leather 174 / Luggage 175 / Shoes and Dresses 175 / Umbrellas 175

SHOPPING STREETS 175

Tottenham Court Road 175 / Oxford Street East 176 / Oxford Street West 177 / Charing Cross Road 178 / Regent Street 179 / New Bond Street 179 / Old Bond Street 180 / South Molton Street 181 / Piccadilly 181 / Burlington Arcade 182 / Jermyn Street 182 / Kensington High Street 183 / Kensington Church Street 184 / Knightsbridge—Brompton Road—Fulham Road 184 / Beauchamp Place 186 / King's Road 187 / Sloane Street 187

Part III
Outside London

15 Bath 191

HOW TO GET THERE 192

WHERE TO STAY 192

DINING 193

SIGHTSEEING 193

EXCURSIONS OUT OF BATH 194

16 Stratford-on-Avon   197
HOW TO GET THERE 198

TOURS 198

DINING 199

SIGHTSEEING 200

WARWICK 201

Dining in Warwick 202

Part IV
The Southern Coast

17 Dover   205

18 Folkestone   206
HOW TO GET THERE 206

WHERE TO STAY 206

DINING 206

19 Rye   208
HOW TO GET THERE 208

WHERE TO STAY 208

DINING 209

20 Hastings and St. Leonard's   210
HOW TO GET THERE 211

21 Eastbourne   212
HOW TO GET THERE 213

WHERE TO STAY 213

DINING 213

Contents xiii

22 Brighton 215
HOW TO GET THERE 217
WHERE TO STAY 217
DINING 219
EXCURSIONS OUT OF BRIGHTON 220
Arundel 221 / Hove 221 / Tunbridge Wells 222

23 The Isle of Wight 223
HOW TO GET THERE 223

Index 225

Note to the Reader

It is very important for you to understand that during the writing of this book the dollar value has been jumping all over the place. When I began it, the British pound was worth $2.50 (U.S. dollars); since then it has continued to fluctuate both up and down. I have used that figure, and all the prices in this book are converted accordingly. It's quite possible that when you get there the value will be higher, in which case you will get even better value for your money than is quoted here.

Furthermore, prices at hotels and restaurants are difficult to predict at this time. Some hotels say they will be raising their prices and others say no; but it is probably safest to assume that they will. Restaurant prices fluctuate with the price of food and at the moment there is simply no stabilization in that area at all. Here again, it seems likely prices will go up in the next year. Anyway, please keep these possibilities in mind, and remember that I am giving you the most up-to-date information available. Use it as a guide and leave a little leeway one way or the other. I watch my budget as carefully as you watch yours; I am always on the lookout for bargains, and want to share as many of them as possible in these days of our Yo-Yo economy.

England Especially for Women

Introduction

The main purpose of this book is to act as a very personal, hand-holding guide for every woman who travels. Not only for single women, but for married women who *think* single, or even for those who may travel with their husbands. It caters to the special interests of women and to the very particular problems a woman encounters while traveling. Without help, some of these problems can be rather disconcerting if you are a novice at the wonderful game of "gallivanting."

Often a woman traveling alone hopes to run into a fascinating man. And why shouldn't she? One of the secondary purposes of this book is to act as a catalyst between those who are seeking and the sought-after, bringing them together, hopefully, for their mutual enjoyment.

You will find that the book is addressed to three different age groups: 18–25 indicated in the listing by letter A, 26–40 indicated by letter B, 40 and up indicated by letter C. If a woman of 40 desires company she will obviously be more likely to find it at the hotels, etc., suggested under that age bracket, rather than that of the 18–25'ers. This does not mean, however, that in reading the book you must concentrate on any one particular age group. The groupings merely act as a guide to help you find the kind of people you are interested in. Nor is this written only for man hunters. But it's nice to know the information is there if you want it.

A woman has particular needs when traveling that are seldom taken into account by travel agencies, tourist bureaus, or guidebooks. She may want to know, for instance, where she can safely have her hair bleached, get a good facial, have a handbag repaired, or have a dress made inexpensively or altered; or even where to find a spa for a week's reducing.

This book will give in detail all the information necessary to make a woman's trip as easy, comfortable, and as much fun as possible. It will cover three price ranges, from budget to luxury class, so that there is something for everyone.

All information is given on a personal, woman-to-woman basis. It is keyed to the particular needs of all traveling females, with or without a man, alone, with a friend, or with several other women.

Since we all have different taste and ideas, you can help me as well as other travelers. If you find some lovely little hotel, restaurant, or shop that you were particularly thrilled with, won't you write me and tell me about it? This research is kept very up-to-date, and I will check out your suggestion for the next edition.

On the other hand, if you have had problems you couldn't find answers to, or complaints about any of the establishments listed here, I would like to hear from you on that, too. Perhaps I can help you with the problems; and I will definitely check into your complaints. Management often changes, and when that happens the service may change as well, so we like to hear about it in order to reevaluate the situation before making a recommendation again.

We recognize how important your vacation time and money are to you and therefore make every effort to suggest only those places we feel you can surely enjoy. But naturally there are places we miss, since it would be impossible to cover every hotel and restaurant in a city. Any suggestions—or complaints—are taken very seriously. With your help, the next edition can be even bigger and better.

PART I
Before You Go

1
Making the Most of Your Trip

Any vacation should be considered an investment in the future. If you'd like to find a man, either as a friend or as more permanent company, make the most of your time. Go where the opportunities are best and then spend every minute of your time as if it were money.

Forget about digging up a friend to go with you. You'll do much better on your own and meet people more quickly and easily. Also, you'll be able to be flexible enough to change your plans and follow his itinerary (if you meet him) without having any guilt about leaving your friend. Furthermore, traveling alone away from home, you can be anyone you wish, and that's kind of fun at times. Break your usual bonds and try a new role for a change. Who will know?

Traveling alone requires a lot of initiative. Don't wait for people to speak to you first; men are sometimes leery of approaching a lone woman. But if you extend a touch of friendliness, say to the businessman sitting next to you on the plane, you will more than likely find a willing escort when you land. And if you are staying on after he leaves he may even introduce you to his friends or business colleagues to squire you around after his departure.

Abroad, the American Express office is a second home to most travelers, a place where they pick up their mail, book their tours, and cash checks. It's a crowded and informal place where somebody interesting could well turn up. Also, around breakfast time, in any city, your hotel lobby is a good place to be when people stand around awaiting their tours and making plans. Some nice, lonely guest may ask you to join him. It happens all the time. If you'd like to meet a drink or mealtime companion, you have to be in the right place at the right time—in this case, the pre-dinner apéritif hour. Hotel cocktail lounges allow female guests unescorted, so don't hesitate to take a table and have a drink or two. You will no doubt meet a lot of American men this way, though rarely Europeans, as they do their imbibing at dinner.

You must decide early on in your travels if you want to find just pleasant company or a serious romance. If it is just company, which is the wisest attitude, accept all offers initially and take the opportunity to see the city with a resident. After all, he can't get past the hotel lobby if you don't want him to. But chances are, he will prove interesting and you will see things firsthand that will enhance your store of knowledge as well as your memory book.

You will seldom find the brashness of the American male, or the savoir-faire of the Frenchman, or the devil-may-care-attitude of the Italian, but it is almost certain you will find an Englishman to be very polite, very conservative, and very reserved. The British are not quite as romantic as the Continentals, but somehow their sincerity is more obvious. They generally do not make passes on the first couple of dates, but then they don't appear to get that interested either. As I said, they are reserved, and this is an attitude that an American woman has to warm up to. The Englishman will talk about all the current political problems, or anything else of interest, but seldom does he get romantic and personal on the first few dates.

Since prices are a bit high in comparison to wages in England chances are that unless he happens to be a well-paid businessman he will not be able to afford to take you to very glamorous places, and you may very well wind up in an interesting and charming little pub. Although he will be most polite in asking you what you would like to see, or where you would like to go, it would be best to let him take the lead as he alone knows the state of his finances, and in England, as elsewhere, this can be a problem.

Don't spend all your time man-hunting or your vacation may be completely lost. Being so intense about the main thing can cause you to lose sight of what you have come for—knowledge and enjoyment of a new country. Try to forget about being an American and learn to accept what you find, no matter where you go. Don't cling to your expectations or fantasies; if you give up your preconceived ideas, you can enjoy the individual personality and charm that each place offers.

Being a good traveler also involves what you might call "tourist manners," the heart of which is really a consideration for others and their ways. Need I remind you that the subject of politics is strictly forbidden? Whatever you may think, keep it to yourself. You cannot hope to change anyone's mind about his own country's policies, and frankly I don't think you have any right to. Furthermore, you are unlikely to be well-informed enough to discuss the subject intelligently.

Be prepared for all sort of delays, changes, and frustrations on your travels and take them good-naturedly. It doesn't help to complain and will only waste your breath or raise your blood pressure. Another good rule is to keep smiling. This will get you through any difficulty whether you speak the language or not. People always welcome an attitude of warmth and friendliness and will go out of their way to make you feel comfortable. And when this happens you will find that traveling is one of the best and most exciting means of broadening not only your knowledge and experience, but also your circle of friends.

2
Tips for Travelers

Traveling can be interesting, invigorating, and fun. It can also be hectic and debilitating if it's your first trip and you still lack the information and knowledge that we veteran travelers have picked up along the way. Having traveled the world under all conditions—from luxury cruise to African safari—I shall now pass on to you my gems of wisdom.

Packing Hints

This may be the most important part of your preparations, because whatever you pack will have to take care of your needs throughout your entire trip, and in some cases serve triple duty.

When selecting your wardrobe, go over the temperature charts provided on page 23 to see what your requirements will be, and then coordinate accordingly. Remember, too, that few people are likely to see you in the same thing twice, so you can virtually repeat the same two or three outfits in every city. Unless you can wear at least part of an outfit for every occasion and it can be intermatched, forget it. That lovely dress for which you need a special pair of shoes is best left at home. It will mean that much more room for goodies you may wish to buy along the way, which, I warn you, will be a strong temptation!

Keeping in mind that you will be living out of a suitcase, packing and repacking it, fishing through it for something when you are in a hurry, or having to find just one little item when you arrive at your destination late and want to flop right into bed, you will understand why I consider your choice of suitcases a major decision.

First you will need two bags: one large and one small. Today's tote bags are not only good and roomy but very convenient. If you play your cards right, you can get a tote bag through the check-in desk without weighing it. Of course, you will have to carry it with you on board the plane, but that's better than having to check it through and pay overweight charges, isn't it?

I put my heaviest things in a tote bag and leave it on a chair somewhere when I check in, then collect it before boarding. It's also convenient to keep some toiletries, cosmetics (you never know when you may meet some gorgeous male and want to freshen up in a hurry to make points before landing), reading material, and stationery for use in-flight.

Another reason a tote bag is convenient is that you may wish to spend a day at the beach or take an overnight trip somewhere, and it is much easier to carry a tote bag than a weekender-size suitcase.

I will get back to the large suitcase in a minute, but first, another suggestion. A lightweight, plastic garment bag is invaluable, either to carry a few dresses in for a weekend trip without all your luggage, or packed full, several dresses on each hanger, to carry on board over your arm if your luggage is too overweight. Just pack it flat in the bottom of your case until you need it. For a trip of several days, you can pack it with all your hanging things, use the tote bag for all the other essentials, and check the rest of your luggage with the hotel bell captain.

Now for the large case. The very best type of bag to use is one made of light but very strong fiber, that has some "give" to it. The locks, too, are important. These must be sturdy and reliable, or you will have your things spilling out all over the off-loading ramps.

After a lot of experimenting with many different types, my favorite (this is not a plug!) is Samsonite's Fashionaire which opens up flat, like a man's suitcase, allowing you to pack all your dresses and hanging things on one side, and lingerie, accessories, cosmetics, etc., on the other.

On the hanging side, I generally put several garments on one hanger to save space and to keep them from jostling around. The cheap wire hangers are best because they are lightweight and convenient. You can lift them right out and hang them up in your hotel-room closet, and pack them just as quickly. Since you will very seldom find enough hangers in your closet, carrying your own is a good precaution.

Pack the dresses flat into the case, lengthwise, folding at the waistline, and alternating the position of each hanger to evenly

8 BEFORE YOU GO

distribute the weight and bulk. Leave your nightie and dressing gown for last so you can get at them easily. Lingerie is best either sorted into coordinate sets and then placed in a plastic bag, or separated according to bras, slips, panties, and stockings, each again slipped by group into a plastic bag. This keeps them all together and all you have to do when packing or unpacking is to slip the bag into your case or a drawer, without having to gather up each piece and fold it. The plastic bags also keep them clean and free of snags.

Two cosmetic bags can separate your toiletries into the things that you use daily, and those that you keep for spares or use only occasionally—suntan lotions, medications, Band-Aids, shampoo, and the like.

A hanging mirror with a magnifying side to use around your neck is a "must." That way, you can see the back of your hair while using both hands, or take it over to a window for a better light to make up by.

A sewing kit, extra bobby pins, a nail kit, Scotch tape, extra plastic bags, and a laundry kit (portable line, inflatable hangers for drying "drip-drys," and packets of soap powder), plus a travel iron with adapters, complete the necessity list. A tube of Duco Cement also comes in handy for mending fingernails as well as dozens of other things.

Under the heading of medical supplies, remember to take your prescriptions and extra medication if possible. Also: Band-Aids, bandages, antacid tablets, aspirin, something for constipation and diarrhea, eye drops, and suntan lotion. A knife, spoon, and fork are also handy for "in-room" snacks and a dozen other uses.

Remember that you are entitled to 66 pounds free baggage allowance in first class and 44 pounds in economy class. Weigh your empty bags first and deduct their total weight from your total allowance. Then eliminate all the things you do not absolutely need, pack the essentials, and leave plenty of room for the irresistibles that you'll find en route.

The moment you arrive in your hotel room you will want to hang all your clothes in the bathroom and turn on the hot water in the tub to steam out the wrinkles. Close the door and leave them in there for at least 15 minutes. Then you won't have to worry about having each dress pressed as you need it. For deep creases, or if there isn't enough steam, wet a face cloth and dampen the creases thoroughly. As the dress dries, the creases will disappear. Be sure, though, that the fabric can stand water.

What to Take

The most important items are a folding umbrella and a raincoat, since you're sure to have some rain. A zip-in-lining coat is very handy, to wear on either chilly or warm days. The go-everywhere type is particularly good, since you can wear it for day or evening.

For the summer you can take light suits, or summer dresses with cardigans or shawls for the evening. For the winter, woolens, sweaters, and a warm coat are necessary. A neutral or coordinated color scheme in your choice of clothes will help to extend your wardrobe. The British enjoy their rather chilly weather, and most buildings are not kept as warm as we might like them to be, so do remember those extra sweaters to slip on. Comfortable, basic shoes and a good roomy handbag that goes with everything are absolutely essential. A variety of turbans, scarfs, or other headgear that can be packed flat and easily carried in your handbag might also be a good idea; if a sudden shower catches you without your umbrella, these cover-ups will come in handy.

Shorts are never worn in the cities even on the hottest day, but slacks are very much in fashion anywhere and everywhere, day or evening.

Being comfortable is most important if you want to relax and sleep on the plane. Avoid wearing tight slacks, dresses, belts, or girdles; a loose-fitting skirt with a jacket or sweater is just the ticket. Take along a pair of slipper socks and put them on as soon as you get on the plane.

Health Hints

Many travelers spoil their trip by failing to observe a few basic dos and don'ts, so take a few moments to go through these tips before you leave home and you should have no problem.

Diarrhea is the usual souvenir of less-than-cautious travelers. Water used to be the number-one problem, but, thank heaven, it is now safe to drink the tap water in just about any major city. This is good news for the budget too, since the bottled water we have always been cautioned to drink at all times, even for brushing the teeth, starts adding up after a while. Mind you, I said *tap water;* that doesn't mean you can safely drink at a quaint little spring you may find in some village. In villages or outlying towns it is still wise to stick with bottled water or wine.

The possibility of food contamination is generally a matter of where you eat. You can tell how clean the kitchen or chefs are by the general appearance of the public areas. If these are less than satisfactory, chances are the kitchen isn't any better. In that case, either leave or stick to basic foods that are thoroughly cooked. A simple sandwich can always hold you until you can scout for something a bit more acceptable.

Stay away from any foods of an indeterminate nature, even in the better restaurants. You wouldn't eat hamburger or meatloaf in some places in the United States; follow that rule in foreign countries and you should be able to avoid food poisoning.

Since pasteurization is still not done everywhere, be cautious. Dairy products such as milk or cream, or even custard or cream-filled pastries, require a good sniff and a careful scrutiny before you eat them. The latter may not have been properly refrigerated; or, left out in the open to entice the customer, may have gone bad.

Shellfish should only be eaten when you know for a fact that it has been freshly caught and refrigerated, and that means either at a seaside resort or a good hotel or restaurant.

No raw vegetables or fruit should be eaten without thorough washing. It's wiser to have them cooked first, and also to peel all fruit (which is the European way, anyway). The best bet is not to eat any fresh, raw vegetables at all. Normally this doesn't present a problem, but it's always better to be on the safe side.

Even with all these precautions one can still get a tummy upset just from the change in eating habits and all the hectic and unaccustomed running around, not to mention a possible change of climate. All those new sauces and wines can also wreak havoc with the intestinal tract. So carry along a bottle of Kaopectate or similar medication, because nothing can make you feel worse than a case of the "tourista trots" when you are on holiday. I want to stress the fact that you should take along your own antidiarrhea medication—*don't* buy it in Europe. It has recently been discovered that some of the most popular medications are dangerous and since they are sold there under several brand names, you won't know what you are buying.

Relax

Nothing is as tiring as sightseeing and shopping. The only way to survive is to stay as fit as possible. Don't rush around like an idiot, trying to see a dozen places in one day—and very likely not remembering a thing about them. Wear comfortable clothes, especially shoes! Sore feet have ruined many a holiday. Try to arrange your sightseeing so that you go first, in the morning, while you are feeling fresh, to a place that requires a lot of walking and stair-climbing; then, in the afternoon, to a place where you can sit or be fairly inactive. Also alternate what you see between the indoors and the outdoors. This will give you enough change of pace and surroundings to conserve your energy and your interest. For lunch, have a light snack: a heavy meal makes you too sluggish afterward to pull your poor body around, especially if you drink wine.

When you return to your room take off all your clothes and stand in the tub. Take the hand shower (most hotels have them) and play a spray of cool-to-tepid water on your legs from the thighs down to the ankles. Use it full force to take full advantage of its therapeutic powers. The heavy spray will relax those knotted muscles, stimulate the circulation, and refresh you to the point where you're ready to go off to your next destination. If there is no hand shower, stand in the tub under the faucet, positioning your legs so that the flow of the water is directed at the calf, gradually working down to the feet.

For summertime sightseeing you may want to dispense with stockings, which is fine, but keep a small tin or box of talc to dust your feet and prevent blisters that can make it too painful to carry on. If you get stuck without it, don't stand on formality—whip out your compact and press it into double duty. Use a tissue to dust the powder on your feet, though—save the puff for your face.

Beauty Hints

I believe in using every moment to advantage while traveling, and that's why I prefer to do my own hair and nails, using the time normally spent in beauty salons for shopping or sightseeing instead.

If you can manage your own hair, you're in luck. Roll it around your fingers, stick in a few bobby pins instead of curlers, and wrap it up in a lovely scarf (luckily they're "in" so you will be right in style). You won't have the obvious lumps of rollers and it won't be uncomfortable to sleep on. Just brush out your hair when you get ready and you'll look fresh and neat instead of a mess.

For those who prefer going to a hairdresser, why not do it the day you arrive in the city instead of before you leave home, so you won't have to squash your hairdo sleeping on the plane. Most large hotels have a beauty salon and you can ask for an appointment when you make your reservation. It would be good timing to have it done shortly after you arrive so the shampoo and massage will relax you after your flight.

Broken nails can be such a bother while traveling when you don't

12 BEFORE YOU GO

want to waste your time with a manicurist. I always carry Duco Cement with me for quick patch-ups. Cover the nail with the glue, then peel off a tiny piece of tissue and pat it over the break. Now put on the nail patch, bringing it right up to the edge on top and on the side to give it more strength. Spread more glue over it. When thoroughly dry, file it down smooth on the top and sides and you're all set. A coat of polish hides all traces of the patch and it will last quite some time.

Rather than carry extra bottles with you that you really don't use every day, take advantage of your hotel room service for your beauty treatments. Here's how:

FACIAL MASK Tighten and refine the pores by covering the face and neck with simple honey. Order it with your breakfast and put the remainder in your medicine chest so the maid won't take it away.

CLEANSER Naturally you will want to carry your own with you, but should you run out, regular cooking oil can be used for the same purpose. When you order a salad ask for vinegar and oil dressing and hang onto the cruets of both.

ASTRINGENT Cucumber will remove the traces of oil and act as the perfect tonic, closing the pores and tightening the skin.

TIRED OR BURNING EYES Here again cucumber comes to the rescue. A slice on each eye will give you soothing relief and take down the swelling. Good for under the eyes, too, when they puff up.

BATH OIL The same salad oil can be used in the bath to moisturize your skin. Have the water quite hot so you open all the pores and allow it to penetrate, so that when you wipe off the excess as you get out of the tub there is a sufficient amount left in the pores to work.

BUBBLE BATH Plain shampoo gives you a rich bubble bath and, depending on the type used, can also moisturize and clean.

SHINY HAIR To give your hair new life, sheen, and body beat up a raw egg with a fork and work it through your hair, letting it sit for a while before washing it out.

HAIR RINSE To remove all traces of oil and soap (very difficult in hard-water areas) use the vinegar left over from your salad for guaranteed "squeaky clean" hair.

DRY, SUN-BLEACHED HAIR Ask your room service to heat a halfcup of salad oil for you, or put it in a glass and then into a basin of hot water. Daub it all over the scalp and the rest of your hair. Wrap a towel around your head for a couple of hours (at least one), then shampoo. You will need two or three sudsings to get it all out, but it will be worth it. Your hair will gleam like a new penny and be as soft as silk.

MOISTURIZING MASK Plain yogurt can do wonders for your skin. Just leave it on as long as you like and rinse off. Your skin will feel soft and silky, and firm.

Extra Tips

Your Duco Cement will also come in handy for dozens of other things: a stone popped out of its setting, a shoe sole or strap that has pulled open, the broken cap of a cosmetic bottle, cracked mirror in a compact—any number of things.

Scotch tape is another indispensable, great for a hem that has come undone until you can fix it. And speaking of hems, like most women you may buy something on your trip that you wish to wear while traveling. If you want to hem it yourself and don't have any straight pins, just use bobby pins to hold it in place while you hem it. They also make good paper clips or bookmarks. When using a guidebook it's a good idea to clip a bobby pin on the top of important pages you want to refer to that day—a map of the city, local transport, certain shops or monuments you may want to see, etc. You can also clip your sales receipts together this way to keep them all in place for the time when you have to make out your customs declaration. Try Scotch-taping a hotel envelope to the inside cover of your guidebook to keep them in. Another on the other cover could hold business cards of people you meet along the way and want to write to later.

To make sure you have handy all the names and addresses of people you want to see, write them in the back of this book so you won't have to look all over for separate slips of paper or address books.

3
From Here to There

Getting to England will be not only your first concern, but your first major expense as well. It's good to shop for the best bargain, so we will try to help you sort this one out. But at this stage I am afraid I must sadly report that there are few bargains around these days. Air fares have reached a new high and I see that another 7% hike may be instituted as well. This is over and above the 15% increase already levied up until now, so it is anyone's guess as to what will happen. Another casualty is the elimination of the budget plans so many tourists took advantage of, especially the student fare.

Let's start with first things first, and that is that all major airlines are required to charge the exact same fares, except for Icelandic, by the International Air Transport Association, which regulates all matters concerning international air travel.

So that leaves only one decision: what airline to use. My preference and suggestion has always been to use the national airline of the country to be visited, to get a feel of that country as soon as possible.

In this case, my suggestion is British Airways, not only because it is Britain's national carrier, but also because of the courtesy and friendliness shown the passengers by the crew over and above their normal duties. I have found the British to be so exceptionally charming and helpful that I am often quite taken aback, accustomed as I am to the somewhat more abrupt attitude of busy America.

You will see what I mean the moment you step aboard the flight. The stewardesses cannot do enough for you and should you request something they will generally cease whatever they are doing to try to fulfill it for you. Most unusual, indeed! They stop at your seat to ask if you need anything, inquire about where you are from, ask if this is your first trip, and carry on a very friendly conversation. They often make good suggestions, too, as to where to get a good bargain, what show to see, or where to dine.

Aside from all the friendly chatting, quick, courteous service, and excellent food—it is also nice to know that they have a good record of safety and reliability. If a flight is scheduled for a certain time, they do everything possible to get it off at that time. If there are delays, they will explain them and cheerfully aid you in overcoming any difficulties they might cause. Experienced travelers will understand what a help this is.

Now let's get down to hard facts—prices! Starting with straight individual travel (no group or special plan) we list below the round-trip fares from New York to major European cities. The first-class fare is the same throughout the year. However, the economy fare is based on three separate seasons:

Peak season, eastbound June 1 through August 31, westbound July 1 through September 30.

Shoulder season, eastbound April 1 through May 31 and September 1 through October 31; westbound April 1 through June 30 and October 1 through October 31.

Winter season, November 1 through March 31.

Fares

FROM NEW YORK TO:	First Class	Economy Class P	S	W
London	$966	$648	$536	$478
Belfast	928	606	494	450
Birmingham	966	636	526	478
Edinburgh	926	600	510	446
Glasgow	918	596	486	442

14-to-21-DAY EXCURSION FARE

For this fare, you must be out of the country no less than 14 days and no more than 21 days; and it allows you quite a saving. You also have the advantage of two additional stopovers permitted in each direction. This means that you would book your ticket to your

16 BEFORE YOU GO

farthest stop, which becomes your "turn-around city," and be allowed two stops on the way from New York to your turn-around city free and another two stops to any city you like on the way back to New York. For example, if Rome were your turn-around city, you could stop at London and Paris on the way to Rome free, staying as long as you like (as long as it's within the 21-day limit). On the return from Rome to New York, you would be allowed another two stopovers anywhere on a direct line from Rome to New York.

There is a weekend surcharge of $15 each way on this fare. That means if you schedule your eastbound flight for between 7 P.M. on Friday and 7 A.M. on Sunday, you will pay an additional $15. That $15 surcharge applies also if you return to the United States between 7 P.M. Saturday and 7 A.M. Monday. So if you want to avoid the additional fee, plan your flights for between Monday and Thursday.

There are only two seasons to contend with on the 14-to-21-day excursion fare:

Peak excursion season, June 1 through August 31.
Basic excursion season, September 1 through May 31.

14-to-21-Day Excursion Fare

FROM NEW YORK TO:	Peak	Basic
London	$492	$420
Belfast	464	392
Birmingham	485	413
Edinburgh	459	387
Glasgow	456	384

22-to-45-DAY EXCURSION FARE

This is similar to the plan above except that you must be out of the country no less than 22 days and no more than 45 days. It represents an even greater saving to the traveler. There are three seasons to contend with:

Peak season, June 1 through August 31.
Shoulder season, April 1 through May 31, September 1 through October 31.
Winter season, November 1 through March 31.

22-to-45-Day Excursion Fare

FROM NEW YORK TO:	P	S	W
London	$386	$302	$282
Belfast	366	293	274
Birmingham	386	302	282
Edinburgh	368	295	276
Glasgow	366	293	274

There are no stopovers permitted on this particular plan and the same weekend surcharge applies as for the 14-to-21 day.

Additional Savings

If you are flying to London from Boston, Chicago, Detroit, Los Angeles, Miami, Philadelphia, or Washington, D.C., via New York, you can save money by booking your ticket direct from your home city rather than using one ticket for the home to New York flight and one ticket for the New York to London flight. These are called Gateway Cities fares, and there is quite a reduction. Your British Airways representative or your travel agent can give you the information on these fares.

Budget Tips for Getting to the Airport

For all New Yorkers, or visitors who happen to spend time in New York prior to going abroad, there is a new service that can save you quite a bit of money. It is called Econo'Limousine, 330 E. 56th St., N.Y., N.Y. 10022 Tel: 371-2460, and is run by a very industrious group of young men who have managed to lop off several dollars on the abominable cab fares now charged to go to the airport. They will pick you up at your home, office, or any place of your choice on the East Side of New York. You may have to share the limousine with a few other people, and then again, you may not—it depends upon the reservations they have. The rates are as follows: La Guardia Airport, $4 for the first passenger, $2 for each additional passenger; JFK Airport, $6 for the first passenger, $2.50 for each additional passenger; for the entire car, $15 (for use up to 2 hours). This is an especially good bargain if you are traveling with several other people, or if you wish to go to the airport to pick someone up and return to the city. There is an additional surcharge for the West Side and for rush hours; but the saving is still considerable.

4
Useful Information

TRAVELING IN BRITAIN

In London, the British Travel Centre on Lower Regent Street near Piccadilly Circus is the place to go for any information or reservations for travel within England.

Air Travel

Regular service between the major cities of England, Scotland, Wales, Northern Ireland, and the Channel Islands is operated by British Airways. Passenger fares are extremely competitive and cheap rates are available off-peak and on night flights. Full information from your local BOAC office, from your travel agent, or from British Airways, Dorland Hall, Lower Regent Street, London, S.W.1.

Train Travel

Ordinary round-trip tickets usually cost double the one-way rate and are normally valid for 3 calendar months, except those tickets issued for use in the London area, which are valid on day of issue only. First-class fares are approximately 50% to 60% above second-class. Each adult passenger is allowed 150 pounds of free baggage in first class, 100 pounds in second class.

You can obtain a discount of as much as 50% if you are making a one-day, round-trip excursion, using Day-Return Tickets. All British railway stations have the information on these.

With Circular Tour Tickets you can save about 10% on round-trip fares for journeys that begin and end in the same city. A break in the journey is allowed for any stop en route. The tickets are valid for three months for tours covering any desired routes that are made up of three or more point-to-point journeys in continuity. Certain road and steamer journeys can be included in the tour. Ask about them at the railway station.

All-Line Railrover Ticket

With this ticket, you can travel anywhere on British Rail routes in England, Scotland, and Wales for as little as £24 ($60) for a period of 7 days or £37 ($92) for 14 days, both via second class. These tickets, which can be used between any British Rail stations, are available from March through October.

Thrift Rail Coupons

These coupons are issued in books valued at $60 and $40, giving a saving on normal fares. The coupons have unlimited validity, and are exchangeable among family and friends. They may also be exchanged at British Rail ticket offices for all types of rail travel tickets in Britain and on British Rail steamer services to Ireland and the Channel Islands. They can also be used in payment for seat reservations, sleeping berth fees, cabin and berth reservations, etc. (They are not valid for tickets on Continental boat trains and steamer services nor for meals in restaurant cars, or on board ships.)

Thrift Rail Coupons are not on sale in Britain, but can be purchased at British Rail offices and certain travel agencies in the United States and Canada.

BritRail Pass

For individual travel and valid up to 12 months from date of issue. Allows unlimited journeys throughout England, Scotland, and Wales—including transatlantic and Continental boat trains and Caledonian Steam Packet Company, steamer services on the Clyde and Loch Lomond.

Prices in the United States and Canada

	First Class	Second Class (Economy)
8 days	$ 66	$ 44
15 days	83	61
21 days	99	77
1 month	127	105

These passes must be purchased before leaving the United States or Canada; they are not on sale in Britain. There is also a BritRail Youth Pass; second class only, which is $35 for 8 days; $50 for 15 days; $63 for 21 days; and $94 for 1 month.

Bus and Coach Travel

The cost works out at between $.03 and $.05 per mile for long-distance coach services to the suburbs or between cities. Information on coach services starting from London (on which it is advisable to book well in advance) is obtained from Victoria Coach Station, London, S.W.1. For local bus routes or long-distance coach routes, information should be obtained at the stations. No advance bookings are necessary on local bus services, which cost between $.07 and $.13 per mile.

Visitors planning to travel extensively by coach can obtain a copy of the *Express Coach Guide* published by the National Bus Company, 25 New Street Square, London, E.C.4. The guide is issued twice a year—summer and winter—and gives detailed timetable information for the majority of services throughout Britain. Help in planning coach itineraries can be obtained through the Publicity Manager, Victoria Coach Station, London, S.W.1.

Green Line Coaches

To reach the surburbs of London and nearby towns take a Green Line Coach. These coaches service all of the little towns as much as 40 miles out of London. All over the city you will see signs indicating a Green Line Coach stop. Many of the coaches are double-deckers, and of course, the top deck is a perfect vantage point from which to see the surrounding country. Information on fares and schedules can be obtained from the London Country Bus Service, Ltd., Bell Street, Reigate, Surrey.

Taxis

Taxis may be hailed in central London streets. When they are free, the "For Hire" sign at the front of the cab is lit.

If you wish to call for a taxi, look under "Taxi-cabs" in the telephone directory. The owner-drivers radio taxi service operates a 24-hour service. Tel: 286-4848. The minimum fare is 15p ($.37) and charges are metered thereafter. For every mile after the initial half-mile of your journey there is an additional 3p ($.07). An extra charge of 3p is made for every additional passenger and 3p for each item of baggage carried on the roof or on driver's platform. For hirings between midnight and 6 A.M., 9p extra is charged.

The average charge for a trip from Heathrow Airport to Piccadilly Circus would be £3.25 ($8.12).

In the provincial towns taxi charges vary from region to region, but the average charge is about 20p ($.50) for the first mile and 10p to 15p ($.25 to $.37) for each additional mile.

A minimum of 5p ($.12) tip for all fares up to 20p ($.50) and roughly 15% of the fare above that is recommended. A larger tip is expected for any special service.

ENGLISH GOVERNMENT REGULATIONS

Passports and Visas

As a general rule, to enter the United Kingdom one must have a valid passport and a visa issued by British consular authorities abroad. However, citizens of the United States do not need visas. Canadian citizens can obtain application forms at post offices, and the completed form should be sent to the Canadian Passport Office, 85 Sparks Street, Ottawa, Ontario, together with a remittance of $10.

Vaccinations

You will be asked to produce an international certificate of vaccination against smallpox and cholera, if you come from an infected area or from certain countries. Otherwise, they are not required for entry into Britain. However, you may need them upon reentry into your country of residence; check before you go. For a while, smallpox vaccinations were not required, but after an outbreak in Europe the United States again demanded proof of vaccination upon reentry into the country.

Customs

When you arrive in Britain your baggage in liable to customs examination. If you are visiting the United Kingdom for less than 6 months, all personal effects that you intend to take with you when you leave are duty-free, except tobacco goods, wine, spirits, and perfume. Visitors are entitled to bring in certain amounts of these items duty-free, and these need not be declared at Customs.

22 BEFORE YOU GO

DUTY-FREE ALLOWANCES
400 cigarettes or 200 cigarillos
100 cigars or 500 grams tobacco
1 bottle of spirits or 2 bottles of wine
50 grams (2 fluid ounces) perfume
¼ liter toilet water
film (movie or regular photographic): reasonable quantity for private use
other goods: £10 worth

The allowances for tobacco and alcoholic goods are for persons over seventeen years of age.

These allowances apply only to goods carried in the baggage that you clear through Customs at the time of your arrival. The allowances don't apply to any articles brought in for sale or for other commercial purposes.

Currency Regulations

ENTERING BRITAIN Travelers may bring in traveler's checks, sterling notes, foreign currency notes, letters of credit, etc., in any currency and up to any amount.

LEAVING BRITAIN Nonresident travelers may take out:

(a) Not more than £25 in sterling notes (If you have more than this in sterling notes as a result of cashing too many traveler's checks or letters of credit, a bank will exchange up to £100 into traveler's checks, usable anywhere in the world.);

(b) The amount of foreign currency notes brought in by you or the equivalent of £300, whichever is the larger;

(c) Traveler's checks, letters of credit, etc., issued to you by authorized dealers in Britain. You may also take out traveler's checks, letters of credit, etc., which you brought with you into Britain but which have not been cashed.

CLIMATE

The weather in Britain is not really as bad as all the jokes about it would have you think. There are no extremes such as the very cold winters and very hot summers we have in America; the temperature does stay at a rather even keel. If it snows it doesn't last very long, and there is never the slush problem that we find in big cities here. Summers can sometimes get a bit hot and humid, but the average summer high is still a very comfortable 77°. Rarely, too,

Weather Chart

	Average Daily Temperature	Average Daily Low Temperature	Average Daily High Temperature	Average Humidity	Average Number of Days of Rain
January	39	35	43	85	15
February	40	35	45	82	15
March	43	36	49	79	14
April	48	40	55	75	13
May	54	45	62	73	12
June	60	51	68	73	12
July	63	54	71	73	13
August	62	54	70	76	13
September	57	49	65	80	12
October	50	44	56	85	16
November	44	39	49	86	16
December	41	36	45	86	16

does one run into the pea-soup fogs that have become associated with London. So it is not really that bad.

I wish I could say that just as the pea-soup fogs have gone abroad so has the rain London is also famous for, but unfortunately this is not the case. It does rain often and steadily, so you can't do without an umbrella at any time of the year.

SIZE CHARTS

Sizes can be a problem in England since European sizes are used in some instances and English sizes in others. American sizes are used only rarely. These charts are just a rough guide, so don't go by them alone. The best thing to do is to try the article on first.

Hosiery

American, Australian, English	European
8½	1
9	2
9½	3
10	4
10½	5
11	6

Shoes

American and Australian	English	European
4½	3	34
5	3½	35
5½	4	35
6	4½	36
6½	5	36
7	5½	37
7½	6	37
8	6½	38
8½	7	38
9	7½	39
9½	8	40

Coats, Dresses, Suits, Skirts

American	European
7–8	38
9–10	40
11–12	42
13–14	44
15–16	46
17–18	48

Junior Misses

American	European
9	34
11	36
13	38
15	40
17	42

Men's Shirts

American	European	English
14	36	14
14½	37	14½
15	38	15
15½	39	15½
16	41	16
16½	42	16½
17	43	17

English sizes in men's pajamas and suits also correspond to American ones.

Men's Sweaters

American	European	English
Small	44	34
Medium	46–48	36–38
Large	50	40
Extra large	52–54	42–44

Children's Dresses and Suits

American	European	English
2	40–45	16–18
4	50–55	20–22
6	60–65	24–26
8	70–75	28–30
10	80–85	32–34
12	90–95	36–38

Children's Sweaters

American	European
10–30	38
12–32	40
14–34	42
16–36	44
18–38	46
20–40	48

WEIGHTS AND MEASURES

Liquid Measure

1 liter = 1.057 quarts
1 pint = 0.56 liter
1 quart = 1.136 liters
1 gallon = 4.54 liters

Weight

1 kilogram or kilo (1,000 grams) = 2.2 pounds
1 metric ton (1,000 kilograms) = 2,204.62 pounds

Area

1 square meter = 10.76 square feet
1 square kilometer = 0.3861 square mile
1 hectare = 2.471 acres

Distance

1 kilometer (1,000 meters) = approx. 5/8 mile
1 meter = approx. 39 inches or 3.28 feet
1 centimeter (.01 meter) = .4 inch
1 millimeter (.001 meter) = approx. .04 inch

TO CONVERT KILOMETERS TO MILES: Divide by three and multiply by 2. Thus, 60 kilometers becomes: 60 ÷ 3 = 20; 20 × 2 = 40 miles.

Time Conversion

England is 6 hours ahead of the Eastern United States. Therefore, when it is 6 P.M. in London, in the United States it is:

EST	CST	MST	PST
12 noon	11 A.M.	10 A.M.	9 A.M.

Useful Information 27

Telephone Service

Public boxes take 2p and 10p coins. The minimum charge for local calls from public call boxes is 2p ($.05). This will buy three minutes Monday through Friday from 8 A.M. to 6 P.M., or six minutes evenings and weekends. Outside of London there are still some telephone booths with the old-type coin boxes, with buttons marked *a* and *b* , from which local calls can be dialed. There are instructions on the box to tell you when to insert your coins and when to push the button. Be sure to read it before you make your call. Only local calls can be made from these boxes.

Calls to the United States and Canada (except Alaska) cost 75p ($1.87) per minute until 8 P.M. The reduced rate of 56p ($1.40) per minute applies Monday through Saturday from 10 P.M. to 10A.M. and all day Sundays. Many U.S. cities can now be dialed direct from the United Kingdom at a much lower rate.

To contact operator: dial 100.

For directory information: dial 142.

To find out the time: dial 123.

For daily information service on main events in London: dial 246-8041.

For London region weather forecast: dial 246-8091.

For conditions on the road within fifty miles of London: dial 246-8021.

For weather on the coast: dial 246-8096 (Essex); 246-8098 (Kent); 246-8097 (Sussex).

To call London from outside the city: dial 01 first.

Postage

Local mail
 1 ounce 5½p ($.13)
Foreign mail
 air mail (½ounce) 8p ($.20)
 air-mail postcard 5p ($.12)
 aerogram 6½p ($.16)

Currency

The exchange rate between pounds and dollars fluctuates daily. As of this writing the rate is generally about $2.50 per £1, and all the prices in this book are figured at that rate. For the exact price check with your local bank or, upon arriving in Britain, at the airport. Many stores and hotels accept U.S. dollars, but it will cost you about 5% more than the exchange would be at the bank.

Currency Conversion Table

British	U.S.	U.S.	British
½p	.01¼	.01	²⁄₅p
1p	.02½	.05	2p
5p	.12½	.10	4p
10p	.25	.25	10p
25p	.62½	.50	20p
50p	$ 1.25	$ 1.00	40p
£ 1	2.50	2.50	£ 1
5	12.50	5.00	2
10	25.00	10.00	4
25	62.50	25.00	10
50	125.00	50.00	20
100	250.00	100.00	40

There are 100 pence to the pound sterling. Copper coins are in denominations of ½p, 1p, and 2p. Silver coins are 2½ p (the same size as an American penny), 5p, 10p, and 50p. Bank of England bills (called "notes") are £1 (colloquially called a "quid"), £5 (or a "fiver"), £10 (a "tenner"), and £20 (a "twenty"). There are two old currency coins you may still see in circulation: the old shilling piece, which is the same size and value as the 5p coin, and the two-shilling piece, which is worth 10p.

There are exchange offices at all of the airports and ports, which are generally opened only upon arrival and departure of all aircraft and vessels. You may also exchange at all hotels and, of course, at banks, during normal banking hours. Banking hours are 9:30 A.M. to 3:30 P.M., Monday through Friday. There is a late opening one day a week, depending on local demand.

Tipping

There are no fixed rules covering tipping and the following advice is intended only as a guide. For advice on taxis, see page 21. For porters, the tip depends on the size of baggage and on the distance carried. It is customary to tip about 5p ($.12) a case.

In restaurants, where a service charge is not included, 10% to 12% of the bill should be given. If special service has been given you, you may prefer to tip even more than that.

In a hotel, for a stay of more than three days leave a tip for the chambermaid of about 20p ($.50) per day on the dresser. If she has done something special for you, adjust the tip accordingly.

In theaters in some European cities you tip the usherette when she takes you to your seat. In London you do not, but you do pay

5p ($.12) for the program and another 5p if she brings you coffee. In beauty salons, an appropriate tip is 20% of the total charge.

VAT Tax

The Value Added Tax (VAT) has been applied as of April 1, 1973. It covers the total costs of services you may buy, including any service charge (in the case of hotels, etc.). When making reservations it is most important to find out if the VAT is included in the rates they quote. If not, you may have an additional 10% to contend with and this does make quite a difference.

Since the way the tax is computed is complicated, none of the prices listed in this book include the VAT tax. So when you're planning your expenses, remember to plan for that extra charge.

Electrical Equipment

Make sure that any electric irons, curlers, or other electrical appliances that you take into Britain can be used on British voltages. The most general current is 240 volts AC, 50 cycles, although variations between 200 and 250 volts may still be found. DC is still used in a few areas. Leading hotels will, on request, supply adapters for these appliances. However, it is best to make sure that your appliances operate on an international current. Always make certain to check the position of the button or lever that adjusts the current on your appliance. If you forget to switch it to the proper current you can very easily blow out your appliance.

POLICE, FIRE, OR AMBULANCE

Dial 999 and the operator will connect you immediately.

5
A Word About Language

Though supposedly Americans and the British speak the same language, we really don't. Many British terms and words are quite different from ours and can lead to some confusion. The following may help a bit.

American	English
apartment	flat
bathing suit	bathing costume
bathroom	water closet, or W.C. or loo
call up	ring up
candy	sweets
cookie or cracker	biscuit
dessert	sweet
elevator	lift
expensive	dear
french fries	chips
napkin	serviette
second floor	first floor
soda fountain	milk bar
stand in line	queue up
subway	underground or tube
ticket office	booking hall
two weeks	fortnight
washcloth	flannel or facecloth

The one phrase that I get the biggest kick out of, and that perhaps shocks most Americans more than any other, is "keep your pecker up"—which merely means keep your chin up.

A Word About Language 31

Street names, too, can be a problem. Here are some that are pronounced quite differently from what you might expect.

Beauchamp is pronounced Beecham
Berkeley " " Barklay
Gloucester " " Gloster
Grosvenor " " Grovener
Leicester " " Lester
Marylebone " " Marlibone

PART II
London

6
Welcome to London

Once a dreary, austere metropolis, shrouded in pea-soup fogs and soggy with a constant rain, London—the largest city in Europe—has in the last couple of decades risen from the ashes of her Victorian past.

Much of her new personality began to develop during World War II when London was repeatedly bombed by the Germans, and Londoners responded with remarkable endurance and courage. In September 1940, Winston Churchill said in a speech, "These cruel, wanton, indescribable bombings of London are part of Hitler's invasion plans, but little does he know the spirit of the British people, or the tough fibre of Londoners." How right he was. Their indomitable spirit and fierce pride gave them the strength to level the rubble of the war and begin a siege of frantic building that goes on even to this day. Skyscrapers and modern blocks of apartments rose on the sites of what were once merely cottages, stables, or shops. Today London is one of the most modern and most important centers of the business world.

One of the major factors responsible for the emergence of a new London was the government's pollution-control edict. The thick, black smoke that belched from thousands of chimneys, covered the city like an impenetrable cloud, and imprisoned the pea-soup fogs beneath it, has disappeared and now one can see one of the clearest blue skies in the world.

Perhaps the banishment of the "black menace" has also caused the revitalization of the populace. They cast off their neutral colors and styles that suited the dreary, foggy, gray atmosphere of yesterday and began to dress in wild colors and way-out fashions. The miniskirt was born; historical costumes and uniforms became the mode of the day. Carnaby Street burst on the scene like a rocket and mod boutiques sprang up like weeds. Other shops and department stores replaced their traditional conservative lines with the latest in Continental fashions in an effort to compete. Radios, record players, and night clubs blasted the silence with ear-splitting rock music. Staid night clubs changed their policies to feature popular, even erotic Continental entertainment. Hotels and restaurants replaced their bland cuisine with that of the finest European chefs.

But, with all this radical change in personality, luckily, Londoners have not lost their native charm, sincerity, good manners, and friendliness. They are still eager to help a stranger and quick to befriend you. Their politeness is incomparable! You will be thanked to death, warmly smiled at by most shop clerks, and given service the likes of which we seldom see in the United States. Neglect to give a New York cab driver a healthy tip and you will hear about it. Forget to tip a London cab driver and he will smile and wish you a pleasant day.

London spreads out endlessly over 620 square miles, but don't worry about that, because we are going to cover only the part of it that best applies to tourists. Though only a few miles, it is quite enough to give you a thorough knowledge of this great city.

London is definitely a woman's city because here she can find every possible interest and can go anywhere she likes without an escort and without fear of being bothered. She can stroll the streets alone at night anywhere in London proper and not have to always look over her shoulder, or question each car that slows down alongside of her at the curb. If she meets a man she fancies she can generally accept his invitation for tea, drink, or dinner, assured that he is not going to try to rape her on the way home, or force his way into her hotel room. Of course, this applies to Englishmen, not to other travelers you are bound to meet here as well. Then you are really on your own.

HOW TO GET AROUND

Double-Decker Buses

They are perhaps the most popular and exciting way of seeing London. For less than $1.50 you can take in almost all the important sights, as the buses worm their way into almost every corner of London. Fares depend upon how far you ride. The conductor comes around after you are seated, asks you where you want to go, and then tells you how much it will be. The cheapest fare on all buses is about 5p ($.12). This applies to the double-decker buses and to the Red Arrow Single-Decker Buses, which are much faster and give practically nonstop service on the busier routes. To obtain your ticket for the Red Arrow Bus you drop a 5p coin into the automatic machine upon boarding the bus.

Subway

The subway in London is referred to as the "tube" or "underground." Its routes cover all of London and it is really the easiest and quickest way to get around. You buy your ticket at the station, with fares depending upon the length of your journey. The cheapest fare is 5p ($.12); a longer trip out into the suburbs may run to 75p ($1.87). Buy your ticket at either the ticket booth or the automatic slot machine located nearby, and hang onto it, as it will be collected when you get off. Some of the stations, especially the new Victoria line, have automatic entry and exit barriers that operate only upon the insertion of your ticket.

Once you select your stop, you will note that it is color-coded. All you have to do is follow the identical colored arrows pointing in the direction you should go. You will also find maps everywhere; so you really should not get lost.

If you are going to be doing a lot of sightseeing for at least four days you will find two budget travel deals available to you which are well worth taking advantage of. The "Go As You Please" plan allows you to travel virtually anywhere within London on the subway or buses. To use the pass all you do is show it at the end of your journey or whenever the conductor comes around. This Plan also includes London Transport's "Round London" sightseeing tour of the city. You can buy a "Go As You Please" ticket from British Railway here in the U.S. for $11 for a four-day pass, or $14.50 for a seven-day pass. You can buy them when you're in England from the London Transport offices, for slightly more.

There is also a one-day special ticket on the Green Rover, which allows you to ride any green "country buses," except the Green Line coaches. This costs 60p ($1.50). The Red Bus Rover ticket gives you access to any of the red buses, and costs 50p ($1.25). Both are good for a full day and begin after 9:30 A.M. They may be bought at most underground stations.

For more information on any of these plans, you can check with the London Transport offices at St. James's Park, Oxford Circus, Piccadilly Circus, Victoria Station, Euston, or King's Cross underground stations.

Taxis

London taxis are the roomiest and most comfortable of any anywhere in the world and are still comparatively inexpensive. All taxis are metered and cost about 12p ($.30) a mile for the first 6 miles, after which the rate doubles. For shorter distances count on about 3p ($.07) for about every quarter mile. Up to 40p tip the driver 5p, and for fares up to 60p tip 10p.

Taxis may be hailed in central London streets. When they are free, the ("For Hire") sign is lit at the front of the cab.

If you wish to call for a taxi see "Taxi-cabs" in the telephone directory. The owner-drivers radio taxi service operates a 24-hour service, Tel: 286-4848. The minimum fare is 15p ($.37), and charges are metered thereafter. For every mile after the initial half mile of your journey there is an additional 3p ($.07). An extra charge of 3p is made for every additional passenger and 3p for each item of baggage carried on the roof or on the driver's platform. For hirings between midnight and 6 A.M., 9p extra is charged.

USEFUL ADDRESSES

Police, Fire, or Ambulance

Pick up the phone, dial 999, and the operator will connect you immediately.

Emergency Medical Service

MIDDLESEX HOSPITAL Mortimer Street, W.1 Tel: 636-8333
  Or the Casualty Department of the nearest hospital.

Dental Emergencies

ST. GEORGE'S HOSPITAL Tooting Grove, S.W.17 Tel: 672-1255
KINGS COLLEGE HOSPITAL Denmark Hill, S.E.15 Tel: 733-1031
  Mornings only.

Eye Treatment

MOORFIELDS EYE HOSPITAL City Road, E.C.1 Tel: 253-3411
  For emergency treatment.
  For general advice and information on eyes, glasses, contact lenses.

Welcome to London

THE EYE CARE INFORMATION BUREAU 55 Park Lane, W.1 Tel: 499-0609

All-Night Pharmacies

BOOTS Piccadilly Circus, W.1 Tel: 930-4761
Open 24 hours.
BLISS CHEMIST 50–56 Willesden Lane, N.W.6 Tel: 624-9000
Open 24 hours.
JOHN BEWL & CROYDEN 50 Wigmore Street, W.1 Tel: 935-5555
Open from 8:30 A.M. to 10 P.M.

All-Night Post Office

TRAFALGAR SQUARE POST OFFICE 22–28 William IV Street, W.C.2 Tel: 930-3308

Travel Information

LONDON TOURIST BOARD 4 Grosvenor Gardens, Victoria, S.W.1
Open Monday through Friday from 9:15 A.M. to 5:30 P.M.
VICTORIA STATION OFFICE (adjacent to platform 15) Victoria, S.W.1 Tel: 730-0791
Open daily from 7:30 A.M. to 11 P.M. Information is available by telephone daily from 9 A.M. to 8 P.M.
FOR HOTEL ACCOMMODATIONS Tel: 730-9845
Monday through Friday from 9 A.M. to 7 P.M., Saturdays from 9 A.M. to noon, Sundays from 10 A.M. to 1 P.M.
LONDON TOURIST BOARD STUDENT CENTER 8–10 Buckingham Palace Road
Open from 8 A.M. to 11 P.M. For student accommodations and information.
LONDON TRANSPORT 55 Broadway, S.W.1 Tel: 222-1234
Information on travel in London. Free maps of bus, tube, and Green Line Coach services are also available at all tube stations.
GROSVENOR GUIDE SERVICE 13A Harriet Walk, S.W.1 Tel: 235-4750
For special tours. They will take you on shopping tours, to Windsor, on other excursions, anything you like.
BRITISH RAIL TRAVEL CENTER Lower Regent Street, S.W.1 Underground: Piccadilly Circus.

Information on passenger-train service for the rest of England is also available from the following stations, depending on what part of the country you're interested in:

Eastern Region

FENCHURCH STREET STATION Tel: 488-3725 Underground: Towerhill

KING'S CROSS STATION Tel: 837-3355 Underground: King's Cross
LIVERPOOL STREET STATION Tel: 283-7171 Underground: Liverpool Street

London Midland Region

EUSTON STATION Tel: 387-7070 Underground: Euston

Southern Region

CHARING CROSS STATION Underground: Strand
LONDON BRIDGE STATION Underground: London Bridge
VICTORIA STATION Underground: Victoria
WATERLOO STATION Tel: 928-5100 Underground: Waterloo

Western Region

PADDINGTON STATION Tel: 262-6767 Underground: Paddington
VICTORIA COACH STATION 164 Buckingham Palace Road, S.W.1 Tel: 730-0202 Underground: Victoria
BRITISH AIRWAYS Air Terminal, Buckingham Palace Road, S.W.1 Tel: 828-9711 Underground: Victoria

AMERICAN EXPRESS 6 Haymarket, S.W.1 Tel: 930-4411; 89 Mount Street, W.1 Tel: 499-4436; 2 Savoy Court, W.C.2 Tel: 836-0508; 82 Brompton Road, S.W.3 Tel: 584-6182

CALENDAR OF EVENTS

Even with all of the rapid building of hotels of the last couple of years London still seems to run short of rooms during certain seasons, especially in July and August when many Britishers take their own holiday and come to London. When there are many shows in town, such as the International Boat Show, or the Ready-To-Wear Show, etc., it is almost impossible to get a room, so it is quite necessary to book well in advance. The following calendar of events should help you to judge accordingly. It will also be a guide as to when you may wish to be in London. I've also included events that occur outside London itself, but that are easy to reach from the city. They're as much a part of London life as Big Ben.

For the exact dates of the various events, check with the British Tourist Authority in your city if there is one, or with the British Airways. They can also tell you where to obtain tickets.

Welcome to London 41

Autumn

HORSE OF THE YEAR SHOW Wembley, Middlesex October
After a year of preliminary trials and eliminations the best jumpers, trotters, and show horses of Britain gather for the supreme test at the Horse of the Year Show in London. Tickets 50p ($1.25) to £2.50 ($6.25).

INTERNATIONAL MOTOR SHOW Earls Court, London October
Probably the world's leading auto show with all leading British, American, and Continental manufacturers putting their best models forward. Tickets opening day and the following Tuesday £2 ($5); all other days 50p ($1.25).

LONDON-TO-BRIGHTON VETERAN CAR RUN November
Ever since 1905 owners of the finest "old crocks" in Britain have gathered with their tenderly preserved old chugging monsters to make the trip from London to Brighton and a grand feast. Speed is not the object: there is a 20-mile-per-hour maximum. No tickets required. Watchers gather at Hyde Park at the pre-run festivities and along the route to watch the fun.

Winter

INTERNATIONAL BOAT SHOW Earls Court, London January
Tickets from £1 ($2.50) for the first two days of the show, to 40p ($1) for the rest.

CRUFT'S DOG SHOW Olympia, London February
The nearest thing in Britain to a national championship and the largest dog show in the world. Tickets 50p ($1.25) at entrance to Exhibition Hall.

Spring

GRAND NATIONAL Aintree, Lancashire March
The four-mile Steeplechase, the most grueling and spectacular in the world. Tickets £7 ($17.50) to £11 ($27.50); unreserved 25p ($.62) to £2.50 ($6.25).

SHAKESPEARE SEASON Stratford-on-Avon, Warwickshire March through December
Five to six Shakespeare plays (changing each year) are presented at this famous festival beside the river Avon near the poet's birthplace. Most of Britain's best actors have trained in this company, which also has an annex in London. Tickets 50p ($1.25) to £2.50 ($6.25).

37th ANTIQUE FAIR Old Town Hall, Chelsea, London March
One of Britain's most splendid antique get-togethers in picturesque Chelsea's town hall. The place to look for Chippendale. Tickets 40p ($1) at entrance to exhibition.

OXFORD AND CAMBRIDGE BOAT RACE Thames, London April
For nearly 140 years this contest has been run (with few exceptions) on the river between Putney and Mortlake, London. A seat in a steamer that follows the race costs £2 ($5).

BATH FESTIVAL Bath, Somerset Late May or early June
Festival of greatly increased importance, now spilled over into Bristol and lovely Wells. Choral and orchestral concerts, recitals, chamber music,

42 LONDON

lectures, exhibitions, and interesting special events. Special late train service from Bath and Bristol to Paddington Station. Tickets 40p ($1) to £3 ($7.50).

BRIGHTON FESTIVAL Brighton, Sussex May
Music, opera, ballets, and exhibitions. Three major British symphony orchestras, and 50 "fringe" events. Tickets 12p ($.30) to £2.25 ($5.62).

CHELSEA FLOWER SHOW Royal Hospital Grounds, Chelsea, London S.W.3 May
On the grounds of Charles II's Royal Hospital in the heart of Chelsea. Leading flower show in Britain and one of the major ones in the world. Tickets 60p ($1.50) to £1.50 ($3.75).

GLYNDEBOURNE FESTIVAL OPERA Glyndebourne, Lewes Sussex May
Opera by the world's best artists in an opera house at a glorious Elizabethan mansion. Lovely gardens where guests picnic in formal evening dress or dine in the restaurant at the intermission. Special train services from Victoria Station in London to Lewes and return. (70% of the tickets are offered first to members of the Festival Society.) Tickets £3.50 ($8.75) to £8 ($20).

Summer

ALDEBURGH FESTIVAL Aldeburgh, Suffolk June
A festival of opera, choral, orchestral, and chamber music, and lectures and exhibitions of all periods and countries, with some emphasis on works of local origin and those which are not too well known. Benjamin Britten has made it famous. Tickets £1 ($2.50) to £3.50 ($8.75).

CHESTER FESTIVAL AND MYSTERY PLAYS Chester, Cheshire June
Concerts, opera, exhibitions, and the oldest English mystery plays performed in a city rich in medieval atmosphere.

THE DERBY AND THE OAKS Epsom, Surrey June
The derby is one of the greatest horse races run on the famous Epsom Race Course in one of the most fashionable sporting events of the year. The Oaks, another classic race meeting, is restricted to fillies only. Special bus service from Epsom Station to the Downs. Admission to Grand Stand and Paddock £3 ($7.50).

ROYAL ASCOT Ascot, Berkshire June
This four-day race meeting, a key event in London's social season, is highlighted by races for the Hunt Cup on the second day and the Gold Cup on the third day. The Royal Party rides in carriages along the course each day. Racing from 2:30 to about 6 P.M. The only seats bookable in advance are in the Grand Stand. Admission to Grand Stand, Paddock, and Tattersalls £3 ($7.50) to £3.50 ($8.58); reserved seats in the Grand Stand may be booked at an additional charge of £1 ($2.50) or £1.50 ($3.75).

SON ET LUMIÈRE ST. PAUL'S CATHEDRAL London, E.C.4 June
Dramatic presentation in sound and light staged inside this historical cathedral. Nightly except Sundays and Mondays. Tickets 50p ($1.25) to £1.50 ($3.75).

Welcome to London 43

TROOPING THE COLOUR Horse Guards Palace Whitehall, London, S.W.1 June
A full-dress parade to celebrate the official birthday of the Queen. Troops taking part are the Household Cavalry Regiment and Mounted Band with detachments of battalions of Foot Guards together with the Massed Bands and Corps of Drums of the Brigade of Guards. Starts at 11 A.M. and lasts for approximately one hour. Tickets £2 ($5).

WIMBLEDON LAWN TENNIS CHAMPIONSHIPS Wimbledon, London, S.W.19 June
The Championships attract the top competitors from all over the world. The major matches are played on the Centre Court and the No. 1 Court. For the Centre Court: two-day book of tickets £4 ($10) (no more than two books sold per person); daily ticket obtainable only at the ground, £1.75 ($4.37). For the No. 1 Court: 12-day book of tickets £13 ($32.50). For the covered stand: 6-day book of tickets £6 ($15). For the open stand: daily ticket, obtainable only at the ground, £1 ($2.50).

YORK MYSTERY PLAYS AND FESTIVAL OF THE ARTS York, Yorkshire June
One of Europe's oldest festivals, centered on the medieval mystery plays, set in the ruined St. Mary's Abbey. Cast of over 200. Choral and orchestral concerts in York Minster. Opera, ballet, pop, and jazz. Tickets 50p ($1.25) to £1.50 ($3.75).

HENLEY ROYAL REGATTA Henley-on-Thames, Oxfordshire July
This world-renowned series of crew races is one of the main events in the London social season and the rowing calendar. Tickets for Regatta Enclosure 50p ($1.25) per day; Saturdays 75p ($1.87). Tickets for Stewards' Enclosure about £2.25 ($5.62) per day; Saturdays £4 ($10); 4-day ticket £8 ($20).

SON ET LUMIÈRE Royal Greenwich Observatory London July
Nightly entertainment in sound and light covering the long history of Royal Greenwich. The Observatory, dating from 1675, will be the backdrop, and voices of actors telling the story include those of Sir Ralph Richardson and Sir Alec Guinness. Tickets £1 ($2.50), £1.50 ($3.75) and £2 ($5).

SON ET LUMIÈRE Bristol Cathedral Bristol August
A presentation of the history of the Cathedral narrated by well-known contemporary actors. Part of the program of celebrations to mark the 600th anniversary of the granting of the Bristol Charter in 1373. Tickets 50p ($1.25) to £1.25 ($3.12).

May through September

CHICHESTER FESTIVAL THEATRE SEASON Chichester, Sussex
This festival was hailed by critic Clive Barnes as equal to Stratford. Distinguished actors and actresses appear for the season and perform four plays. Attractive modern theater with an open stage. Tickets 50p ($1.25) to £2 ($5).

7
Where to Stay

There was a time not too long ago when getting a room in London was a real production, a matter of knowing someone, who knew someone else who knew a porter at a hotel who knew a room clerk well enough to get you a room. But today, thank heaven, due to a rash of recent building, there is a bit more of a choice, except at those periods of the year when there happens to be an auto show, trade show, or other goings-on. You still should book as far in advance as possible.

Most of the new hotels are in the upper price bracket, and, believe me, London hotels in general are very pricey indeed. I inspected as many establishments as possible, and tried to find the best accommodations within a reasonable bracket. Places differ in décor, etc., but my main concerns are cleanliness, comfort, safety, convenience, and service.

In each hotel listing you will see A, B, or C or maybe all three together. This is my special code system to tell you the age group that frequents the establishment. It allows you to choose the ambiance you prefer. Here is what the symbols mean:

A = 18-to-25-year age group   B = 26 to 40   C = 40 and up

Most English hotels are pretty stingy with soap and washcloths so I generally collect an extra little bar here and there in the less stingy places and keep it handy. A small sponge serves as a washcloth and can be kept in a plastic bag if it is damp when you pack.

There is a bit of confusion at present about taxes since the VAT tax is a new addition. Some hotels include taxes and others do not, so you have to ask. There is a service charge, usually 15%, and 10%

government VAT tax, so it does add up. The prices given here do not include VAT taxes or service charges.

Breakfast is sometimes included as well but generally only in the more traditional hotels. It will probably be what is called a Continental breakfast; rolls, jam, and tea or coffee. The typical English breakfast is really a stick-to-the-ribs affair and not recommended if you are on a diet. You will start with hot or cold cereal, then go on to eggs or an omelet with bacon, ham, sausage, or smoked fish, toast and jam, and tea, coffee, or hot chocolate. If you sleep late this kind of eye-opener will get you right through to high-tea time, in mid-afternoon.

Unlike most large cities, London does not have a hotel rating system, so I have elected to use the traditional star system: five stars = deluxe, four stars = superior first-class, three stars = first-class, two stars = second-class.

There is also something called a bed-and-breakfast place that is rather nice. These are not hotels in the true sense of the word, with public rooms, restaurants, etc., but generally old rooming-type houses, and they serve breakfast. In many cases this is the typical English breakfast described above, which can save you an additional $2.50, which is what it would cost. Bed-and-breakfast places are quite a bargain if you are only going to be in your room to sleep, and are well worth using rather than some of the higher-priced hotels so you can use your money for other things.

You will find it easiest to select a hotel if you first decide what part of London you wish to be in. If shopping is your pleasure, you may want to be near Bond Street, Oxford Street, or Knightsbridge. Or, you may wish to be near museums or a park. Don't worry about my suggesting a hotel out in the suburbs because it is available at a budgety price; you will find only the more popular parts of London listed here. I have concentrated on the heart of the city, rather than the industrial or residential areas.

HYDE PARK HOTELS

Deluxe

THE CARLTON TOWER Sloane Street and Cadogan Place, S.W.1 Tel: 235-5411 B-C
Near excellent shopping right off Sloane Street at the top of Sloane Square. It gets a lot of businessmen, senior executives, and diplomats. Single: £11.50 to £13.75 ($28.75 to $34.35); double £17.50 ($43.75); twin: £18 ($45); single occupancy of a twin room: £16.25 ($40.60); not including

breakfast, VAT, or service. The rooms are medium to large with phone, radio, color TV, wall-to-wall carpeting, air-conditioning, and 24-hour room service. All are furnished in lovely English traditional style. There is no coffee shop, but the Chelsea Lounge is open 24 hours a day for drinks, coffee, and sandwiches. The Rib Room, a London landmark especially famous for its roast beef, gets a great number of celebrities. Fixed-price lunch £2.20 ($5.50); dinner main course £1.75 to £3.75 ($4.37 to $9.37). The Chelsea is an elegant restaurant overlooking the park and serves French cuisine. There is a pianist from 3 to 6 P.M. and a trio at night. Main course £1.80 to £2.60 ($4.50 to $6.50). There are also two bars. The concierge is said to be the very best in London, which is good news, so he can help you with anything you wish. Besides that, the service is excellent and every room was newly refurnished in 1974.

Four Star

BELGRAVIA ROYAL 20 Chesham Place, S.W.1 Tel: 235-6040 Cable: BELROYAL B-C

Near King's Road and Knightsbridge Road. Gets a lot of businessmen and single people. Single: £11 to £14 ($27.50 to $35); double: £14 to £23 ($35 to $57.50); not including breakfast, VAT, or service. Rooms have phone, radio, color TV, wall-to-wall carpeting, makeup table, air conditioning, large bath, bidet, large mirror, and sitting alcove. There is 24-hour service. Continental breakfast 80p ($2); English breakfast £1.20 ($3). The rooms are large and furnished in modern style. The coffee shop is open from 8 A.M. to 11 P.M. The dining room is open for lunch and dinner, with main course £1.20 to £3 ($3 to $7.50). There is a bar as well. There is 24-hour service on laundry and dry cleaning, and there is a beauty salon right around the corner.

THE CAPITAL HOTEL 22 Basil Street, S.W.3 Tel: 589-5171 Cable: HOTELCAP B-C

Right next to Harrods, this is a small hotel but very well situated. It gets a lot of businessmen and you really have to book well in advance. New as of 1971 but they are running almost 100% occupancy already, primarily because of their excellent restaurant and the convenient location. Single: £10.75 ($26.85); double: £16 ($40); not including breakfast, VAT, or service. Every room is large, beautifully decorated in orange, beige, and brown shades with thick wall-to-wall carpeting and leather tufted boudoir chairs. The baths are very modern with colored fixtures, heated towel racks, and terry-cloth robes. All rooms have a phone, radio, and color TV. There is 24-hour room service; which comes through the restaurant. No coffee shop. The restaurant has gotten such fantastic reviews that you must book at least a week in advance if you want to eat between 8 and 9:30 P.M. So eat earlier—or later if you can hold out. Main dishes £1.85 to £2.50 ($4.62 to $6.25). There is a bar but no other facilities. They will send out all your dry cleaning, pressing, and any repairs that need to be done.

THE HYDE PARK HOTEL 66 Knightsbridge, S.W.1 Tel: 235-2000 Cable: HIGHCASTE A-B-C

In this case the four stars indicate a truly superior, first-class hotel. The front of the hotel faces Knightsbridge and the back Hyde Park—an excellent location. The clientele is mixed, including every age group and type of person. In the summertime, especially, you will find a preponderance of the A group. Single with bath: £12.40 to £14.80 ($31 to $37); twin with bath: £16.75 to £20.75 ($41.85 to $51.85); not including breakfast, VAT, or service. Continental breakfast 75p ($1.87).

English breakfast £1.90 ($4.75). Every room has a phone, radio, color TV, wall-to-wall carpeting, and 24-hour room service. No air conditioning at the moment but all rooms are expected to have separate units within the next year or two. All rooms are spacious and very well furnished in a traditional manner.The bathrooms are large and very convenient, with heated towel racks and many with bidets, and of course the large English tubs are a joy. Most singles and doubles face the front, Knightsbridge Road, while the suites face the park. There are a few singles and doubles that face the park as well at no additional cost. If you prefer one of these, write at least a month in advance and specify a park-side room; you probably will be able to get one this way. All rooms have an anteroom; half the rooms at the moment have separate makeup tables that are very handy. This is truly a beautiful hotel with elegantly traditional entrances and public rooms. Though it is about 80 years old, it was newly renovated in late 1971 in keeping with the traditional style that makes you feel most comfortable and at home. The corridors are large and beautifully carpeted with old grape-cluster crystal chandeliers throughout. There is no coffee shop, but coffee and drinks are served in the tea lounges 24 hours a day. There is also 24-hour room service. The Cavalry Room Restaurant, done in superb old English style with low-beamed ceilings, is rather masculine but interesting. It features a cold buffet at lunchtime, specializing in roast beef. Open for lunch from noon to 3 P.M. and for dinner from 7 to 11 P.M. The main dining room itself is lovely, facing right on the park; it is open from 6:30 to 10 P.M. There is a beauty salon in the hotel.

LOWNDES HOTEL 1921 Lowndes Street, S.W.1 Tel: 235-6020 Cable: LOWNDES B-C

The clientele here is couples and businessmen. Single: £13.50 ($33.75); double: £17.50 ($43.75); not including breakfast, VAT, or service. They take no singles except in the off-season. Every room has a phone, radio, TV, and wall-to-wall carpeting. There is 24-hour service. The rooms are medium size and furnished in good English traditional style. The Adam Room Restaurant is open for breakfast from 7:30 to 10 A.M., for lunch from noon to 3 P.M., and for dinner from 6 to 9 P.M. There is a bar but no other facilities. All cleaning, laundry, etc., are sent out. Unfortunately, though the hotel is rather nice and comfortable, it is terribly overpriced; in fact, it charges almost the same price as the Carlton Tower with nowhere near the service or facilities. The room service, especially, is not very good. There is a nice little shopping arcade right next to the hotel with antiques, jewelry, gifts, and "cosmetics à la carte" where you can have all cosmetics made to order.

PENTA HOTEL Cromwell Road, S.W.7 Tel: 370-5757 Cable: PENTOTEL A-B-C

Not exactly in the heart of a good shopping area, but it isn't all that far away, about a half-mile from Harrods and just opposite the West Side Air Terminal. The hotel is brand new and I find it very convenient and comfortable. It gets a lot of businessmen, as do most modern American-style hotels. Single: £7 ($17.50); double: £10.50 ($26.25); including Continental breakfast and service, but not VAT. All rooms have phone, radio, TV, and wall-to-wall carpeting. There is 24-hour service. Rooms are

48   LONDON

medium to large, furnished in the modern style with mauve and hot-pink color scheme. The best part of it is that all rooms have an automatic dispenser for drinks, coffee, juice, and breakfast, an oven/warmer, and a fridge. So, you can keep either hot or cold food handy, which is certainly a treat when you consider the price of eating out in London today. Thirty-six of the doubles have a combination of a double bed and one standard single bed, while the rest of the 675 twins have just twin beds. There is a 24-hour coffee shop and self-service cafeteria with a very good selection of dishes. The Beefeater's Grill Room is open for lunch from noon to 3 P.M. and for dinner from 6 to 11 P.M. It has a proper charcoal grill, and main dishes run £1.10 to £2.10 ($2.75 to $5.25). In the Lounge tea, coffee, drinks, and sandwiches are served from 10 A.M. to 2 A.M. Then there is a typical English pub serving "pub grub"—the English version of hot or cold snacks. Just outside the pub is the outdoor patio for drinks and sandwiches. The Zodiac Cocktail Lounge features a pianist and is modern and comfortable. There is a beauty salon on the premises.

SKYLINE PARK TOWER   101 Knightsbridge, S.W.1   Tel: 235-8050   Cable: PARKTOWER   A-B-C

A new, modern, circular hotel, opened in June 1973. It is conveniently located, just opposite the Hyde Park Hotel. It caters to businessmen. Single with bath: £13 to £15 ($32.50 to $37.50); double with bath: £17 to £19 ($42.50 to $47.50); not including VAT. Singles are really twin-bedded rooms; this is a single-occupancy price. Every room has a phone, radio, color TV, wall-to-wall carpeting, and air conditioning. There is 24-hour service. Rooms are large and very modern with two main color schemes: green tones, and beige and brown. The lobby is done in hot pinks, oranges, and violets, and has huge brass ginger-jar lamps and gorgeous Scandinavian-style woven and embroidered wall hangings. The coffee shop is a dream, all pink, lime green, and white brick, garden-style; it makes you want to sit and linger through the day as you watch the people go by. The service is excellent, and the waitresses are really very kind. Le Trianon Restaurant is open for dinner only from 6:30 P.M. to midnight. Its ceiling and walls are covered with a magnificent flowered fabric that has been woven to match the carpeting. Star-burst chandeliers flicker over the walls, making an especially beautiful sight at night. The whole room is done in rose and lilac tones with olive. The terrace is lovely when weather permits its use. French cuisine dominates and main courses run £1.90 to £2.50 ($4.75 to $6.25). Very large wine selection. There is music for dancing. A lovely place for single women because you are inconspicuous here. The Top-of-the-Park Cocktail Lounge is very modern, with a view of Chelsea and Belgravia; dinner-dancing. The modern décor is not all that interesting but in any case you wouldn't want to go there unless you are with someone, whether a male escort or other women.

Three Star

THE BASIL HOTEL   Basil Street, Knightsbridge, S.W.3   Tel: 730-3411   Cable: SPOTLESS   A-B-C

Just behind Brompton Road, near Harrods and all good shopping. An old hotel, but really quite comfortable. It caters mostly to British and especially to single women; in fact, that is about all I saw in the hotel, with the exception of one or two men. From April 1 through October 31, single with bath: £9.56 ($23.90); single without bath: £6.90 ($17.25);

double with bath: £16.30 ($40.75); double without bath: £12.95 ($32.35); including Continental breakfast, VAT, and service. English breakfast 50p ($1.25). The rooms are small and very clean, with old-fashioned but quite adequate furnishings. Every room has a phone and wall-to-wall carpeting; 60% have bathrooms (quite pleasant, with wall-to-wall carpeting), 40% have just a wash basin. There are 6 or 8 very large doubles, all at the same price as the regular double. Room 315A was particularly nice, with bay windows, fireplace, anteroom, and dressing room. The all-in-one coffee shop, snack bar, self-service restaurant is open from 10 A.M. to 10 P.M., closed Sundays. The dining room is rather large and there are always fresh flowers on every table. It is open for breakfast from 8 to 10 A.M., for lunch from 1 to 3 P.M., and for dinner from 7 to 10 P.M. It has an international menu with fixed-price meals: lunch £2.60 ($6.50); dinner £3.20 ($8). There is a bar and a TV room. The hotel has a very special service called the Parrot Club. This is a large lounge essentially for women who want to come in to relax or meet their friends, have parcels delivered here, etc. Women from all over London make arrangements to meet their husbands here, come in the morning, leave their clothes for the evening, go shopping, and come back to change. You can use their electric curlers and have a foot massage free. A rather thoughtful service, free to hotel guests, and even when you are not staying at the hotel, it might come in handy. Snacks are also available. The hotel has a beauty parlor, open Monday through Friday.

CADOGAN HOTEL 75 Sloane Street, S.W.1 Tel: Cable: NAGODAC B-C

Just opposite Cadogan Place (Park). The hotel is quite well situated as it is near to all shopping on Sloane Street. It gets a lot of single businessmen and no long-hairs. Single with bath: £10.50 to £13 ($26.25 to $32.50); single without bath: £5.50 ($13.75); double with bath: £15.50 to £17 ($38.75 to $42.50); not including breakfast, VAT, or service. Continental breakfast 65p ($1.62); English breakfast £1 ($2.50). All rooms are medium size, very nicely done, and have phone, radio, wall-to-wall carpeting and color TV. There is 24-hour room service. The baths are new, with large Italian tiles from floor to ceiling, and very well done; 70% of the rooms have bidets and 60% have fridges, very handy for snacks if you don't feel like going out to eat. Originally, the west wing of the hotel was Lily Langtry's personal home, which the hotel added onto their main building about 85 years ago. The light oak paneling throughout the public rooms of the hotel creates a great deal of warmth and surprises one after a gander at its very old-fashioned exterior. All in all, it is very quiet, comfortable, and most charming. The upstairs quarters are very bright and gay with red fabric on the walls and shiny white woodwork with gold balustrade and elevator cage. The Lily Langtry Lounge and Restaurant is open for breakfast from 7:30 to 10:30 A.M., for lunch from noon to 2:30 P.M., and for dinner from 6:30 to 10:30 P.M. The à la carte menu is predominantly French and the entrées run £1 to £1.75 ($2.50 to $4.37). The restaurant looks Gay '90-ish with its rose velvet chairs and Austrian curtains.

Bed-and-Breakfast Hotels

A bed-and-breakfast hotel is very convenient if you just want a place to put your luggage and sleep. All of the prices given here include breakfast, too.

50 LONDON

The Bucks, the Cloverly House, and the Knightsbridge are on a beautiful tree-lined cul-de-sac just behind Harrods and all the good shopping on Brompton Road. The buildings are all white row houses with pillars in front and little balconies on the second floor, set on a beautiful, most charming street. They were all private homes at one time so you enjoy a rather homey atmosphere and certainly not the hustle and bustle of a hotel.

BUCKS HOTEL 33 Beaufort Gardens, S.W.3 Tel: 584-5252 B-C

This charming hotel gets a lot of businessmen, particularly during the winter, especially Australians and South Americans, and a good number of diplomats. Single with bath: £6.10 ($15.25); double with bath: £9.50 ($23.75); including English breakfast, but not VAT. The rooms are quite small but well done in modern style and very comfortable. All the baths are new with colored fixtures. The singles have just a shower, the doubles have a tub. Every room has a phone, radio, and wall-to-wall carpeting. There is no coffee shop but they do have 24-hour room service with coffee, tea, etc. There is a TV lounge. The breakfast (served from 7:30 to 10 A.M.) is a very full breakfast indeed. They brag about the fact that they use back bacon rather than the fatty strips, with two eggs instead of one, and so forth. They are very proud of their service and apparently justifiably so. They will send out your dry cleaning and pressing. I really found this to be the most charming and the friendliest of all the bed-and-breakfast choices. I enjoyed the people—they certainly put themselves out.

THE CLOVERLY HOUSE 14 Beaufort Gardens, S.W.3 Tel: 589-4740 A-B-C

A lot of American businessmen in the B and C age group. Single with bath: £4 ($10); single without bath: £3.50 ($8.75); double with bath: £5.80 ($14.50); double without bath: £5.40 ($13.50); including full English breakfast, but not VAT. The double rooms are large, the singles medium size, very simply but adequately furnished. There is a TV lounge. The hotel is being fully renovated. Fourteen rooms have private baths and there are 16 without. Book three to four weeks in advance. Breakfast is served from 7:30 to 9:15 A.M.; no other room service.

THE DIPLOMAT 2 Chesham Street, S.W.1 Tel: 235-1544 B-C

Single: £4.50 ($11.25); double: £7 ($17.50); not including VAT. Large, comfortable, well done rooms, 11 with private baths. The staff is very kind and the service good. They get a lot of diplomatic people here so you'll have interesting company.

HEADFORT PLACE HOTEL 17 Headfort Place, S.W.1 Tel: 235-2607 B-C

Single: £3.25 ($8); double: £6.50 to £7.50 ($16.25 to $18.75); not including VAT or service. A very charming little hotel in a mews, which makes it rather traditionally English. Large and comfortable bedrooms, four with private baths. Breakfasts are marvelous.

KNIGHTSBRIDGE HOTEL 10 Beaufort Gardens, S.W.3 Tel: 589-9271 Cable: KNIFORT B-C

A lot of businessmen come here, especially in September and March. Single with bath: £6.05 ($15.12); single without bath: £3.63 ($9.07); double with bath: £8.80 ($22); double without bath: £7.26 ($18.15); including English breakfast, VAT, and service. The doubles with bath are very large, with a phone and wall-to-wall carpeting. The singles are small, with rather modern furniture, simple but adequate. Breakfast is served from 8 to 9:30 A.M. and there is room service for sandwiches, coffee, drinks, etc., from 10 A.M. to 10 P.M. There are a bar and two TV lounges. From March through October they are fully booked so you must book one month in advance. There are 8 rooms with bath or shower, and 12 without bath, but there is one bath for every four rooms.

THE SIXTY-NINE HOTEL 69 Cadogan Gardens, S.W.3 Tel: 589-9196 B-C

Single: £4 to £5.50 ($10 to $13.75); double: £7 to £10 ($17.50 to $25). Rooms are rather nice, all different, with only 9 private baths, but the public bathrooms are fair enough. Breakfast is served in the room.

THE SLOANE HALL HOTEL 6 Sloane Gardens, S.W.1 Tel: 730-5733 B-C

Single: £3 to £4 ($7.50 to $10); double: £5 to £8 ($12.50 to $20); including Continental breakfast, but not VAT or service. English breakfast 50p ($1.25). Very lovely home with beautiful private gardens, rooms are large enough and include electric heaters and equipment to make your own tea and coffee.

WILLETT HOTEL 32 Sloane Gardens, S.W.1 Tel: 730-0634 B-C

Single: £2.75 to £3 ($6.87 to $7.50); double: £4.50 to £6 ($11.25 to $15); not including VAT. A quiet, very nicely furnished hotel with bright bedrooms and thick carpeting. The rooms are small, and there is only one bathroom for every two rooms, but the dining room is rather cozy.

The next few hotels are a bit further out along the Cromwell Road area known as South Kensington and Earls Court. They are not quite as convenient as those mentioned above but there is good bus service to take you wherever you want to go in a short time; and the prices are low.

THE ANDORA 44–48 West Cromwell Road, S.W.5 Tel: 373-4546 B-C

Single: £3.50 to £4 ($8.75 to $10); double: £5.50 to £6.50 ($13.75 to $16.25); not including VAT or service. This is a combination of four adjoining houses. The rooms are nice-sized and quite adequate, Most have a private bath and stall showers. There is a TV lounge and bar, open until 2 A.M. Breakfast, luncheon, and dinner are served. The service is excellent.

CONCORD HOTEL 155–157 Cromwell Road, S.W.5 Tel: 270-0151 B-C

Single: £2.75 to £3.25 ($6.87 to $8.12); double: £4.50 to £5.50 ($11.25 to $13.75); not including VAT or service. Open 24 hours a day, which is nice if you arrive late at night. The bedrooms are large and well kept. Some of the smaller ones have fitted modern furniture. Not all have private showers, you must ask in advance. The service is quite good.

KENSINGTON COURT HOTEL 33–35 Nevam Place, S.W.3 Tel: 370-5151   B-C
Single: £5 ($12.50); double: £7.50 ($18.75); not including VAT or service. Very well done, large rooms, all with private bath, TV, and radio. They have a good restaurant for breakfast and dinner and a lounge/bar.

PARK HOUSE HOTEL 126 Queens Gate, S.W.7   Tel: 589-9628   B-C
Single: £1.75 to £3.50 ($4.37 to $8.75); double: £4 to £7 ($10 to $17.50). The rooms are large, very clean and well equipped; good-sized bathrooms. The hotel is well managed, and has a lounge and breakfast room.

RICHMOND COURT 5 Courtfield Gardens, S.W.5   Tel: 373-5322   B-C
Single: £4.50 ($11.25); double: £6 ($15); not including VAT or service. A quiet, friendly little place on a quiet square. The bedrooms are simply furnished. There is a TV lounge and a breakfast room, with a very good breakfast.

SORBONNE HOTEL 39 Cromwell Road, S.W.7   Tel: 589-6636   B-C
Single: £3 to £4.75 ($7.50 to $11.87); double: £5 to £6 ($12.50 to $15). Close to the BOAC Terminal and the museums, nice enough for perhaps one night or two. Rooms are very simple, but adequate enough.

MARBLE ARCH–OXFORD STREET AREA HOTELS

Deluxe

CLARIDGE'S Brooks Street, W.1   Tel: 629-8860   B-C
Near Bond Street and Oxford Street. An old landmark and always full of the best people. Single: £12.50 ($31.25); double: £19 ($47.50). All rooms have phone, radio, wall-to-wall carpeting, 24-hour service, and are deluxe with turn-of-the-century décor. The restaurants are excellent, as one might expect at a place like this. Your afternoon coffee or tea will be accompanied by a string orchestra. The hotel is frequented by people who come back year after year after year, so reservations are necessary.

THE CONNAUGHT HOTEL Carlos Place, W.1   Tel: 499-7070   B-C
Near Bond Street and Oxford Street. Very posh, popular, and selective. Businessmen abound. They take only individuals, no groups. Single: £11.50 ($28.75); double: £15 ($37.50); not including VAT or service. All rooms are rather large and include phone, radio, and wall-to wall carpeting; furnished with antiques or copies of antiques. Tearoom lounge, bar, and dining room. The clientele here is a steady one, people who come back year after year, so if you want to stay here you really must make a reservation well in advance.

THE MONTCALM Great Cumberland Place, W.1   Tel: 082-4288   B-C
This elegant hotel has a lot of businessmen and diplomatic types. Single: £15.50 ($38.75); double: £19 ($47.50); twin: £20.50 ($51.25); including VAT and service. Rooms have phone, radio, color TV, wall-to-wall car-

peting, air conditioning. There is 24-hour room service, available through the restaurant. The baths are very nice with bidet, marble sinks, free talc, and Blue Grass soap. The single rooms are rather small; the double rooms are a bit larger, and are modern and quite nice. There is no coffee shop. The restaurant is open for breakfast from 7 to 11 A.M., for lunch from 12:30 to 2:45 P.M., and for dinner from 6:30 to 10:45 P.M. The average main course at lunch runs £1.75 to £2.85 ($4.37 to $7.12); dinner £2.20 to £3.20 ($5.50 to $8). It is a very new hotel, open as of September 1973, with a very posh lobby—all gold, beige, and brown, lovely antiques, soft leather chairs, and lounges.

Four Star

BROWN'S HOTEL Dover Street and Albemarle Street, W.1 Tel: 493-6020 B-C

Single: £10 to £12 ($25 to $30); double: £15 to £20 ($37.50 to $50); not including VAT or service. Full English breakfast: £1 ($2.50). Most rooms are quite large, though there are a few small ones; all have been newly (and beautifully) redecorated in the traditional English style. The rooms are quite comfortable and have radio, telephone, and wall-to-wall carpeting. The Byron Lounge has coffee, tea, and drinks. During the winter there is a lovely fire to drink in front of. Two dining rooms with excellent service and cuisine. This very popular hotel was created by James Brown, once valet to Lord Byron, in 1837. The flavor of that era still lingers in all the appointments, service, and attitude, which probably accounts for its popularity.

THE CHURCHILL HOTEL Portman Square, W.1 Tel: 486-5800 B-C

This hotel gets a lot of businessmen. Just two short blocks from Oxford Road and facing on Portman Square. Single: £10.50 ($26.25) and up; double: £14 ($35) and up; including breakfast, but not VAT or service. All rooms are good size, with phone, radio, color TV, wall-to-wall carpeting, and 24-hour service: they are very well done in traditional English style. The corridors are bright yellow, white, and gray. There is a coffee shop. The Number Ten dining room is decorated with velvet chairs, good paintings (all originals) of English hunting lodges and historical places. Lovely atmosphere, excellent food and service, and a very extensive menu. Open for lunch from noon to 3 P.M. and for dinner from 6 to about 10:30 P.M. Average main dish for dinner £1.50 ($3.75). The Coffee Lounge in the lobby is a delight and whether or not I stay at the hotel, I always manage to drop by to have coffee or to meet people. It is a sunken lobby done, like the rooms, in beautiful bright yellow and gray and white, with soft couches and lounge chairs. You can have coffee, tea, and drinks here all day long and a choice of delicious pastries from the pastry cart. The atmosphere is one of quiet contentment and elegance. There is a beauty salon.

THE CUMBERLAND HOTEL Marble Arch, W.1 Tel: 263-1234 B-C

Just opposite the Marble Arch and at the head of Oxford Street, across from Park Lane. About 50% of their clientele is businessmen and the hotel is very large, so if you want to meet anyone it is quite easy. Single: £10 ($25); twin: £15.60 ($39); including full English breakfast and VAT, but not service. The single rooms are small but quite convenient; the doubles are large. All rooms include phone, radio, TV, wall-to-wall carpeting. There is 24-hour service. Each room has a massage unit for the bed at 10p ($.25) per 15-minute session. A coffee shop is open from breakfast on, until 1:30 A.M. A restaurant, the Carvery, is open 7 days a week, for lunch from noon to 2:30 P.M. and for dinner from 5:30 to 9 P.M. A very, very popular place: they have an eat-as-much-as-you-like policy with several roasts that you carve yourself, for £2 ($5). L'Epée d'Or, another restaurant, is open for dinner from 6 to 11:45 P.M. and specializes in brochettes; the average main dish runs from £3 ($7.50). They also have three Maison Lyons restaurants, a grill room, and a café, so you can get something to eat at any hour—especially handy for women traveling on a budget. The beauty salon is open Monday through Friday from 9 A.M. to 6 P.M. Shampoo and set from £1.65 ($4.12); cut from £1.95 ($4.87); manicure 65p ($1.62). There is a sauna open Monday through Friday from 9 A.M. to 8 P.M. It runs £1.75 ($4.37); for a half-hour massage £2 ($5); for a one-hour massage £3.25 ($8.12); suntan £1.20 ($3); infrared for aches and pains and skin problems £2.50 ($6.25). They renovate 8 floors of the hotel annually, so it is kept up nicely. As there is very little group business, it is relatively quiet. There are a few ice and shoe-polish machines on every floor. This hotel is actually a very good deal; and it is convenient to all the important areas for women.

HOLIDAY INN 134 George Street, W.1 Tel: 723-1277 Cable: HOLINMARCH A-B-C

Several blocks from Marble Arch, convenient enough. As a Holiday Inn, of course, it gets a lot of businessmen. Single: £11.50 ($28.75); double: £15 ($37.50); not including VAT or service. All single rooms have a double bed. Extremely lovely with white soft leather furniture, formica-topped dressing tables, and big baths with three-mirrored walls. All have phone, radio, color TV, wall-to-wall carpeting, and air conditioning. There is 24-hour service. The coffee shop is open from 8 A.M. to 11 P.M. The restaurant is open for breakfast from 7 to 10 A.M., for lunch from 12:30 to 3 P.M., and for dinner from 7:30 to 10:30 P.M. A very bright and pretty room with lots of plants. The fixed-price menu is £2.30 ($5.75). There is no beauty salon in the hotel but His and Hers is nearby, Tel: 262-4419, open Monday through Saturday from 9 A.M. to 6 P.M. There is a bar; also a free sauna (open from 9 A.M. to 7:30 P.M.) and indoor pool (same hours), which is really very nice. They will provide an iron in your room if you need one. The hotel opened in May 1973 and appears to be quite well run.

THE PORTMAN HOTEL 20 Portman Square, W.1 Tel: 406-5844 Cable: INHOTELCON B-C

In wintertime there are a lot of businessmen here, the rest of the time many couples. Single: £9 to £10 ($22.50 to $25.00); double: £12.50 to £13.50 ($31.25 to $33.75); not including VAT or service. This is an Intercontinental hotel, situated just two short blocks from Oxford Street. All rooms are large and done in modern décor, with phone, radio, TV, and wall-to-wall carpeting. There is 24-hour service. The single is as large as the double room with a sofa bed large enough for two people. They have an information tape in the radio that gives you all pertinent information on the hotel and tourist information, in five languages. The 24-hour coffee shop is a good place for American-style hamburgers. The Captain's Bar, open 24 hours a day, 7 days a week, has American-style desserts. It is charming, decorated as the interior of a ship. The Vassery is a round-the-clock hangout for Londoners. The Rotisserie Normande will transport you to the French countryside; it is a beautiful room that will make your dinner quite an experience. Sundays it features an excellent buffet with different entrées every week. The beauty salon is open Monday through Friday from 9 A.M. to 6 P.M., Saturdays from 9 A.M. to 1 P.M. They will give you every sort of beauty treatment or facial in your room if you like, including a body massage. A facial runs about £2 ($5); massage £3.50 ($8.75).

THE SELFRIDGE HOTEL Orchard Street, W.1 Tel: 408-2080 A-B-C

Just behind Selfridges Department Store on Oxford Road, very convenient indeed. They get a lot of businessmen, middle-aged and up. Single: £9.90 ($24.75); double: £16.50 ($41.25); including VAT, but not breakfast or service. Continental breakfast 85p ($2.12); English breakfast £1.20 ($3). Every room has a phone, radio, color TV, wall-to-wall carpeting, air conditioning, modern all-tiled bath. There is 24-hour service. Single rooms are small, but doubles are about medium size, all furnished in traditional English style. A nice, quiet hotel. The coffee shop is open 7 A.M. to 1 A.M.; and there is a lounge where coffee, drinks, and sandwiches are served 24 hours a day. The restaurant is open for lunch from 12:30 to 2:30 P.M. and for dinner from 7 to 11 P.M. There is a bar but no other services. The hotel opened in July 1973.

WESTBURY HOTEL New Bond Street at Conduit, W.1 Tel: 629-7755 Cable: WESTBUROTEL B-C

Near Oxford Street and Bond Street for good shopping, also near Savile Row, famous for men's suits, which means women's slacks can be bought as well, and beautifully tailored at that. Businessmen stay here. Single: £11.50 ($28.75); double: £15.50 to £18 ($38.75 to $45); not including breakfast, VAT, or service. Continental breakfast 66p ($1.50); English breakfast £1.50 ($3.75). All rooms are medium size and furnished in traditional style, rather nice and comfortable; all have phone, radio, color TV, wall-to-wall carpeting, heated towel racks in bathroom. There is 24-hour service. The coffee shop is open from 7 A.M. to midnight. The restaurant is open for lunch from noon to 2 P.M. and for dinner from 6 to 11 P.M. The Grey Room is open only for lunch, from noon to 2 P.M. The beauty salon is open from 9 A.M. to 5 P.M. There is also a Dorothy Gray Salon nearby at 45 Conduit Street, Tel: 734-7885; sauna £1.50 ($3.75); sauna and massage £3.60 ($9).

Three Star

CLIFTON-FORD Welbeck Street, W.1 Tel: 486-6600 B-C
Near Oxford Street. This hotel gets a lot of businessmen. Single with bath: £8 ($20); double: £11.50 ($28.74); including service, but not VAT. All rooms have phone, radio, TV, wall-to-wall carpeting. There is 24-hour service. Rooms are small to medium with modern furniture and very nicely done. In my estimation this is the best of the entire three-star group. The Beefeater Restaurant is open for lunch from 12:30 to 2 P.M. and for

dinner from 6:30 to 10 P.M. It is a very popular restaurant, with prices £1.70 to £2.30 ($4.25 to $5.75). There is also a bar.

THE LONDONER Welbeck Street, W.1 Tel: 935-4442 Cable: SUPERTEL A-B-C

Near Oxford Street. Single with bath: £8 ($20); double: £11.50 ($28.74); including Continental breakfast and service plus VAT. All rooms have phone, radio, TV, and wall-to-wall carpeting. They are small, modern, and quite nice. There is 24-hour service, and a free shoe valet on every floor. This hotel is a good value, one of the nicest in this range, so you must book in advance. The Four Seasons Restaurant is open for lunch from 12:30 to 2 P.M. and for dinner from 6:30 to 10 P.M. It runs 90p to £2 ($2.25 to $5).

MANDEVILLE Mandeville Place, W.1 Tel: 935-5599 Cable: MANVILHOTE A-B-C

Near Oxford Street and good shopping. Single with bath: £7 ($17.50); single without bath: £5.25 ($13.12); double with bath: £11.00 ($27.50); double without bath: £4.30 ($10.75); including Continental breakfast, VAT and service. All rooms have phone, radio, wall-to-wall carpeting, and heated towel racks in the bathrooms. There is 24-hour service. All rooms are medium size, simple, with modern furniture—quite nice enough. Rooms without bath are in other respects exactly the same as those with. There are two sections, one new and the other old. The rooms in the old section are furnished just as nicely as the new section; however, the corridors do show their age. The Queen's Restaurant is open for lunch from 12:30 to 2 P.M. and for dinner from 6:30 to 10 P.M. Lunch £1.25 to £1.40 ($3.12 to $3.50); dinner £1 to £2.66 ($2.50 to $6.65). There are two bars, but no other facilities.

THE MOUNT ROYAL HOTEL Marble Arch, W.1 Tel: 629-8040 Cable: MOUNROY A-B-C

Right on Oxford Street, one block from Marble Arch, and very convenient for all shopping. Many businessmen stay here during the winter. Single: £7.70 ($19.25); twin room for single occupancy: £9.90 ($24.75); double room: £11.55 ($28.85); including Continental breakfast, VAT, and service. Most rooms have a shower and a dressing room; all have phone, radio, TV, and wall-to-wall carpeting. There is 24-hour service. The rooms are large and quite adequate, with modern furniture, but small baths. The coffee shop is open from 8 A.M. to 1 A.M. A restaurant with eighteenth-century atmosphere is open for breakfast from 7 to 10 A.M., for lunch from 12:30 to 2:30 P.M., and for dinner from 6:30 to 10:30 P.M. There is also the Irish Bar. Free shoeshine machine on every floor. This is sort of a Times Squarish type place, large and old, but very convenient.

MOSTYN HOTEL Portman Street, W.1 Tel: 935-2361 Cable: MOSTYNHO A-B-C

A small hotel, just one tiny block off Oxford Street, so it is really very convenient without as much noise as there is on Oxford. Single with bath: £6.20 ($15.50); single without bath: £4.50 ($11.25); double with bath: £9.50 ($23.75); double without bath: £7.50 ($18.75); including Continental breakfast and service, but not VAT. All rooms have phone and radio, and there is 24-hour service. The single rooms are medium-sized, the twins are large. All are simply furnished and most baths are modern. There is just a restaurant, open for lunch from noon to 2:30 P.M. and for dinner from 6:30 to 9:30 P.M. Entrées run about £1 to £1.80 ($2.50 to $4.50).

STRATFORD COURT 350 Oxford Street, W.1 Tel: 629-7474 Cable: STRAFORT A-B-C
Near Bond Street and the lower end of Oxford Road, good for shopping. Single: £8 ($20); double: £11.50 ($28.74); including Continental breakfast, VAT, and service. Every room has a phone, radio, TV, and wall-to-wall carpeting. There is 24-hour service. The rooms are small to medium, very simple but adequate. Baths are nice enough. The Bib and Tucker Restaurant is open for lunch from 12:30 to 2:30 P.M. and for dinner from 6:30 to 10 P.M.; entrées 60p to £1.35 ($1.50 to $3.37). There is a TV lounge and a bar but nothing else. The elevators are absolutely claustrophobic—two skinny people fit if you are lucky enough to get one. Other than that, the rooms are nice enough, but this hotel is not one of my preferences.

Bed-and-Breakfast Hotels

BECKWELL HOUSE 11 Welbeck Street, W.1 Tel: 935-7069 B-C
Single: £2.75 to £3.75 ($6.87 to $9.37). This is rather old fashioned but very stately and British in its way. Continental breakfast in your room.

THE PARKWOOD 4 Stanhope Place, W.2 Tel: 262-9484 B-C
Single: £2.35 to £3 ($5.87 to $7.50); double: £5 to £6.50 ($12.50 to $16.25); not including VAT or service. Bright rooms, quite well furnished. Not all have a bath or shower. Nice TV lounge and bar.

THE STRAND HOTELS

Deluxe

THE SAVOY Victoria Embankment Gardens, W.C.2 Tel: 836-4343 B-C
Overlooks the Thames. Single: £12 ($30); double: £16 ($40); not including VAT or service. All rooms are large and Italian in décor, with phone, radio, and wall-to-wall carpeting. There is 24-hour service. There are two restaurants for lunch and dinner, the Savoy Grille and the Savoy Restaurant. Both are extremely popular, so a reservation is needed for dinner. Excellent service, courteous staff, and an elegant clientele make this hotel one of *the* places to go.

Four Star

THE ROYAL TRAFALGAR HOTEL Whitcomb Street, W.C.2 Tel: 930-4477 A-B-C
Near the Strand. Single: £7 ($17.50); double: £11 ($27.50); including Continental breakfast, but not VAT. English breakfast 60p ($1.50). This happens to be a particularly good hotel for single people because it has 38 single rooms, very unusual for hotels today, which usually cater to double occupancy. All rooms, though small, are splashed in color, and very convenient with all kinds of built-in furniture. In the Steak Room Restaurant you will find an excellent steak for £1 to £1.50 ($2.50 to $3.75). There is also a pub where light snacks are served, as well as tea and coffee in traditional London style.

58 LONDON

STRAND PALACE HOTEL The Strand, W.C.2 Tel: 836-8080 A-B-C
Just a few minutes' walk from many theaters, from Fleet Street, Trafalgar Square, and Piccadilly. Single: £6.20 ($15.50); double: £10.50 ($26.25); including a good English breakfast, VAT, and service. The hotel has just been all renovated and all the rooms are fresh and bright. Each contains a radio, telephone, and wall-to-wall carpeting. There is 24-hour service. The coffee shop looks like a bit of old Broadway in New York. The Mast Bar is good for a casual drink. The Carvery is another eat-all-you-wish type of place with delicious beef, lamb, and pork roast. The Terrace Room features a fixed-price dinner for about £3 ($7.50).

PARK LANE AREA HOTELS

Deluxe

THE DORCHESTER Park Lane, W.1 Tel: 629-8888 Cable: DORCHOTEL B-C
Right opposite Hyde Park. This hotel has a varied and very wealthy clientele. Single: £5 to £15 ($12.50 to $37.50); double: £18 to £19 ($45 to $47.50); not including VAT or service. All rooms are large and have phone, radio, TV, and wall-to-wall carpeting. There is 24-hour service. Rooms are simply furnished in the traditional English style. The baths are large, with heated towel racks. The Grill Room is open for breakfast from 7 to 10:30 A.M., for lunch from 12:30 to 2:30 P.M., and for dinner from 6 P.M. to 1 A.M. The beauty salon is open Monday through Friday from 9 A.M. to 7 P.M., Saturdays from 9 A.M. to 1 P.M. Shampoo and set £3.45 ($8.62); cut £2.50 ($6.25); manicure £1.15 ($2.87). Elizabeth Taylor and Richard Burton always stayed here when they were in town. It is a lovely place.

GROSVENOR HOUSE Park Lane, W.1 Tel: 499-6363 Cable: GROVHOSS B-C
The clientele here is 70% American businessmen. Single: £12 to £15 ($30 to $37.50); double: £16.50 to £21 ($14.25 to $52.50); not including breakfast, VAT, or service. Continental breakfast 85p ($2.12); English breakfast £1.25 ($3.12). All rooms are large, and all have phone, radio, TV, wall-to-wall carpeting, and anterooms. The baths are large with typical English tubs and heated towel racks. The rooms are simply furnished in traditional English style. La Fontaine Restaurant is open Monday through Saturday for lunch from 12:30 to 3 P.M. and for dinner from 7:30 to 11:30 P.M.; it runs £2.05 to £5.30 ($5.12 to $13.25). La Piazza Restaurant is open from 7 A.M. to midnight and runs £1.25 to £1.90 ($3.12 to $4.75). At the Vidal Sassoon Beauty Salon, a cut starts at £3.60 ($9). They also have a sauna, a pool, a gym, and two bars. Snacks and drinks are served at the pool, which costs about $1. The sauna is £1 ($2.50).

THE INN ON THE PARK Park Lane and Hamilton Place, W.1 Tel: 499-0888 Cable: INNPARK B-C
On Hyde Park. The clientele includes a lot of businessmen and celebrities. Single: £15 ($37.50); double: £20.50 ($51.25); not including breakfast, VAT, or service. Continental breakfast 60p ($1.50); English breakfast

£1 ($2.50). All rooms have phone, radio, color TV, wall-to-wall carpeting, and air conditioning. There is 24-hour service. Beautiful baths, with marble tops, good makeup alcove, and bidets. The rooms are done in beautiful traditional English manner and have a large picture window with a sitting area in front of it. Really one of the nicest I've seen on Park Lane. The second-floor rooms have sliding doors onto a patio. There is an extra TV channel in the room that plays films on various topics of interest for tourists. The Vintage Room is open for breakfast from 7 to 10 A.M. and then from 8 P.M. to 3 A.M. The Four Seasons Restaurant is beautifully done, with silver service plates and crystal. It is open for lunch from noon to 3 P.M. and for dinner from 6 to 11 P.M., with an à la carte menu, £1.75 to £3.65 ($4.37 to $9.12). There are also two bars, and a very nice lounge for coffee and drinks, available in the afternoon. Really a lovely hotel, new as of 1970. It is truly one of my favorites.

LONDONDERRY Park Lane, W.1 Tel: 493-7292 Cable: LONDHOTEL B-C

Right on Hyde Park. Many businessmen stay here. Single: £14 ($35); double: £18.60 ($46.50); not including VAT or service. All rooms have phone, radio, TV, wall-to-wall carpeting, and are furnished in modern décor. There is 24-hour service. The baths have heated towel racks and bidets. The singles are rather small, the doubles are large. The coffee shop is open 24 hours. L'Ile de France is open for lunch from 12:30 to 3 P.M. and for dinner from 7 to 11 P.M., with a pianist in the evening and an à la carte menu. There is a bar as well, though I did not find it as deluxe as the others on Park Lane and was not at all impressed with the service.

LONDON HILTON Park Lane, W.1 Tel: 493-8000 Cable: HILTELS B-C

Lots of American businessmen! Single: £13 to £16 ($32.50 to $40); double: £17 to £19 ($42.50 to $47.50); not including VAT or service. All rooms have phone, radio, TV, wall-to-wall carpeting, and air conditioning, with bidets in the bath. There is 24-hour service. The rooms are furnished in the usual modern deluxe manner that would be expected at the Hilton. The double rooms are a bit small but all are very nice. There is a coffee shop, the 18th-century London Tower, for breakfast, lunch, and dinner; the Scandinavian Sandwich Shop, open all day; Trader Vic's Polynesian restaurant; the Roof Restaurant for dancing; and the International Restaurant with music, which is very comfortable for women alone. The Patio is open for drinks, tea, or coffee, 24 hours a day. There is a night club, the "007," and the St. George Bar, which serves a large buffet on weekdays. There is a beauty salon, and an international shopping arcade.

PICCADILLY AREA HOTELS

Deluxe

THE RITZ HOTEL Piccadilly Tel: 493-8181 Cable: RITZOTEL A-B-C

Near Piccadilly, Green Park, and Buckingham Palace through the park. Many businessmen stay here. Single: £11 ($27.50); double: £19 ($47.50); not including breakfast, VAT, or service. All rooms have phone and wall-to-wall carpeting. There is 24-hour service. Rooms are quite large and pleasant, furnished in the old-fashioned, traditional English manner, with silk spreads and drapes; all closet doors are mirrored. Almost all double baths have bidets, heated towel racks, fireplace, and dressing table. TV rental is available. There is the Palm Court Lounge and Tea Room, which is open from 10:30 A.M. to 11 P.M., a beautiful, very Waldorfish type of lounge with crystal chandeliers, which makes you feel very old-worldly and very, very British. There is a lovely restaurant, all done in bright green and pinks with lots of murals, golden garlands hanging from the ceiling, chandeliers, and flowers on the tables. It is open for lunch from 12:30 to 3 P.M. and for dinner from 7:30 to 10 P.M.; prices run £1.50 to £2.50 ($3.75 to $6.25). The restaurant overlooks a lovely courtyard. For the woman alone it is the ideal place to have dinner without feeling conspicuous.

Four Star

BRISTOL HOTEL Berkeley Street, W.1 Tel: 493-8282 Cable: BRISTOTEL B-C

Near Piccadilly, Green Park, and Berkeley Square. Single: £12 ($30); double: £18 ($45); including VAT and service, but not breakfast. Continental breakfast 90p ($2.25); English breakfast £1.50 ($3.75). All rooms have phone, radio, TV, wall-to-wall carpeting, and air conditioning. There is 24-hour service with coffee, drinks, and sandwiches. Rooms are large and very nicely furnished in orange and brown tones, with bamboo chairs and a comfortable sitting area. All baths have heated towel racks. The restaurant is open for breakfast from 7 to 10 P.M., for lunch from 12:30 to 3 P.M., and for dinner from 6:30 to 10:30 P.M. Prices run £1.80 to £2.90 ($4.50 to $7.25). The hotel is new as of 1972 and is very nicely done—quiet, comfortable, and convenient. A lot of single men here if you want to meet someone, particularly businessmen, but they won't bother you. The restaurant is particularly nice, and a lovely place for one to eat alone without problems.

CAVENDISH HOTEL Jermyn Street, S.W.1 Tel: 930-2111 Cable: ROSATEL B-C

Near Piccadilly Circus. Many businessmen. Single: £13 ($32.50); double: £19.20 ($48); including Continental breakfast, VAT, and service. English breakfast £1.20 ($3). All rooms are medium size, furnished rather simply, but light and comfortable; all have phone, radio, TV, and wall-to-wall carpeting. There is 24-hour service from the lounge for coffee, drinks, and sandwiches. There is also 24-hour service at the Subrosa Bar and the Riddlesdale Room. The lounge and lobby are quite impressive, but the rooms seem a bit makeshift to me. However, it is conveniently located.

DUKE'S HOTEL 35 St. James's Place, S.W.1 Tel: 493-2366 Cable: Dukeshotel B-C

Near Piccadilly, and five minutes from Green Park. Many English businessmen among their clientele. Single: £12 ($30); double; £20.50 ($51.25); including VAT and service, but not breakfast. All rooms are rather small but very comfortable, furnished in the traditional English manner; with phone, radio, TV, and wall-to-wall carpeting. The baths are modern. Most of the doubles have bidets; all have heated towel racks. There is no coffee shop, but there is 24-hour room service from the restaurant. The restaurant is open for breakfast from 7:30 to 10 A.M., for lunch from 12:30 to 2:30 P.M., and for dinner from 6:30 to 10:30 P.M.; it runs £2.50 to £3.50 ($6.25 to $8.75). There is a beauty salon open from 9:30 A.M. to 6 P.M., and a bar. Fruit baskets are put in each room upon your arrival. This is a small, traditional hotel, quiet and convenient.

THE MAY FAIR HOTEL Berkeley Street, W.1 Tel: 629-7777 Cable: MAYFAIRTEL A-B-C

Near Piccadilly, Green Park, and Berkeley Square. Many Continental and American businessmen stay here. Single: £10.50 ($26.25); double: £16 ($40); not including breakfast, VAT, or service. Continental breakfast 60 p ($1.50); English breakfast £1.20 ($3). All rooms are medium size, nicely furnished in modern décor, and have phone, radio, TV, and wall-to-wall carpeting. There is 24-hour service. In 1969 the sixth and seventh floors were added, and the rest of the hotel was renovated in 1973. The twins are huge! They have large sitting areas and large, fully mirrored areas. The bathrooms are beautiful—all with colored fixtures, tiles, and heated towel racks. There is a coffee shop, open from 8 A.M. to midnight. The restaurant, Chateaubriand, is open for lunch from 12:30 to 2:30 P.M. and for dinner from 6:30 to 11 P.M., with prices £1.45 to £2.55 ($3.62 to $6.37). The Beachcomber Nightclub and Restaurant, specializing in Polynesian food, is open from 7 P.M. to 2 A.M., except Sundays. This hotel is a very good value for the money. I highly recommend it.

HOTEL MEURICE Bury Street, S.W.1 Tel: 930-6767 B-C

Near Piccadilly. It gets a lot of businessmen. Single: £10.30 ($25.75); double: £15.50 ($38.75); not including VAT or service. All rooms are large, furnished traditionally and very nicely, with phone, radio, wall-to-wall carpeting, and dressing table. There are only five singles and they are really not as nice as the doubles. All the front doubles are air-conditioned. There is no coffee shop, but room service from 7 A.M. to 11 P.M. Quaglino's Restaurant is very famous, which is part of the reason why the hotel is so popular. It is open for lunch from 12:30 to 2 P.M. and for dinner from 7:30 to midnight. Although the hotel is considered quite deluxe, I personally don't think it is worthy of that label, as it really doesn't have the services to offer; nor are the rooms all that great, though they are very comfortable and pleasant. I also think it is overpriced.

Three Star

PICCADILLY HOTEL Piccadilly, W.1 Tel: 734-8000 Cable: PIQUDILLO B-C

On Piccadilly Circus, close to shopping. Single: £9 ($22.50); double: £14 ($35); including breakfast, but not VAT or service. All rooms have phone, radio, TV, and wall-to-wall carpeting. They are medium size, simply furnished; really not too bad. This is a big barn of a place, and the service, I must say, is not very good at all, but it is convenient. There is 24-hour room service, a restaurant, a beauty parlor, and a bar.

STAFFORD HOTEL 16 St. James's Place, S.W.1 Tel: 093-0111 Cable: STAFOROTEL B-C

Many English and American businessmen stay here. Single: £10.50 ($26.25); double: £13 to £16 ($32.50 to $40); not including breakfast,

VAT, or service. Continental breakfast 90p ($2.25); English breakfast £1.30 ($3.25). All rooms have phone, radio, wall-to-wall carpeting, and dressing tables. TV may be rented at 75p ($1.87) per night. Rooms are very large and well done. Bathrooms include heated towel rack and bidet. There is 24-hour service; no coffee shop, but a nice lounge and restaurant. At the restaurant, main dishes run £2.50 to £3 ($6.25 to $7.50). There is also a bar, and very nice lobby and public rooms. This place can give you a nice, warm, comfortable feeling, and the people here are very friendly.

Two Star

THE REGENT PALACE Piccadilly Circus, W.1 Tel: 734-7000 A-B-C
No baths or toilets in any of the rooms. Single: £5.60 ($14); double: £9.60 ($24); including full English breakfast and service, but not VAT. Every room has phone, radio, wall-to-wall carpeting, and a basin. Rooms are medium size and clean. There is 24-hour service. Garry's Coffee Shop is open from 11:30 A.M. to 1:30 A.M. Also in the hotel are the Regent Grill and the Stetson Bar, an old Western-style saloon. A beauty salon is open from 8 A.M. to 8 P.M., Monday through Friday. Hundreds of people are milling around in this hotel all the time, Times-Square-style, and the service is not very good.

Bed-and-Breakfast Hotel

EROS HOTEL 67 Shaftesbury Avenue, W.1 Tel: 734-8781 A-B-C
Near Piccadilly Circus. Single: £3.50 to £4.25 ($9.25 to $10.50); double: £5.50 to £6.50 ($15.75 to $16.25); Not including VAT or service. The bedrooms are quite adequate and comfortable; some have private baths and some do not. There is room service, and Continental breakfast in your room or in the public room. Also TV lounge.

SOUTH KENSINGTON HOTELS

Four Star

THE KENSINGTON HILTON 179 Holland Park Avenue, W.11 Tel: 683-3355 B-C
Single: £8.50 ($21.25) to £10 ($25); double: £11 ($27.50) to £12 ($30.00). A lot of businessmen holding Hilton charge cards stay here. All rooms are nice-sized, done in modern décor and bright colors, and have phone, radio, color TV, wall-to-wall carpeting, taped music, refrigerator bar, and air conditioning, and some even have little balconies. This is a typical Hilton hotel, but the rates are lower than the one on Park Lane. It is a good bargain if you like the typical American service of the Hilton hotels.

Three Star

THE KENSINGTON PALACE HOTEL De Vere Gardens, W.8 Tel: 937-8181 A-B-C

Single: £10 ($25); double: £15 ($37.50); not including breakfast, VAT, or service. Continental breakfast 60p ($1.50). All the rooms are medium size with phone, radio, TV, and wall-to-wall carpeting. They are simple but quite nice; some are paneled, some are not; but all are rather bright and fresh. There is 24-hour service, and a coffee shop for 24-hour snacking. The Barrie Grille, the dining room, is open for lunch and dinner—a very bright, pleasant place done in gay yellow. Main courses average about £3.50 ($8.75). This is near Cromwell Road for shopping.

8
Wining and Dining

With the exception of roast beef and Yorkshire pudding, which they have excelled in, the English have always been known as notoriously bad cooks. Their food has been tasteless and devoid of spices, with all dishes tasting the same: dull, unimaginative, bland.

Recently, however, a culinary revolution has completely reversed the situation, and it is safe to say that one can get a good meal just about anywhere. Today the fare at any of the moderate-priced and expensive restaurants would be on a par with food in cosmopolitan cities anywhere in the world. The reason for this, of course, is tourism, which has become a major industry worldwide. Since every city wants its fair share of tourism, restaurant and hotel owners have brought in top chefs to command their kitchens and train their staffs.

Of course, this is all very well for travelers with thick wallets, but for the budget diner there are still a few problems. In this group the best thing is to frequent foreign restaurants—Italian, Chinese, Greek, Indian, German, etc.—of which there are a multitude. Their prices generally are budget to moderate; and they are often run by a family that projects all the zest and gusto of its native land into its cuisine. Then, too, there are little shops that sell sausage rolls, quiche Lorraine, steak and kidney pies, and the like. There's no strain on the tummy or the budget.

One place I do *not* recommend is the chain of Wimpy's hamburger restaurants, all over the place. Americans homesick for a good hamburger have learned the hard way that this is not the place to find one. They are paper-thin, tough, and fried to a greasy crispness that in no way resembles our national favorite.

Most restaurants, aside from coffee shops and snackeries, are only open for lunch and dinner; from noon to 2:30 P.M. and from 7 to 10 or 11 P.M. In addition, you can get tea, coffee, pastry, and sandwiches at teatime from 4 to 6-ish in the lounges of most hotels.

An area that abounds with foreign restaurants is Soho. It also abounds with sex shows, so don't go there alone at night; not that anything will happen to you—it won't—but you just won't be as comfortable.

In general, two women unescorted can go to any restaurant without problems, whereas a woman alone may feel out of place in some. Hotel restaurants are usually the easiest; there will generally be other women alone there as well, and you will be well taken care of and made to feel quite at ease.

The restaurants listed here will only be those in which you can feel very comfortable, with the exception of a few that are simply too good to miss; in these cases, I have noted that an escort is necessary.

Some places add an automatic service charge of 10–15%, in which case no additional tip is required unless you feel you've had exceptional service and wish to add more. If the service has not been added, add between 10% and 15%, depending on the class of restaurant and the service.

A word of caution: If for any reason you sign your check, as you might at the restaurant in your hotel, always make sure the bill has been totaled and all taxes added before you sign it. It's not uncommon for waiters later to add expensive wines and other goodies, which they make off with while you pay through the nose and don't even realize it.

Restaurants are listed according to price, in three categories, Expensive: £2.25 ($5.62) and up; Moderate: £1 to £2 ($2.50 to $5); Inexpensive: up to £1 ($2.50).

SOME ENGLISH SPECIALTIES

English food is often much like American food; and, of course, London is such a sophisticated city that it has all kinds of cuisine available.

These are some typically English dishes that you really should try while you can. After all, what's the fun of visiting a country if you don't at least taste its own food?

bangers and mash sausages and mashed potatoes (I must say I find this very tasteless)
fish and chips fried fish and French fries

66 LONDON

pudding sometimes known as just plain "pud"; Christmas plum pudding and others similar to it

sausage roll a length of bulk sausage rolled inside a flaky pastry crust, served warm

scones generally served at teatime; similar to our own baking-powder biscuits

trifle a dessert composed of pound cake or cookies, pudding, fruits, and some kind of sauce, all mixed together

Yorkshire pudding not a pudding at all but like our popovers; delicious

RESTAURANTS

Expensive

A L'ECU DE FRANCE 111 Jermyn Street, S.W.1 Tel: 930-2837

Near Piccadilly Circus. This elegant French restaurant is right in the heart of theaterland and a perfect place to stop for dinner either before or after the show. It specializes in French cuisine. The *mousse de saumon fumé* is wonderful, as is the *filet de boeuf en croûte*. Open for lunch from 12:30 to 2:30 P.M. and for dinner from 6:30 to 11:30 P.M. Closed Saturdays and Sundays for lunch, and all day Christmas Day and Good Friday. Average three-course meal £3.75 ($9.37).

AU JARDIN DES GOURMETS 5 Greek Street, Soho Square, W.1 Tel: 437-1816

An old, established French restaurant with some elegant new rooms, for film moguls or budding stars only. Since they do have to pass by you, you're bound to get a look at some glamour gal as she disappears into the inner sanctum. Meanwhile, the food in the public areas is excellent indeed. There is a very good and expensive à la carte menu featuring excellent seafood dishes. Among the favorite specialties are *crêpes d'homard au Cognac, suprême de volaille Edouard VII,* and all game in season. Open for lunch from 12:15 to 2:30 P.M. and for dinner from 6:30 to 11:30 P.M. Closed Saturdays for lunch, and all day Sundays and bank holidays. Average three-course meal £2.75 ($6.87).

BROMPTON GRILL 243 Brompton Road, S.W.3 Tel: 489-8005

Very near to Harrod's, Brompton Oratory, and the museums. An excellent restaurant and very convenient for lunch if you're shopping in the Knightsbridge area. It specializes in French cuisine. Some specialties are *ris de veau aux champignons, veau flambé,* and *noisette d'agneau à l'estragon.* Open for lunch from noon to 3 P.M. and for dinner from 6 to 11 P.M. Closed Sundays and bank holidays for lunch, and all day Good Friday, Christmas Day, and Boxing Day. Average three-course meal £3.25 ($8.12).

CALEDONIAN SUITE Northumberland Avenue, where the Strand meets the Mall Tel: 930-7255

For a real Scottish fling this is the place to be. There are even Scottish kilts available for brave patrons who wish to go all the way. And the food is right out of the Scotch highlands, with cock-a-leekie soup, Scotch

Wining and Dining 67

salmon, and the Aberdeen Angus beef the Scotch are so proud of. The food is delicious and the portions are most generous, not to mention the unlimited wine that accompanies the meal. The brand of generosity and friendliness is set with an offer of a free Scotch before you even order your meal. And after your tummy is full, there are the bagpipes and wild Scottish dancing to entertain you. So gay is the entertainment that the audience is invited to participate—and very, very few refuse. You need not worry about making a fool of yourself because the ambiance is that of a warm family gathering where everyone joins in.

CAPRICE Arlington House, Arlington Street, S.W.1 Tel: 493-5154

Close to Bond Street and St. James's Street. Caprice has always been London's theater restaurant, where one goes to see and be seen. In the meantime they also serve excellent international cuisine. Some of their specialties are *homard Merio, escalope de veau St. James, poulet Souvarof*. Open for lunch from 12:30 to 2:30 P.M. and for dinner from 6:30 to 11:30 P.M. Closed Sundays, Christmas Day, and Good Friday. Average three-course meal £3.75 ($9.37).

CARRIERS 2 Camden Passage Tel: 226-5353

Near Sadler's Wells and Camden Passage Antique Centre. Owned by the world-famous author of cookbooks, Robert Carrier, this is the perfect choice for a meal at any time. Not only is the food as excellent as one might expect, under his watchful eye, but the décor, too, is just lovely. I love the little garden room with greenery growing all over the place, pink cloths, cane chairs, and candles. There is also an exotic "red" room. Aside from all these distractions, the main star of the place is still the excellent cuisine, generally French. Open for lunch from 12:30 to 3 P.M. and for dinner from 7:30 to 11:30 P.M. Fixed-price lunch £2.75 ($7.37); fixed-price dinner £3.95 ($9.87); both are three-course meals. Specialties include *brandade* of smoked trout, Fillet of Beef in Shirtsleeves with horse radish Chantilly, lamb in Greek pastry, and Mr. Carrier's Special Chocolate Fancy to top it off.

LE CARROSSE 19–21 Elystan Street, S.W.3 Tel: 584-5248

Close to King's Road and the Victoria and Albert Museum. A very chic, intimate, personally run Chelsea restaurant elegantly designed by David Hicks. The high-class French cuisine is supplemented by interesting international specialties such as lamb Shrewsbury, *scallopines au pistou*, and *petit pot au chocolat*. Open for dinner from 7 to 11:30 P.M., weekday evenings only. Closed most bank holidays and for two weeks in August. Average three-course meal £2.65 ($6.62).

CONNAUGHT RESTAURANT at the Connaught Hotel, Carlos Place, W.1 Tel: 499-7070

Situated in one of the world's most famous hotels, this restaurant is equal to the best anywhere in the world. The atmosphere is very staid and conservative, much like an exclusive English club, but the service is absolutely superb. Every dish from the pâté to the desserts is a culinary masterpiece. If you happen to be with a companion, do come early and have a drink at the bar where you can ogle the celebrities who make this a regular meeting place. Open for lunch from 12:30 to 3 P.M., and for dinner from 6:30 to 11 P.M. Fixed-price lunch from £2.75 ($6.87); fixed-price dinner from £3 ($7.50).

68 LONDON

LE COQ D'OR Stratton Street, W.1 Tel: 629-7807
Close to Shepherd's Market. Spacious, elegant atmosphere enhanced by genuine French tapestry walls. The restaurant has efficient, friendly service and offers classical French desserts. Open for lunch from 12:30 to 3 P.M. and for dinner from 7 to 11 P.M. Closed Sundays and all bank holidays. Average three-course meal £3.50 ($8.75).

DORCHESTER GRILL AND TERRACE RESTAURANT in the Dorchester Hotel, Park Lane, W.1 Tel: 629-8888
The kitchen is manned by a Swiss chef, Monsieur Kaufeler, who rules his staff with an iron hand. Nothing less than perfection is allowed to leave his kitchen, and the cuisine ranks at the top of the list in London. In one of the most popular hotels in London, many of the dinner guests are bound to be recognizable personalities. The Grill Room is done in a beautiful Spanish motif and is open for lunch from 12:30 to 2:30 P.M. and for dinner from 7 to 11 P.M. The Terrace Room is open from 12:30 to 2:30 P.M. and from 6 P.M. to 1 A.M. Closed Sundays. Should you feel like soft dinner music or dancing this is the place, as the Terrace Room is one of the few left in London with such pursuits. A good but expensive à la carte menu.

THE GARDEN 9 Henrietta Street, W.C.2 Tel: 240-0088
Close to the National Gallery, Trafalgar Square, Royal Opera House. A strikingly modern restaurant designed by David Hicks, in the heart of Covent Garden. English specialties with Continental overtones, such as: stuffed escallope of veal, homemade terrines, and lemon chicken with tarragon. Open for lunch from 12:30 to 2:30 P.M. and for dinner from 7:30 to 11:45 P.M. Closed Saturdays for lunch, all day Sundays and bank holidays, and for three weeks in August. Average three-course meal £2.65 ($6.62).

LE GAVROCHE 61 Lower Sloane Street, S.W.1 Tel: 730-2820
Managed by two brothers, Michel and Albert Roux, one of whom acts as the chef and the other the maître d'. The chef never ceases to maintain his high standard of perfection and attends to even the smallest detail himself. One of London's top restaurants, where the excellent service equals the excellence of the cuisine. Open for dinner only from 7 P.M. to midnight. Average dish runs about £2 ($5). Closed Sundays and bank holidays.

THE GAY HUSSAR 2 Greek Street, W.1 Tel: 437-0973
Close to Soho Square and theaterland. A tiny, intimate, restaurant with food based on mid-19th-century Hungarian recipes, such as Transylvanian stuffed cabbage, roast gosling, red cabbage, wild cherry soup, and chicken paprika. Open for lunch from 12:30 to 2:30 P.M. and for dinner from 5:30 to 11:30 P.M. Closed Sundays and bank holidays. Average three-course meal £2.25 ($5.62).

GENNARO'S Dean Street, W.1 Tel: 435-3950
London has a vast number of Italian restaurants, but there is only one Gennaro's. In its cooking, wine, and service and in its elegant Roman patrician décor and spacious elegance, it is the most distinguished of all. It is also one of Princess Margaret's favorites, as well as that of other celebrities. The menu displays an immense variety with 12 different pasta dishes alone and a similar abundance of choice in other areas, too. Many of the specialties come from the most refined gastronomic region of Italy,

Wining and Dining

the Emilia Romana, where cream and herbs are used. The excellent wine list contains a remarkable range of Italian wines, logically classified by wine regions.

THE GRANGE 39 King Street, W.C.2 Tel: 240-2939

Close to the British Museum and the Royal Opera House. A distinguished restaurant designed by David Hicks. Well known for generous fixed-price menu that includes wine and service. The homemade pâtés and the beef Wellington are perfect. Open for lunch from 12:30 to 2:30 P.M. and for dinner from 7:30 to 11:45 P.M. Closed Saturdays for lunch, and all day Sundays and some bank holidays. Average three-course meal £3 ($7.50).

INIGO JONES 14 Garrick Street, W.C.2 Tel: 836-6456

Close to the Royal Opera House and theaters. Its proximity to cinema and theaters makes it very popular for late-night dining. The atmosphere is very interesting, with brick walls and arches, candlelight, greenery, etc. Very romantic. Try the *blinis au saumon* (thin buckwheat pancakes with smoked salmon, covered with cream sauce) or the *carré d'agneau en croûte* (boned saddle of lamb in a puff pastry). Open for lunch from 12:30 to 2:30 P.M. and for dinner from 6 P.M. to midnight. Closed Saturdays for lunch and all day most bank holidays. Average three-course meal £4 ($10).

KEATS Downshire Hill, Hampstead N.W.3 Tel: 435-1499

Close to Keats House (where the romantic poet lived for two years) and the Heath. Using only fresh ingredients and specializing in serious cooking of the highest order, it claims to be able to cook any classical dish to order. Especially good with fish and game. Don't let the simple provincial-type atmosphere throw you, the food is of the highest level, surprisingly enough for such a small restaurant. The truffles are flown in and the chestnuts are preserved in brandy. The live trout, prawns, and lobster are fresh from a tank so you can see exactly what you're getting before your dish is prepared. Open weekdays for dinner only from 7 P.M. to midnight, and for lunch Sundays. Closed Christmas Day and Boxing Day. Average three-course meal £3 ($7.50).

LEITHS 92 Kensington Park Road, W.1 Tel: 229-4481

Close to Portobello Road (and the street antique market). An elegant Victorian house in a residential street, it reflects Prudence Leith's highly personal taste in a short, *soigné* menu that changes seasonally. No gimmicks, no rules on dress. Atmosphere is extremely pleasant and comfortable, and the food and service flawless. Try Leith's duckling with almonds or its sweetbreads with cream and Calvados, which is a new treat. For dessert, how about Grand Marnier orange pancakes? Open for dinner only from 7 P.M. to midnight. Closed Christmas Day and Boxing Day. Average three-course meal £3.75 ($9.37).

MAISON PRUNIER 72 St. James's Street, S.W.1 Tel: 493-1373

Close to St. James's Palace. The same concern runs the two famous Prunier Restaurants in Paris, and this one is no less excellent than its two pace-setting twins. It specializes in French cooking, particularly seafood; try the *soufflé de turbot* with Hollandaise sauce, or the *filet de sole Prunier*. Open for lunch from noon to 2:30 P.M. and for dinner from 6 to 11:30 P.M. Open Sundays, but closed bank holidays. Average three-course meal £4 ($10).

MARIO AND FRANCO'S TRATTOO 2 Abingdon Road, W.8
Tel: 937-4448

Close to Kensington High Street Shopping Centre. Unusual, exotic garden atmosphere created by a theater designer, with lots of greenery and little intimate tables. Piano bar in the evenings. They specialize in Italian food, but one dish that is not Italian and is certainly my favorite is Satay Malayan (marinated pork strips, skewered, with hot sauce and cool cucumber). *Penne alla carbonara* is also good. This is a thick pasta with a sauce of egg, cheese, and crispy bacon. Open for lunch from noon to 3 P.M. and for dinner from 7 P.M. to 1:30 A.M. Average three-course meal £2.50 ($6.25).

MILO AND FRANCO'S TIBERIO 22 Queen Street, Mayfair W.1 Tel: 629-3561

Luxuriously appointed, elegance combined with daring and some unique décor features. Their specialty is classical Italian and every dish is mouth-watering. Try the Neapolitan seafood salad for starters, or the young lobster with melted butter and garlic mayonnaise. Whatever you choose, I can assure you you won't be disappointed. Open for lunch from noon to 3 P.M. and for dinner from 7 P.M. to midnight. Closed Saturdays for lunch, and all day Sundays. Average three-course meal £4 ($10). They have dancing in the evening.

MIRABELLE 56 Curzon Street, W.1 Tel: 499-4636

This is not only one of the most beautiful restaurants in London, but the most popular as well. Who wouldn't wish to dine in their lovely, romantic garden in the summertime? That of course, is why it is so difficult to get in and it is recommended that you book well in advance. Dining at the Mirabelle is well worth a special place in your memory book, and you will no doubt come back every time you're in London. The cuisine is exquisite, matched only by the service. Open for lunch from 1 to 2:15 P.M. and for dinner from 7:15 to 11 P.M. Closed Sundays and bank holidays. Average individual dish £1.50 ($3.75).

L'OPERA 32 Great Queen Street, W.C.2 Tel: 405-9020

Close to the British Museum and Royal Opera House. A plush Edwardian restaurant in the heart of theaterland, very convenient for dinner prior to, or after, the show. They specialize in French Mediterranean-style food such as *bouillabaisse, couscous à la façon du chef, shiskebab à la Turque*. Open for lunch from 12:15 to 2:30 P.M. and for dinner from 6 to midnight. Closed Saturdays for lunch, and all day Sundays and bank holidays. Average three-course meal £2.50 ($6.25).

THE PARK RESTAURANT Hyde Park Hotel, Knightsbridge, S.W.1 Tel: 235-2000

The most elegant dining room in London. Large terrace windows open onto Hyde Park and through the trees the brightly colored sails on the Serpentine and the occasional pageantry of the Queen's Cavalry riding by can be seen. A distinguished clientele enjoys, in spaciousness and luxury, the unobtrusive and friendly service that enhances the classical French cuisine. The chef will prepare a number of *spécialités de la maison,* such as *suprême de turbot Hyde Park* (braised in champagne, with lobster and caviar in a sauce) or *poulet poêle Serpentine* (the sauce is made with brandy, *foie gras,* truffles, and cream). The cellars are noted for having some of the finest wines in London.

Wining and Dining 71

QUAGLINO'S Hotel Meurice, 16 Bury Street, St. James's S.W.1 Tel: 930-6767
Real live trees, displays of rare *objets d'art* and old master paintings add distinction to the elegant, new décor of this world-famous restaurant. The bright, cheerful setting created by the simulated daylight at lunchtime changes to glamorous dimness at dinnertime for dancing to the music of two bands. The great traditions of superb French cuisine, the finest wine, and impeccable service go naturally with this elegant setting. Of the great specialties of the house, only a couple need to be mentioned as examples to set the standard: *Felices de Sole Madrilène* (sole fillets on a bed of *aubergines,* with sauce Bercy, purée of mushrooms and shallots), and *suprême de volaille Côte d'Azur* (cooked in butter with *courgettes, aubergines,* tomatoes, and peppers). Open until 1:30 A.M. Closed Sundays.

LE RELAIS Café Royal, 68 Regent Street, W.1 Tel: 437-9090
Founded in 1865 by the Frenchman Daniel Nicol, the Café Royal continues its supremacy based on the finest traditional cuisine. For many years it has been known as one of the top restaurants in Europe, with one of the best cellars in existence, and as the London meeting place of the famous. In 1968, when the Automobile Association first made a classification of restaurants, it was one of the only two to merit the top rank of Five Crossed Knives and Forks. Le Relais specializes in French regional cuisine, featuring a selection from a different province each month. The rest of the à la carte menu is based on a French bourgeois cuisine.

THE RIDDLESDALE ROOM Cavendish Hotel, Jermyn Street, S.W.1 Tel: 930-2111
This is one of the very few restaurants in London that remain open 24 hours a day, seven days a week. It has an attractive modern décor, equally friendly and welcoming at night and in the daylight. The menu is international and British, including such favorites as calves' liver with bacon and onions, chicken pancake *Princesse,* chicken Marion, lamb cutlets Reform, and sirloin steak *au poivre.* A wide choice of freshly cooked vegetables is served from a special heated trolley, and the service is remarkably quick and efficient. An ideal place for meeting friends when shopping, on business, or before and after the theater, for it is but a stone's throw from Piccadilly Circus.

SAVOY HOTEL RESTAURANT at the Strand, W.C.2 Tel: 836-4343
This is definitely the place for a very romantic dinner, with its crystal chandeliers, red plush seats and true elegant atmosphere. From here there is a beautiful view of the river, if you decide to come for lunch. For dinner you can enjoy an excellent cabaret show. The menu is primarily French and each dish is well prepared. Open for lunch from 12:30 to 2:30 P.M. and for dinner from 7:30 P.M. to 3 A.M. Closed Sundays. Fixed-price lunch £2.50 ($6.25); dinner from £4 ($10).

THE STABLE 123 Cromwell Road, S.W.7 Tel: 370-1203
Close to London museums and Albert Hall. A relaxed and unusual candle-lit atmosphere, with quiet alcoves, old wood beams, hay wagons and a Spanish singer and guitarist, makes this a perfect choice for a lovely, comfortable evening. Open for lunch from noon to 2:30 P.M. and for dinner from 7 P.M. to 2:30 A.M. Closed Sundays and bank holidays. Average three-course meal £3.50 ($8.75).

72 LONDON

THE SUMMIT RESTAURANT St. George's Hotel, Langham Place, W.1 Tel: 580-0111
Next to Broadcasting House and only a stone's throw from Oxford Circus and Harley Street, this restaurant, on the 14th floor of the hotel, has a magnificent view over the rooftops of London. Decorated in a welcoming contemporary style, it is designed on two levels so that an attractive view can be enjoyed by all the guests. There is a large classical French menu with an addition of a different roast on the trolley each day. One of the most popular house specialties is the *suprême de volaille Marina*, which is cooked in butter with mushrooms, tomatoes, brandy, cream, and parsley. Wines carefully selected from Europe's principal wine-growing areas are available at reasonable prices.

THE TEMPLARS GRILL Waldorf Hotel, Aldwych, W.C.2 Tel: 836-2400
Built on the probable site of the medieval jousting ground of the Knights Templar, its traditional connection with The City is commemorated in several attractive features: there is a row of bow-fronted shops of bygone days, the now-defunct street vendors of London are depicted and the old Forge represents one installed on this site in 1235. Other mementoes include a milk cart, ingeniously converted into a refrigerated buffet. The location is ideal, close to many theaters and Fleet Street, the western gateway to the City. It is ideal for after-theater suppers. The Templars Grill offers a unique selection of city of London specialties—in addition to the rest of its mainly British traditional repertoire including wardin pie, salmon banker-style and Lemon Powset with King Harry's shoestrings. Open until midnight.

TOP OF THE TOWER Maple Street, W.1 Tel: 636-3000
Situated at the top of the Post Office Tower, 580 feet above London, the restaurant *revolves* once every 30 minutes. You'll find it an ideal place from which to view all London. Modern décor and a good French menu. Their specialties are *scampi en plein ciel, filets de sole sur les toîts*. Average three-course meal £3 ($7.50).

TRADER VIC'S Hilton Hotel, Park Lane, W.1 Tel: 493-7586
Trader Vic's is known, I think, throughout the world, but certainly to Americans, and this one is very much like all the others. There is always the luxurious, romantic, Polynesian atmosphere and exotic drinks. For the atmosphere alone it is worth having a meal here, but the food certainly measures up to the highest standards. The menu is huge and it is almost impossible to decide what to have. Of course the best way to settle that problem is to order several different dishes and share them with your companion if you're lucky enough to have one. Whether your selection is French, Western, Chinese, or Polynesian (cooked in smoke in a typical Polynesian-style oven), one dish is every bit as delicious as another. Open for lunch from noon to 3 P.M. and for dinner from 6:30 P.M. to 1 A.M. Average individual dish £1.50 ($3.75).

THE WALDORF RESTAURANT Waldorf Hotel, Aldwych, W.C.2 Tel: 836-2400
Spaciousness, tall windows with flowing drapes, and glittering chandeliers create an atmosphere of Edwardian opulence in this elegant restaurant. It offers not only perfectly balanced set luncheons and dinners, but also a wide choice from an expensive, classical à la carte menu. This includes

a number of the chef's specialties, such as *Escalope de veau Elizabeth*, which is dramatically finished at the table. Pre-theater dinners are a specialty. At lunchtime this is an ideal place for meeting friends or after shopping or before a matinee. Open Sundays.

WHITE TOWER RESTAURANT   1 Percy Street, W.1   Tel: 636-8141

Not a White Tower as we know it in America, but truly a Greek temple of exotic cuisine. In fact it is considered Britain's finest Greek restaurant. Its owner, Mr. Stais, spares no effort to keep it that way. The menu is quite a masterpiece in itself, not only for the wide variety of excellent dishes it lists, but also for the romantic, detailed descriptions of each. My favorite is the moussaka, a succulent casserole sort of affair with ground beef, eggplant, spices, and a topping of mashed potatoes. But then all of the dishes are mouth-watering, including the non-Greek dishes. If you are on a diet, there are even good English grills to keep you happy. Open for lunch from 12:30 to 3 P.M. and for dinner from 6:45 to 10:30 P.M. Closed Sundays and bank holidays. Average à la carte dish about £1.60 ($4).

WILTON'S   27 Bury Street, S.W.1   Tel: 930-8391

This lovely Victorian-style restaurant goes way back to the days of William IV. It is presided over by the sparkly-eyed, 90-year-old Mr. Marks, who is only too happy to regale you with charming stories of years gone by. Frequented by denizens of the financial world—you may even pick up a good stock market tip or two. Oysters, Scottish salmon, and the lamb are excellent, as is everything else. The accent is on English-style cooking. Open for lunch from noon to 3 P.M. and for dinner from 6 to 10:45 P.M. Closed Saturdays, Sundays, and bank holidays. Average dish about £1.75 ($4.37).

Moderate

THE CARVERY   Cumberland Hotel, Marble Arch, W.1; Regent Palace Hotel, Glasshouse Street, W.1; Strand Palace Hotel, the Strand, W.C.2.

So successful was one that there are now three in three different hotels. They are the perfect place to enjoy the typical roast beef that the English are so famous for. But you're not limited to roast beef as they also have roast pork and roast spring lamb. The beauty of it is you eat all you want and you serve yourself. When you sit down at your table you are served a bowl of salad, a bowl of soup, a slice of melon, or a shrimp cocktail. Then you go to the carving table and help yourself to whatever roast you wish, plus roast potatoes and a good selection of vegetables. Naturally, there is the famous Yorkshire pudding that you shouldn't miss. If you are more in the mood for a cold luncheon, there is also a good selection of cold meats and salads that you may indulge in. If you have any room left after a huge meal, you have an excellent selection of desserts from the rolling trolley. And in the end your bill will be a mere £1.65 ($4.12), no matter how much you have eaten.

CASA PEPE   52 Dean Street, W.1   Tel: 437-3916

In the center of theaterland this too is a favorite of theater-goers and performers. Though I don't like the way all the tables are lined up one next to the other along the wall, I do like the Spanish décor and especially the flamenco entertainment. The food of course is also Spanish and they do serve an excellent *paella, zarzuela,* and *pollo con sanfaina.* Open for lunch from noon to 3 P.M. and for dinner from 6 to 11:30 P.M. Closed Sundays, Christmas Day, and Good Friday. Average three-course meal £1.75 ($4.37).

CASSE CROUTE 1 and 1A Cale Street, S.W.3 Tel: 352-4711
Near King's Road in Chelsea. A very old, established and intimate restaurant specializing in high-quality French cuisine. The linens are soft and luxurious, the lights are dim, and there are shuttered doors with greenery here and there—in short, a very romantic atmosphere. The cuisine of course is French and some of their specialties are *coq au vin* and duck *à l'orange.* Open for lunch from noon to 3 P.M. and for dinner from 7:15 P.M. to midnight. Closed Mondays for lunch. Average three-course meal £2.20 ($5.50).

CHRISTOPHE 9 St. Christopher's Place, W.1 Tel: 486-1851
This has a splendid mirrored décor with a lovely garden atmosphere that is bound to please any woman. One doesn't usually expect to see this kind of place in the heart of London and it is always well appreciated. There are tables and a long counter on one side where all the dishes are set out to tempt you before ordering. Open for lunch from noon to 2:30 P.M. and for dinner from 7 to 11 P.M. Closed Saturdays for lunch, and all day Sundays and bank holidays. Average three-course meal £2 ($5).

CHEZ SOLANGE 35 Cranbourn Street, W.C.2 Tel: 836-5886
Near Trafalgar Square. There are three different floors here: a Victorian ground floor; a cellar with French bourgeois cuisine; a chalet-type ground floor. They have a large cellar with many lesser-known French wines. Some of these specialties are *gratin de crabe frais Côte d'Emeraude, cassoulet toulousain,* and *entrecôte* with sauce bordelaise. Open for lunch from noon to 2:15 P.M. and for dinner from 5:30 P.M. to 12:30 A.M. Closed Sundays and bank holidays. Average three-course meal £1.95 ($4.87).

DIZZY DINER 25 Basil Street, S.W.3 Tel: 589-8444
Just at the back of Harrods Department Store in Knightsbridge. An eating house dedicated to Disraeli, Queen Victoria's famous prime minister, with a real old-fashioned setting. The menu is listed on a blackboard and it changes every two weeks, with 15 starters, 15 main courses, and 15 sweets. Featuring international bistro-style dishes. Open for lunch from noon to 3 P.M. and for dinner from 7 to 11:30 P.M. Open Sundays, but closed Christmas Day and Boxing Day. Average three-course meal £1.75 ($4.37).

FLANAGANS 3 Leicester Place, W.C.2 Tel: 437-5164
Just off Leicester Square, this is a turn-of-the-century seafood house and most charming. The décor looks more like an attic of discarded memorabilia with stuffed animals, old street signs, and silly antiques. They even have the old-fashioned piano player who in no time at all has the entire place singing old-time ditties. You'd better be hungry—the portions are most generous. Should you be in doubt as to what to order, your hostess will be only too happy to recommend lobster Lily Langtry, which she insists was Edward VII's favorite. The unroyal cost is only £1.90 ($4.75); and the other dishes, as generous as they are, are even less expensive. Open for lunch from noon to 3 P.M. and for dinner from 6 P.M. to midnight.

Wining and Dining 75

Open Sundays. Fixed-price lunch 62p ($1.55). Also at: 37 St. Martin's Lane, W.C.2; 11 Kensington High Street, W.8.

L'ESCARGOT BIENVENU 48 Greek Street, W.1 Tel: 437-4460

In Soho and close to most West End theaters. A restaurant originated in 1892 by Georges Gaudin, with old-fashioned French provincial décor and opening hours suited to theater diners. Specialties include *carbonnade de boeuf* and *sardines grillées.* Open for lunch from noon to 2:30 P.M. and for dinner from 6 to 11 P.M. Closed Saturdays, Sundays, and bank holidays. Average three-course meal £2 ($5).

THE HUNGRY HORSE 196 Fulham Road, S.W.10 Tel: 352-7757

Near Chelsea's Kings Road. A very cute, country-type place specializing in good typical British food such as steak, kidney and mushroom pie, Scotch roast beef and Yorkshire pudding, and fresh salmon fishcakes. All the foods are pleasingly arranged on a black-and-white checked tile buffet counter for your selection. Open for dinner from 6:30 P.M. to midnight. Lunch is served only on weekends, from 1 to 3 P.M. Closed Christmas Day, Good Friday, and the last two weeks of August. Average three-course meal £2 ($5).

THE IVY 1 West Street, W.C.2 Tel: 836-4751

In the Ivy, a favorite of stage and screen personalities, you might easily rub elbows with Rex Harrison and the like. Every day the chef features a different specialty. One of my favorites was the Aylesbury duck with Curaçao liqueur and oranges at £1.60 ($4). Other specialties are *escalope de veau Delysia* and *tournedos Dini.* And to top it all off there is a dessert trolley wheeled to your table with a mouth-watering selection of desserts. Open for lunch from noon to 3 P.M. and for dinner from 6 P.M. to midnight. Closed Saturdays for lunch, and all day Sundays and Christmas Day. Average three-course meal £2 ($5).

MAGGIE JONES'S 6 Old Court Place, Kensington Church Street, W.8 Tel: 937-6462

Close to Kensington Palace, Kensington Park, and Kensington High Street shops. An authentic English farmhouse restaurant with old oaken tables, high-backed benches, and candlelight. Good hearty English food such as chicken and artichoke pie and steak and mushroom pie, with English "puds" and trifle for dessert. Open for lunch from noon to 2:30 P.M. and for dinner from 7 P.M. to midnight. Closed Sundays and some bank holidays. Average three-course meal £2 ($5).

MR. CHOWS MONT PELIER GRILL 13 Mont Pelier Street, S.W.7 Tel: 589-0032

In Knightsbridge near Harrods. With a name like this, naturally you are expecting Chinese food. Wrong! Would you believe Italian? Yes, Italian, and, furthermore, *good Italian.* Before I go into a description of the food I'd better explain the name. Michael Chow comes from a very famous Chinese theatrical family and was at one time an actor himself. But I guess he had had enough Chinese food in his lifetime, so he decided to settle for good Italian food. The first level features a Spanish décor (to further enhance the international flavor) and the level above has a very springy gardenlike atmosphere with fresh flowers and a skylight. Their specialties are seafood and steak, but the seafood is really something to see. It's prominently displayed so that you can select exactly what you wish. Average three-course meal £2.50 ($6.25); but the portions are so generous that any of the individual dishes is quite sufficient. Open for lunch from 12:30 to 3 P.M. and for dinner from 7 P.M. to midnight. Open every day. Their fame has spread, so it is wise to make a reservation.

NICK'S DINER   98 Ifield Road, S.W.10   Tel: 352-5641 (day), 352-0930 (evening)
Close to Earls Court, this is one of the first small, friendly bistros specializing in unusual food and cheerful informality. Their specialties are deviled spare ribs and *filet de boeuf en croûte*. Their hamburger in a very special sauce is also very good. Open for dinner from 7:30 to 11:30 P.M. Closed Sundays and bank holidays. Average three-course meal £2.25 ($5.62).

SIMPSON'S-IN-THE-STRAND   100 Strand, W.C.2   Tel: 836-9112
An old traditional landmark that never skimps on its food or service. Thick slices of beef or mutton are carved right before your eyes on a trolley at your table, and of course this comes with a full complement of Yorkshire pudding and vegetables—for only £1.30 ($3.25). The waiters wear long, stiff, white aprons and walrus moustaches, and serve you quickly and efficiently. This is a very famous restaurant and it is a good idea to have a reservation. Closed Sundays.

TRAT WEST   143 Edgware Road, W.2   Tel: 723-8203
Close to Marble Arch. Cool décor in the Sardinian fashion with a host of Scarfe caricatures and an interesting selection of bronzes. Their specialty, *bistecca alla pizzaiola*, is particularly good, as are the barbecued spare ribs. Open for lunch from noon to 3 P.M. and for dinner from 6 P.M. to midnight. Closed Sundays. Average three-course meal £2.30 ($5.75).

VECCHIA RICCIONE   11 Upper St. Martin's Lane, W.C.2   Tel: 836-5121
Near Trafalgar Square. To me this is one of the gayest, most entertaining places in all of London, and at the top of the list of my favorites. All the waiters and the owners sing constantly and make friends of every guest. The proprietor, Otello, is quite a showman himself with a carnation behind his ear that he bestows upon some lucky lady. When you leave, everyone shouts their goodbyes as though you're really parting from a family, which, I suppose, is the greatest description of the place—just one big, happy home. Of course it is noisy, but you would expect that in an Italian family. You simply cannot help but join the spirit of the place and you cannot be anything but cheerful here. Not to come here would be to miss a glorious experience. The antipasto is fabulous, a big cart of goodies: shrimp or crab cocktail, stuffed mushrooms, tomatoes, eggplant, peppers, and artichokes. You name it, it's there. Then you can start on the main course! The dinner comes with braised celery, brussels sprouts, potatoes, etc. They really nearly force-feed you. The dessert cart, too, is an experience—all sorts of cakes, fruits in wine, their own *marrons glacés*, fruit salad, fresh strawberries in cream, and so on. If you like, they will give you a mixed plate of all the desserts for 50p ($1.25). You need never fear coming here alone—they treat women like royalty! This is one place I guarantee you will enjoy, no matter what your taste or personality. It is a small cellar of a place with barrels on the ceiling and frescoes on the wall, and they often just turn off the lights, turn up the music, and

Wining and Dining

everyone sings. Open for lunch from noon to 3 P.M. and for dinner from 6 to 11:30 P.M. Closed Sundays. Average à la carte dish about £1.20 ($3).

Inexpensive

ALVARO PIZZA E PASTA 57 Haymarket, S.W.1

A very rustic type of place, featuring a huge, round brick oven where they bake the pizza. The décor is right out of some little Italian village, with straw chairs and scrubbed wooden tables. There are ten different types of pizza plus several different pasta choices, each 38p ($.95).

ANDREA'S CONTINENTAL RESTAURANT 22 Charlotte Street, W.1

Excellent and inexpensive Greek cuisine; very popular among those who know the difference. Try their *dolmades* (grape leaves stuffed with lamb or beef, rice, spices, and tomatoes), 50p ($1.25). If you have any room left, try the typical Greek pastries, of which *baklava* is the most typical; it is extremely rich, made with honey and nuts, all dripped gooily over flaky pastry. Open for lunch from noon to 3 P.M. and for dinner from 7 P.M. to 2 A.M.

THE BAKER AND OVEN 10 Paddington Street, W.1 Tel: 935-5072

Back around the beginning of the century, this was a real-life bakery. What was once the ovens are now brick-lined alcoves into which tables have been placed for your dining pleasure. A proper dining room is also to be found on the lower level, in what was once the basement. They serve typically English food and very good, at that (though the onion soup may hardly be classified as English). The steak, kidney, and mushroom pie is one of their specialties at 77p ($1.92). Whatever you have, you must try to save room for dessert, which in this case is hot apple pie with whipped country cream poured over it—that is, if you can afford the calories. Open for lunch from noon to 3 P.M. and for dinner from 6 to 10 P.M. Closed Saturdays for lunch, all day Sundays and bank holidays, and for three weeks in August.

BARQUE & BITE on Regent's Canal, opposite 15 Prince Albert Road, N.W.1 Tel: 485-8137

An actual riverboat tied to the dock in Regent's Park, this is a real fun place, aside from its excellent British-style cuisine. The menu is huge, with even a few French dishes scattered among the English specialties. Chicken Kiev goes for 95p ($2.37). The mouth-watering desserts are bound to put you off your diet. Open for lunch from noon to 3 P.M. and for dinner from 6 to 10 P.M. Closed Saturdays for lunch and all day Sundays.

BELGRAVIA 9 Williams Street, S.W.1

Near Harrods Department Store and Hyde Park. In this charming, friendly place everyone is given a big welcome and delightful service. It is a favorite for shoppers in the area who know where to get a good meal quickly at a good price. The toast chicken in bread sauce goes for 65p ($1.62), and there are several good fish dishes at various prices. Closed Sundays.

LE BISTINGO 57–59 Old Compton Street (near Soho theaters and cinemas) Tel: 437-0784; 117 Queens Way, W.2 (close to Hyde Park) Tel: 727-0743; 7 Kensington High Street, W.1

78 LONDON

Tel: 937-0932; 65 Fleet Street, E.C.4 (close to law courts and St. Paul's Cathedral) Tel: 353-4436; 332-334 King's Rd., S.W.3 Tel: 352-4071; 56 Old Brompton Road, S.W.7 Tel: 589-1929

This is a chain of excellent bistros with the typical informal bistro atmosphere that draws a gay informal crowd. The menu is written on a blackboard and features French provincial cooking, plus English and Scotch steaks and fresh trout. Each has a different décor, but a three-course meal in any of them will cost £1.10 ($2.75). They are all open for lunch from noon to 3 P.M. and for dinner from from 6 P.M. to midnight.

THE BUDAPEST 9 Greek Street, W.1

A very simple but excellent restaurant specializing in Hungarian dishes. The menu features almost every Hungarian dish you can think of. The main dishes run from 80p ($2). The veal goulash is succulent, with its tender dumplings, at 90p ($2.25). For dessert, try the walnut pancake. I first had this in Hungary; and the one I had here at the Budapest is identical—a rich crêpe butter loaded with chopped walnuts. After that, all you have to do is worry about some way of getting away from the table because you'll hardly make it under your own steam! Open until 10:30 P.M.

THE CASSEROLE 338 King's Road, S.W.3 Tel: 352-2351

One of the oldest King's Road restaurants, packed with atmosphere and with an avant-garde clientele. They specialize in good English cuisine such as beef Victoria, roasted spare ribs, shepherd's pie, and roasted crown of English lamb. Open for lunch from 12:30 to 3 P.M. and for dinner from 7:30 P.M. to 12:30 A.M. Closed four days at both Christmas and Easter. Average three-course meal £1.50 ($3.75).

THE CATHAY 4 Glasshouse Street, Piccadilly Circus, W.1

The owner tells me this is the oldest Chinese restaurant in London and, judging from its popularity, it probably is. There are two floors done in typical Chinese style, but the second floor, with its huge windows overlooking Piccadilly Circus, is by far preferable. If you enjoy Chinese food, you will find your own favorites among the extensive list on the menu. However, if not there are five separate fixed-price menus, starting at £1.25 ($3.12).

CHESHIRE CHEESE 145 Fleet Street, E.C.4 Tel: 353-6170

An old ale house that goes back for many centuries and is an extremely popular place with sawdust on the floor, wood paneled walls, and (would you believe?) Wedgwood china. They serve good, hearty English-style food and one of the favorites is, of course, the roast beef with Yorkshire pudding for 90p ($2.25). Open for lunch from noon to 3 P.M. and for dinner from 6 to 11 P.M. Closed Saturdays for dinner, and all day Sundays.

THE COCKNEY PRIDE Piccadilly Circus, W.1

Victorian décor with velvet banquettes, brass oil-lantern light fixtures, cut-glass mirrors, etc., quite in contrast to the Cockney menus, which you will never understand! There is simply no other way to order except to have the waiter go down the list, explaining one dish after the other. However, everything is good and the portions rather generous. This is also a favorite spot of swinging London screen stars. Open for lunch from noon to 3 P.M. and for dinner from 6 to 11 P.M. Open every day.

Wining and Dining 79

THE CORDON BLEU RESTAURANT 31 Marylebone Lane, W.1 Tel: WE1-2931 Just off Wigmore Street.

The restaurant is run by the school of the same name and the food is prepared by those who have been lucky enough to complete the advanced courses. One would expect to pay a fortune for a meal here but you may be surprised to find that it really does fit into our budget category. There is a cold buffet table should you prefer a salad, cold meats, and the like or you may choose any one of the hot dishes, which begin at 80p ($2). There are generally a lot of unusual dishes, aside from the standard entrées, and it is great fun to try them, especially the sweets. Open only for lunch, from noon to 3 P.M., and for afternoon tea.

CRANK'S SALAD BOWL Marshall Street, W.1

Right around the corner from Carnaby Street. You'll be happy here if you are on a nature kick or a diet, since nothing but natural foods are served. Breads, cakes, and rolls are made from whole meal, stone-ground English flour. The vegetables, too, are nature's own with no artificial fertilizers. They even have tiger's milk, and, of all things, dandelion coffee! It is a favorite of London's dollies and, of course, models and other figure-conscious types. Salads from 25p ($.62). Open Monday through Friday from 10 A.M. to 8:30 P.M.

DANISH FOOD CENTER 2–3 Conduit Street, Mayfair, W.1

As you might imagine, the bill of fare consists solely of the open-faced sandwiches that Danes are so famous for. Wait until you are good and hungry before stopping here. Then order one of many different varieties, because otherwise it is impossible to make a selection from among these mouth-watering sandwiches. The prices run from 12½p ($.31) and up. Open Monday through Friday from 10 A.M. to 5 P.M., Saturday from 10 A.M. to 12:30 P.M. Closed Sundays.

THE DICKENS INN London Street, W.2

A replica of an old Elizabethan tavern, the likes of which you are unlikely to see anywhere else. The booths have velvet curtains on brass rods to pull if you prefer privacy. Naturally this is ideal if you have interesting dates! There are two bars in front, one of which is the Lamplighter's Doubles Bar where they serve double shots for almost the price of one. Food is typically English, and good and most generous. The usual kidney-and-steak pie goes for 70p ($1.75). Coffee lovers will be in their glory here for there is a choice of 8 super-special types to delight you. They are served in large goblets and ladled with fresh cream. Each 30p ($.75). Open for lunch from noon to 3 P.M. and for dinner from 7 to 10:30 P.M. Open Sundays.

THE DUMPLING INN 15A Gerrard Street, W.1   Tel: 437-2567

In Soho. I must say right from the beginning that the name is extremely misleading. Although you might expect German stews with dumplings, etc., this restaurant specializes in Peking cuisine! And if that doesn't present enough confusion, there is also the décor of the place, which is anything but Chinese—the Venetian murals, for instance. However, once you straighten out all these incongruities, you can settle down to some of the best Mandarin cooking in town. It is a good idea to go with one or two people so you can share the dishes and realy get an idea of what this style of cooking is all about. Don't hesitate to order several dishes as the portions are rather small. Do try the Chinese crêpes, filled with spiced minced meat, which is absolutely delicious at 40p ($1). They could serve as an appetizer, followed by the sliced duck with mushrooms for 80p ($2) as your main course.

FIORI'S   3 Edgware Road, Marble Arch, W.2
An excellent Italian restaurant with oak ceiling beams and sentimental touches interspersed among the modern décor. The *escalope bolognese* (veal sautéed in butter with ham and cheese) is delicious, at 75p ($1.87). Open for dinner only from 5:30 P.M. to 2 A.M. It is a popular spot for after theater for a vigorous night of dancing.

FORTNUM AND MASON   181 Piccadilly, S.W.1
This is actually one of the poshest gourmet food stores in all of England, in fact in all the world. You are served by clerks in tails, believe it or not! Established in 1707, and the clientele you see here is right out of Burke's Peerage. One would think the prices would be sky high in such an establishment; however, it is quite possible to have a snack here on a budget. At Fortnum's fountain you can have a sandwich for about $1 or select a "sweet" from the exquisite pastries available, with coffee. It is interesting just to dawdle over a snack or coffee and watch the rest of the clientele drift in and out. Open from 10 A.M. to 11:30 P.M.

FRIGATE   1 Upper St. Martin's Lane, W.C.2
This nautical restaurant is an interesting monument as well. It has three floors, all decorated as the interior of a four-masted clipper ship. There are bars and dining rooms on every level and everything is available, from a sandwich to a good hearty dinner, washed down by an "pint." A grilled rump steak complete with baked potato and mushrooms goes for 82p ($2.05), a bargain at half the price. Before choosing your dining room, wander around the place to get the feel of each room and check out the other diners—one may offer more interesting possibilities in terms of meeting someone than others.

THE GREAT AMERICAN DISASTER   335 Fulham Road, S.W.10
If you are lonesome for a good old American hamburger, this is the spot to try. But I mean a *real* hamburger, not the Wimpy's type that you'll find about the city. Real because the place was founded by an American, Peter Morton, who knows what a real hamburger should taste like. It is always jammed, especially with screen personalities such as Mia Farrow, Twiggy, Warren Beatty. Everybody befriends everyone else so this is a good place to meet some new people to see London with, especially Americans. A quarter-pound beefburger with French fries costs a mere 50p ($1.25) and it is charcoal broiled. You can also find American-style cheese cake, apple pie, and my favorite of favorites, good chocolaty, fudgy cake. You may drink all you wish of the good hearty American coffee, paying only for the first cup. There is another branch in Knightsbridge at 9 Beauchamp Place, S.W.3, Tel: 589-0992.

LONDON STEAK HOUSE   116 Baker Street, W.1   Tel: 935-1932
There are many of these steak houses but I rather like this one because of its green-and-yellow décor—exactly that of my own apartment—which makes me feel very much at home! There are oak-beamed ceilings and old fashioned gas-type lanterns, all of which makes for a very warm,

Wining and Dining

friendly ambiance. Steak is the star here, but there is also a list of seafood dishes. Everything is à la carte, though the prices are extremely good for the generous portions of food. Steak Diane costs a mere £1.20 ($3) and the sirloin fillet and rump steak come in three different sizes depending upon your appetite, 60p to £1.15 ($1.50 to 2.87). An extra-special, nice touch is the powdered pastries that are served free with your coffee. Open for lunch from noon to 3 P.M. and for dinner from 7 to 11 P.M. Open every day. Also at 31 Basil St., 17–20 Kendall St., and 29 Ebury St. as well as a good dozen scattered elsewhere around London.

MARIO AND FRANCO'S KING BOMBA 37 Old Compton Street, W.1 Tel: 437-4699

Near Soho and Shaftesbury Avenue. Old-style provision and delicatessen store turned into a chic fish and burger restaurant. Unusual, inexpensive evening specialty menu. They also serve real beefburgers and chili con carne in case you are homesick. Open from noon to midnight. Closed Sundays. Average three-course meal 86p ($2.15).

MR. CHOW 151 Knightsbridge, S.W.1 Tel: 589-7347

Close to Harrods. An extremely modern place, all done in white woodwork, floors, chairs, tablecloths, ceilings, etc., with modern aluminum light fixtures. A collection of modern painters is exhibited throughout. They specialize in Peking-style cooking. Open for lunch from noon to 3 P.M. and for dinner from 7 P.M. to midnight. Closed Christmas Day and Boxing Day. Average three-course meal £1.50 ($3.75).

MR. FOGG 66 Regent Street, W.1 Tel: 930-2473

There are 3 restaurants and 4 bars, all decorated in the theme of the Jules Verne film, *Around the World in 80 Days*. Each restaurant serves a different type of food. (More expensive, really not in this budget category, is the one called My Apartment where you actually grill your own steak right at the table. The steak costs £2.45 ($6.12), and they'll tell you exactly how to cook it.) In the budget category, you'll find chicken-in-the-basket in the Balloon Bar for 35p ($.87); and for a good juicy beefburger, try the Steam Packet, where a quarter-pound burger will cost you 40p ($1); spare ribs there are 62p ($1.55). In the Iron Horse, which is split into two levels, you sit in little railway compartments while you eat. Here salads start at 40p ($1). The Pizzeria offers a good selection of pizza pies, 40p to 68p ($1 to $1.70). If you are feeling more romantic, try the beaded-curtained Raj Bar, which will transport you right back to colonial India without the flick of an eyelash. Naturally the fare to be savored here is the authentic Indian curries from 35p ($.87) up. All in all, this is a great place to wander around, meet interesting people, and spend a pleasant couple of hours. Why not have lunch or dinner in one room, dessert and coffee in another, and an after-dinner drink in still another, to truly savor the flavor of the entire complex? The bars are open from 11 A.M. to 3 P.M. and from 5:30 to 11 P.M. The restaurants are open for lunch from noon to 3 P.M. and for dinner from 6 P.M. 1 A.M.

MUMTAZ 56 Edgware Road, W.2 Tel: 723-3243

A must if you like Indian food. The Mumtaz, with its very romantic and classical Indian décor, makes me feel as though I were back in India again. It has the little private alcoves and the bright colors so commonly used in India. There is even a special clay oven imported from India to cook the tandori dishes. Every possible kind of curry is available, but my favorite is the stuffed onion leaves with minced chicken at 30p ($.75), which I highly recommend. It is not at all too spicy for the average palate.

THE OLD KENTUCKY 54 Haymarket, S.W.1
It is just across the street from the American Express Office, which probably accounts in part for its popularity. If you are homesick for good old American-style food, this is the place for you. You can choose anything from pizza to pancakes. On the first floor there is the pancake parlor and the snack bar for more run-of-the-mill fancies; downstairs you will find the pizza parlor, where they also serve spaghetti. I wouldn't say the hamburgers are as good as some of those we have at home, but nevertheless they certainly are a treat in hamburgerless London. Everything is very budget priced which is no doubt the second reason for its popularity. Open every day until 11:30 P.M.

LA PAESANA 40 Uxbridge Street, W.8 Tel: 229-4332
Close to Portobello Road Antique Market. A good place to stop in after exploring the area. It is a fast-service restaurant but is often a good value for the money. Very gay, friendly surroundings, with checkered tablecloths, murals, vaulted ceilings, and Italian Continental cuisine. Open for lunch from noon to 3 P.M. and for dinner from 6 P.M. to midnight. Closed Christmas Day and Boxing Day. Average three-course meal £1.50 ($3.75).

PASTICCERIA AMALFI 31 Old Compton Street, W.11
Extremely good low-priced Italian restaurant, run by its owner, Mr. Sassano, who sees to it that everything is right up to snuff. Being in Soho, it is very convenient for an after-theater snack or dinner. Lasagne is my favorite at 30p ($.75), and the portion is so generous you really can't eat much else. Open for lunch from noon to 3 P.M. and for dinner from 6 P.M. to midnight.

THE PLACE 17 Dukes Road, W.C.1
On the top floor of an artist's studio, a favorite of the young hopefuls in the theatrical world, dancers, musicians, actors. It is a self-service place but the atmosphere is what makes the trip worthwhile. At lunch the menu starts at 20p ($.50) and in the evening at 50p ($1.25). The food is good and the portions generous. Drinks are reserved for members only; however, the membership fee is only 40p ($1).

THE RAW DEAL 65 York Street W.1
This is supposed to be London's only vegetarian restaurant. The proprietress, Mrs. Solley, takes the greatest of pride in developing new ways of using fresh vegetables, and the accent is on the organically grown. There is a counter in the back where you make all your selections, and then you sit at a bare wooden table on a bench. There is even a bulletin board with announcements of the current music concerts and other events of interest to this particular type of crowd. On Thursdays and Saturdays, there is folk music for entertainment, but there is a small cover charge of 10p ($.25).

ROLLEY'S 113 Jermyn Street, W.1
Just off Piccadilly Circus, a very quaint turn-of-the-century place with tiled walls, frosted globe light fixtures and plants all over the place. There is even an old-fashioned overhead ceiling fan. Drop in for a sandwich, milkshake, cake and coffee, or a plate of spaghetti if you like. The menu

offers something for everyone at any time of the day or night. Open every day until 1 A.M. A favorite for after theater or cinema.

ROMANO SANTI 50 Greek Street, W.1 Tel: 437-2350

Near Soho. A friendly restaurant claiming the best values in town, it specializes in shish kebab pilaff, moussaka d'Aubergines, and châteaubriand with Bernaise Sauce, plus other English and Continental dishes. Open for lunch from noon to 3 P.M. and for dinner from 6 to 11 P.M. Average three-course lunch £1 ($2.50); dinner 1.50 ($3.75).

THE SALISBURY 90 St. Martin's Lane, W.C.2

A quaint old Victorian pub that is very popular with British theatrical people. Here you can hear actors buzzing about the plays they were in, and in, or hope to be in, and watch the young hopefuls trying to meet the right people to break into the business. If you prefer privacy you can sit in the old-fashioned banquettes and eat at a copper-topped table, but the fun is really at the third bar, snacking with all the friendly regulars. There is a grill room, a proper dining room and a saloon. At the buffet, roast will cost you 55p ($1.37).

SAN LORENZO 22 Beauchamp Place, S.W.3 Tel: 584-1074

Specializing in Italian cuisine, the décor is anything but. It's very modern, with white brick walls and wooden tables and a sliding roof through which a tree grows. It is very popular and gets a lot of the young "with it" set, so it might be wise to book a reservation. There is a wide selection of dishes, all falling well within the budget rate of this category.

SCHMIDT'S 43 Charlotte Street, W.1

On the outer fringe of Soho. There is no sign out front so you will have to look for this. Inside, you will find a whole series of individual dining rooms, done in wood paneling, with beer mugs and Bavarian paintings for decorations. The portions are huge, yet the prices are mini, so this is a good bet for anyone on a budget. Wienerschnitzel is a favorite here, but you really have to be hungry to eat it. It comes accompanied with noodles, potatoes, two vegetables, rolls, and butter, all for the small pittance of 45p ($1.12)! Open every day until 10:30 P.M.

J. SHEEKEY, LTD 29–31 St. Martin's Court, W.C.2 Tel: 836-4118

Just next to the Wyndham and New Theatres, this is a great place for an after-theater snack and it is a favorite of London's stage and theater people, as the autographed photos on the wall will testify. A very gay, friendly, and sometimes noisy place that gives you the feeling of being in the middle of everything that is important at the moment. Dover sole at 90p ($2.25) is not only a good diet selection but a very good bargain as well, but that is just one of the dishes on the extensive list of seafood available. You can be sure it is all fresh, as this restaurant has been here since 1896 and has quite a reputation for its food. Open Monday through Friday from 12:15 to 8:30 P.M., and Saturdays from 12:15 to 3 P.M.

THE SHERLOCK HOLMES 10 Northumberland Street, W.C.2 Tel: 930-2644

If you have been intrigued by all the Sherlock Holmes books, plays, and movies, this is the place for you. They actually have an authentic replica of the living room of Sherlock Holmes from his home at 221B Baker St., mentioned so often in his novels. Typical English cuisine is served, in plain

84 LONDON

but generous portions. English dishes and grills begin at 60p ($1.50). Open for lunch from noon to 3 P.M. and for dinner from 6 to 10 P.M.

SHEZAN 16–22 Cheval Place, S.W.7 Tel: 589-7918

A large, colorful, very sophisticated restaurant, it is considered one of the world's best and most authentic. It is so comfortable that you may have a tendency to linger here, perhaps too because the food is so exquisite that you eat far more than you can really hold. You haven't lived until you've tried the tandori chicken! Open for lunch from noon to 3 P.M. and for dinner from 7 P.M. to midnight. Closed Sundays. Average individual dish 95p ($2.37).

STRAND CORNER HOUSE the Strand, W.C.2

Off Trafalgar Square. Belonging to the famous Lyons chain of restaurants, this is a complex of several different restaurants, something for every budget. There is the Trafalgar Room on the main floor where you can have a roast with all the vegetables, etc., for about 46p ($1.15). Upstairs you will find the carving room, similar to the one we mentioned earlier at the Cumberland Hotel. You serve yourself and eat as much as you like, going back to the carving table two and three times if your tummy can hold it. You are served either a shrimp cocktail or soup at your table, then you go to the carving table and help yourself. The total bill will be £1.60 ($4), which is just a bit over our budget rate—but I still consider this a bargain.

THE VICTORIA TAVERNS Strathearn Place, W.2 Tel: AMB-4554

A charming place incorporating three separate little havens. On the main floor you find a Victorian-type pub where you can sit in front of the fireplace or at one of the plushy window seats while you enjoy a pre-meal drink. After working up a nice glow, you can go downstairs to the Our Mutual Friend, which is very unique, intimate, and enjoyable. A 19th-century street has been re-created and the restaurant opens off of it, as does a curiosity shop. There is even an old gas lamplight to cast its bright shadows on the narrow street. As I said, most unusual. The food is simple but excellent English fare with a sirloin steak going for 85p ($2.12). But before you settle down to order dinner, do see the Theatre Bar on the top level, which is a mélange of interesting souvenirs of the famous Gaiety Theatre; sit in the white-and-gold boxes and chairs and let your mind drift back to what the theater life must have been in London back in the late 1800s.

THE VENUS KABOB HOUSE 2 Charlotte Street, W.1

An excellent restaurant specializing in Greek cuisine at budget prices. Kabobs, naturally, are the big thing here and lamb or pork kabobs served in a trio goes for 50p ($1.25). In the summertime you can sit outdoors and cool off with a large Greek salad for only 25p ($.62). Open every day from noon to 11:30 P.M.

CHAIN RESTAURANTS

Just as we have our McDonald's hamburger restaurants, Kentucky Fried Chicken, International Pancake House, etc., so the

Wining and Dining

British have their own chains. In fact, I'm quite sure they originated the idea in the first place. Since there are so many of them, they are budget-priced and the food is good, I feel they are worth mentioning here.

CHICKEN INN
There are five or six such inns around London, but the one you will probably find most to your liking, since it is open until midnight, is at 14 Leicester Square. The décor is adorable and looks just like an old country barn with plows and farming equipment all over the place as decorative items. You almost expect a chicken to pop onto your table and lay an egg while you are sitting there. Service is fast and the food is extremely good with generous portions, all at budget prices.

JOLYON
There are too many locations to mention addresses. They are literally all over London, almost as numerous as the famous pubs that dot the city. They are good for quick snacks and sandwiches. The food is good and the prices budget-geared.

KARDOMAH
With a name like this one might expect an Indian menu; on the contrary, they specialize in just plain good English food at budget prices. I wasn't able to track down the origin of the name other than to find out that it originated in 1844 in Liverpool and since then has spread all over London.

LYONS
The most famous and most numerous of the chains, they are scattered all over the city, in fact on just about every other corner. In any of them you can be sure of a good meal, fast but efficient service, and a moderate bill.

There are two Lyons complexes that you won't want to miss as they offer every possible kind of restaurant service you may be looking for. One is the Strand Corner House, Charing Cross Road, just off Trafalgar Square, which includes five restaurants running from budget to expensive, and even a night club. There is a hamburger snack bar on the ground floor and the Trafalgar Room for grills. On the first floor you have a choice of several restaurants: the Trident, for excellent seafood; the Carving Room, where you can eat all you wish of roast beef or lamb with all the trimmings; the Grill Room for the usual steak, chops, etc. All are very moderately priced and obviously this is a good place for just about anything you might have in mind in the way of good, solid, stick-to-the-ribs kind of food.

Next we have the Maison Lyons, conveniently located at the Marble Arch. Here again you have a choice of six different restaurants all with quaint names such as the Thingummajig for light snacks, Wimpy for hamburgers and frankfurters, though I am afraid I can't recommend the hamburgers. The Restful Tray is a self-service cafeteria-type of place for quick meals, and you have the Star Grill and the Red Carpet for more traditional-type meals. The Hayrack serves a budget three-course meal with only two prices on the menu. Any way you look at it, this is another diner's haven with such a selection of restaurants to choose from. If one is busy, you can always pop into the other.

QUALITY INN

They serve a good solid English-style meal as a rule, though they do have a few foreign selections from time to time. In good weather the one at 310 Regent Street is a good bet because of the outdoor café, a rarity in London. Open until 9 P.M. only. This is primarily the kind of place you would want to pop into for lunch, snack, or an early dinner. The food is good and the prices are very modest.

MEDIEVAL RESTAURANTS

These are places that take you back to the Middle Ages and serve you in exactly the same way that diners were served at that time—on long wooden tables with big mugs to drink from, huge roasts from which you will be served a large portion, wenches dressed in peasant blouses and dirndl skirts. This is the kind of place you go to for a full night of entertainment, because they do have singing and court jesters and everything to make your evening memorable. In other words, you don't go there just to eat and leave.

1520 A.D.   8081 St. Martin's Lane, W.C.2   Tel: 240-3978
This is a sixteenth-century room with the oak-beamed ceilings and entertainment that takes you back to the time of King Henry VIII, with jesters, dancing bears, and other spectacles of that era. The minstrels prevail upon the diners to join in. If you refuse, they will put you in the stocks and everybody will throw soft pieces of bread at you! The atmosphere is very lively and there is no embarrassment at all even when that happens. Price for the entire evening expensive, about £3 ($7.50). Open from 8 A.M. to 3 A.M., Sundays 7:30 P.M. till midnight.

MEDIAEVAL FEESTES   The Strand Corner House at Charing Cross, near Trafalgar Square, W.C.2   Tel: 930-7243
The name as well as everything on the menu is spelled as it was back in 1273 and it is all quite fun. Open Monday through Friday from 7:30 to 11 P.M. Dinner takes place in the banqueting hall with beamed ceilings and all the accompanying décor one would expect in such a place. The meal goes on and on and on and the court jesters and musicians perform continually, often persuading the guests to participate in the fun. Reservations are necessary. Prices are expensive but worth it.

RIVERSIDE RESTAURANTS

The river Thames has long associations with brilliant and, alas, sad events and its ever changing moods and daily bustle has fascinated onlookers through the ages. On long summer evenings it is pleasant to enjoy a leisurely meal at one of the many restaurants overlooking the Thames, while the dusk and twinkling lights of

Wining and Dining 87

autumn and winter lend their own mysterious enchantment. The following is a selection of restaurants and inns where a snack or a more relaxed meal may be enjoyed while watching the Thames flow by.

The Regent's Canal has a charm of its own, providing a respite from busy London. Some places to eat at along the canal are also listed here. Fixed-price three-course dinner runs from about £3.50 ($8.75); including wine, coffee, service, and taxes. It is advisable to phone for a lunch or dinner reservation.

THE ANGEL 21 Rotherhithe Street, Bermondsey, S.E.16 Tel: 237-3608
A quaint riverside tavern with historical associations, it has an excellent river view, particularly attractive in the evening. It is fun to just wander around on its several different levels from one bar to the other or one dining area to the other. The usual dark wood paneling as typical of pubs, low-beamed ceilings, and a charming ambiance. Open Monday through Friday for lunch and dinner. Closed Saturdays for lunch, and all day Sundays.

BARQUE & BITE on Regent's Canal, opposite 15 Prince Albert Road, N.W.1 Tel: 485-8137
Near London Zoo. A barge moored right on the canal. Open Monday through Friday for lunch and dinner, Saturdays for dinner only; closed Sundays. Also operates an evening dinner cruise on *The Lady Rose*. They usually just book parties on *The Lady Rose;* however, it you call their offices at 286-6101 you can very easily be allowed to join the party.

CITY BARGE 27 Strand-on-the-Green, Chiswick, W.4 Tel: 994-2148
Royal barges stopped at this attractive Elizabethan inn on the way to Hampton Court. Many historical touches add to its charm. Serves lunch Monday through Friday, and snacks every day.

FATHER THAMES Cadogan Pier, Chelsea Embankment, S.W.3 Tel: 402-4725
A restaurant-ship with a panoramic acrylic roof and a discotheque on the lower deck called the Guard's Room. Plies between Greenwich and Hampton Court. Open for lunch from 12:30 to 3 P.M. and for dinner from 8 to 11:30 P.M.

FESTIVAL GARDENS Battersea Park, S.W.11 Tel: 228-2226
Attractive gardens and fountain, cafeteria, fun fair, dolphins, children's zoo. On Chelsea Embankment.

KING'S HEAD AND EIGHT BELLS 50 Cheyne Walk, Chelsea, S.W.3 Tel: 352-1820
A popular Chelsea pub overlooking the Embankment. Serves lunch and dinner Tuesday through Saturday, lunch only on Saturdays, and snacks throughout the week.

THE MAYFLOWER 117 Rotherhithe Street, S.E.16 Tel: 237-4088
Restored after the 1940 blitz and reopened in 1955, it was originally called "The Shippe". From nearby, the *Mayflower* sailed in 1620 to the New

88 LONDON

World. Interesting relics of the past adorn the interior of the inn. Open Monday through Friday for lunch and dinner. Closed Saturdays for lunch, and all day Sundays.

OLD CALEDONIA Waterloo Pier, Victoria Embankment by Waterloo Bridge W.C.2   Tel: 240-2750

A paddle steamer moored at the Waterloo Bridge. Great fun. Open Monday through Sunday for lunch and dinner. Also cafeteria service from 10 A.M. to 10 P.M.

OLD SWAN   Battersea Church Road, S.W.11   Tel: 238-7152

A pleasant restaurant with attractive views of the river. Lunch and dinner Tuesday through Saturday, snacks throughout the week.

PRINCES ROOM   Tower Hotel, St. Katherine Way, E.1   Tel: 709-0840

Some tables in the restaurant have a river view. The Thames Bar and Terrace serve drinks and have a good view of a stretch of the Thames, overlooking the Tower Bridge.

RIVERSIDE   Southwark Bridge, E.C.4   Tel: 248-5586

Modern pub on the city side of the riverbank beside Southwark Bridge with a riverside terrace. Open Monday through Sunday for lunch and dinner.

ROYAL FESTIVAL HALL   Southbank, S.E.1   Tel: 928-2829

The restaurant offers superb views of the river Thames. At night it is a very romantic place, especially if you have an escort. Open Monday through Friday for lunch and dinner. Closed Saturdays for lunch. Also self-service restaurant, open Monday through Saturday from 10 A.M. to 11 P.M., Sundays from noon to 11 P.M., serving hot dishes, salads, tea, coffee, wine, etc.

SAMUEL PEPYS AT BROOKE WHARF   48 Upper Thames Street, E.C.4   Tel: 248-3048

This restaurant features the life of Samuel Pepys and overlooks the stretch of the river Thames that was described in Pepys's account of the fire of London in 1666. Specializing in Sunday roasts. Open for lunch and dinner, Saturdays for dinner only.

SAVOY HOTEL   Victoria Embankment, W.C.2   Tel: 836-4343

A restaurant with good views of the river Thames and a quiet ambiance. Open Monday through Saturday for lunch and dinner.

SLOOP JOHN D. at Cadogan Pier, Chelsea Embankment, S.W.3   Tel: 223-3341

Free-floating sloop near Battersea Festival Gardens. Open Tuesday through Saturday for dinner only, and for lunch only on Saturdays.

9
Nighttime Entertainment

London has probably the greatest nightly feast of entertainment staged in any city of the world. You have a choice of some 50 live theaters—and they give you everything you want, ranging from the classics (both old and new) at the Old Vic (across the river in South London) and the Aldwich to the avant-garde world of the Royal Court and the Round House.

Theaters like the Drury Lane, the Palace, and Her Majesty's specialize in lavish musicals, while the Palladium and the Victoria Palace are two homes of variety. At the Talk of the Town, there is dining and dancing as well as revue.

And everyone knows the famous names on the London stage—Laurence Olivier, Alec Guinness, Peter Ustinov, Ralph Richardson, Alastair Sims, Claire Bloom, Maggie Smith, Glenda Jackson, and many others.

The London daily, evening, and Sunday newspapers give details of programs at theaters and cinemas; and there is bound to be a copy of the weekly *London Theatre Guide* available at your hotel. Another source of information is the British Travel Association's publication, "This Month in London," which will also tell you what's going on.

The evening tours, listed in Chapter 10, can be a very enjoyable way to see the city by night, and meet some new people too, especially if you're traveling alone.

Special Note

THE DUET, DEHEMS PUB, Macclesfield Street (just off Shaftesbury Avenue), W.1 Underground: Piccadilly Circus. (Walk up Shaftesbury Avenue on the right; Macclesfield Street is just a little alleyway, going to Gerrard Street, which runs parallel to Shaftesbury.)

This is a very interesting club that is absolutely ideal for women traveling on their own. Its purpose is for people to get to know other people, whether they are strangers in town, lonely individuals, or whatever. This does not mean that it is a lonely hearts' club, because it is not. It is merely a very good club that specializes in the little extras that make it easier to form new relationships. Basically, the place is a pub in Soho, but it is run more like a private party that you may have been invited to. You are met at the door by your host, introduced around, and then left to carry on in whatever area you prefer. You can play darts—a typical accessory in almost every English pub—dance, play cards, or sit and drink at the bar if you like, though it is not at all necessary. The main thing is that here you will meet people! I think this is a good place to visit very early in the trip so that you have other people to go out with the rest of the time you are there. Who knows what will happen?! I do know that some very interesting relationships have developed in this way and many women have found perfectly acceptable and interesting escorts. Monday through Friday, people start arriving about 6 P.M. and the party ends at 11 P.M. (standard pub hours, you know). On Saturdays it is open from 7 to 11 P.M., Sundays until 10:30 P.M. Admission fee 50p ($1.25).

BOOKING OFFICES

If you don't mind paying a slight fee for the convenience of booking your tickets through a booking agent, the following will assist you in getting tickets for the theater, ballet, opera, and concerts:

KEITH PROWSE GROUP 155 Charing Cross Road, W.C.2 Tel: 434-1171; 24 Store Street, W.C.1 Tel: 637-3131; 233 Shaftesbury Avenue, W.1 Tel: 240-2891

HARRODS DEPARTMENT STORE (4th floor) Knightsbridge, S.W.1 Tel: 730-1234

ARMY AND NAVY STORES (ground floor) 105 Victoria Street, S.W.1 Tel: 834-1234

EDWARDS AND EDWARDS Palace Theatre. Shaftesbury Avenue Tel: 437-4695

KENT THEATRE TICKETS Hilton Hotel. Park Lane Tel: 493-4406

SIMPSON, LTD. 202 Piccadilly Tel: 734-2080

WEBSTER & GIRLING 211 Baker Street, N.W.1 Tel: 935-6666

BALLET

The principal theaters are those listed below:

THE AUSTRALIAN BALLET London Coliseum St. Martin's Lane, W.1 Tel: 836-7666 Underground: Trafalgar Square. For information, Tel: 836-3161.

Nighttime Entertainment 91

THE ROYAL BALLET NEW GROUP Sadler's Wells Theatre Rosebery Avenue, Islington, E.C.1 Tel: 837-1672 Underground: Angel.
THE ROYAL BALLET Royal Opera House Covent Garden, Bow Street, W.C.2 Tel: 240-1066 Underground: Covent Garden
MUDRA London Coliseum W.1 Tel: 836-7666 Underground: Trafalgar Square

OPERA

ROYAL OPERA HOUSE Covent Garden Bow Street, W.C.2 Tel: 240-1066 Underground: Covent Garden
SADLER'S WELLS OPERA London Coliseum St. Martin's Lane, W.C.2 Tel: 836-3161 Underground: Trafalgar Square
ENGLISH OPERA GROUP Sadler's Wells Theatre Rosebery Avenue, Islington, E.C.1 Tel: 837-1672. Underground: Angel
Details of opera and ballet are also given in the daily newspapers. The main centers are those listed above, all of which are open almost all the year around. Visiting opera and ballet companies can be seen at the Sadler's Wells Theatre.

CONCERTS AND RECITALS

Music lovers will have absolutely no trouble finding something to their liking, from jazz to philharmonic performances. Again, the best place to find the current program is to check either with the reception clerk at your hotel or the daily listings in the newspapers.

The most important and most beautiful of all the halls in London is a musical center completed in 1965 on the south bank of the Waterloo Bridge. The complex consists of the Queen Elizabeth Hall, the Purcell Room, the Royal Festival Hall, the National Film Theatre, and beautiful gardens. The acoustics are marvelous and bring out the very best of all performers, who are more than anxious to appear at this particular center. There are stage productions, films, the London Philharmonic Orchestra, the Royal Philharmonic, the London Symphony, and the BBC performing regularly throughout the season. Tickets run 50p to £2 ($1.25 to $5), depending upon the seat and the performance, though in these particular halls, almost every seat is a good one. For program listings or information on tickets, call the Royal Festival Hall Box Office (Tel: 928-3191) or book through any of the booking agents. Underground: Waterloo Station

ROYAL ALBERT HALL Kensington Gore, S.W.7 Tel: 589-8212. Underground: South Kensington

A gigantic music hall that at one time offered far less comfort and acoustical benefits than it now has. Luckily, there have been extensive renovations and the acoustics have been improved tremendously so that now one can enjoy the finest concerts in the greatest of comfort. Here, too, the programs are varied, everything from rock groups to brass bands, BBC concerts, and top orchestras. Tickets run about 30p to £4 ($.75 to $10).

WIGMORE HALL 36 Wigmore Street, W.1 Tel: 935-2141 Underground: Bond Street

A smaller hall where you will feel the intimacy and the finer nuances of the most marvelous concerts or recitals. It is an excellent room for piano concerts, string quartets, and vocalists who prefer the intimacy of this hall to some of the larger ones mentioned above. Seats from 30p to 90p ($.75 to $2.25)

THEATERS

London has long been revered as the capital of legitimate theater, thanks to the likes of Sir Laurence Olivier, Alec Guinness, beloved Margaret Rutherford, and the adorable Robert Morley. The beauty of it is that all these great stars can still be seen "treading the boards" today, and though most have also expanded into cinema, there is something very special about the performances they give when on a legitimate stage, and one has to see them perform in order to understand this. Sir Laurence Olivier still directs The Old Vic—though it has now changed its name to the National Theatre Company.

Much has been said about the dry English humor and I have heard many Americans say that they are leery about seeing an English comedy for that reason. Nothing could be further from the truth, as the English humor is as understandable as our very own American brand and the American audiences always enjoy the comedies immensely.

The British are not as staid as one might think. You may have quite a surprise when you find that the dialogue of the new plays is every bit as sexually blatant as some of our own sex-oriented films.

The least expensive seats, are, of course, in the gallery. In some theaters they do allow you to reserve them in advance on the same day as the performance; this means you can drop by during the day to pick up your ticket and then come back in time for the performance. However, many theaters do not offer this service, so check with your reception desk at the hotel first. Matinees are on Wednesdays, Thursdays, and Saturdays, and are always fairly crowded. Check, too, to see the curtain time of the play you wish to see as some of the theaters are now raising the curtain at 7:30 P.M.

Nighttime Entertainment

Here are some average prices for tickets: orchestra ("stalls") £3 ($7.50); mezzanine ("dress circle") £2 ($5); balcony ("gallery") 75p ($1.87). Prices are not graded strictly according to sections, so check out the chart before paying for your seat.

We don't have the space to list all the legitimate theaters in London, but the following list includes at least the better known. When you check the theater listings in the newspapers to see what play you want to see, you will have all the further information you need.

THE NATIONAL THEATRE Waterloo Road, S.E.1 Tel: 928-7616 Underground: Waterloo

Formerly known as the "Old Vic," this is probably the most important theatre in London. As I mentioned earlier, it is under the direction of Sir Laurence Olivier, and he often plays the lead role in some of his favorite plays. Naturally you will expect to see the classics such as Shakespeare and Chekov, to mention just two of the most important, but it does offer a modern program from time to time as well. Gallery seats go for 15p to 20p ($.37 to $.50), believe it or not! Circle seats go for 40p ($1). These are certainly bargain rates! Curtain time Monday through Friday evenings at 7:30 P.M.; matinees Thursdays and Saturdays at 2:15 P.M.

ADELPHI Strand, W.C.2 Tel: 836-7611 Underground: Strand or Trafalgar Square

Generally you will find excellent musical and light comedies here. Curtain time Monday through Friday evenings at 7:30 P.M., Saturday evenings at 8:30 P.M.; matinees Thursdays at 3 P.M. and Saturdays at 4 P.M.

AMBASSADORS Cambridge Circus, W.C.2 Tel: 836-1171 Underground: Covent Garden

Curtain time Monday through Friday evenings at 8 P.M., Saturdays at 5 and 8 P.M.; matinees Tuesdays at 2:45 P.M. Currently playing *The Mouse Trap*, the longest running play of its kind in the entire history of British theater.

CRITERION Piccadilly Circus, W.1 Tel: 930-3216 Underground: Piccadilly Circus

Perhaps the best located theater in London, right in the center of Piccadilly Circus with all its snack bars, restaurants, etc. Curtain time Monday through Friday evenings at 8 P.M., Saturdays at 5:15 and 8:30 P.M.

DRURY LANE (THEATRE ROYAL) Catherine Street, Aldwych, W.C.2 Tel: 836-8108 Underground: Covent Garden

One of the oldest and most famous theaters in London next to the Old Vic, noted for the association of Nell Gwynne, King Charles's cockney mistress, with it. It is said that her ghost still haunts the place. The Drury Lane has been home to almost every famous British legitimate actor and they generally have a very soft spot in their hearts for it. Musicals seem to be the specialty, though good dramas are not at all unusual. Curtain time Monday, Tuesday, and Thursday evenings at 8:30 P.M., Fridays and Saturdays at 6:15 and 8:30 P.M. Tickets 50p to £2.50 ($1.25 to $6.25).

FORTUNE Russell Street, Covent Garden, W.C.2 Tel: 836-2238 Underground: Covent Garden

Another of the picturesque old theaters in the Covent Garden Market area. Curtain time Monday through Friday evenings at 8 P.M., Saturdays at 5:30 and 8:30 P.M. Tickets 50p to £1.50 ($1.25 to $3.75).

HER MAJESTY'S Haymarket, S.W.1 Tel: 930-6606 Underground: Piccadilly Circus or Trafalgar Square

Very posh and elegant, Her Majesty's is one of the most popular theaters for musical productions. Curtain time Monday through Friday evenings at 7:30 P.M.; matinees Fridays and Saturdays at 5 P.M. Tickets 80p to £2.50 ($2 to $6.25); slightly less expensive at matinees.

MERMAID Upper Thames Street E.C.4 Tel: 248-7656 Underground: Black Friars Station

Although one of London's newest theaters, it has a rather historical attachment, since this area was the local stamping ground of Shakespeare himself. The Mermaid is more than just a theater: there is a lovely restaurant right on the bank of the Thames, a tavern, a coffee bar, and two other bars, plus a souvenir shop. It is a good spot to spend an entire evening. The prices are reasonable and the theater offerings are generally risqué comedies or up-to-date modern dramas.

ROYAL COURT Sloane Square, Chelsea, S.W.1 Tel: 730-1745 Underground: Sloane Square

Actually this is two theatres in one. The one on the main floor specializes in the usual drama or comedy and is open to the public. The Theatre Upstairs is a new concept in theater, a club specializing in the avant-garde, and you have to be a member to get in. In the main theater, curtain time Monday through Friday evenings at 8 P.M., Saturdays at 5 and 8:30 P.M. Tickets 25p to £1.80 ($.62 to $4.49).

ROYAL SHAKESPEARE COMPANY ALDWYCH THEATRE Aldwych Tel: 836-6404 Underground: Holborn or the Temple

The home theater of this repertory company is Stratford-on-Avon, of course. However, it is not always so easy to get out to that part of the country, so this branch of the theater has been very successful. One might think that Shakespeare plays would be the only ones presented here but other authors are honored as well, such as Sean O'Casey and the controversial Harold Pinter. Tickets 60p to £2.10 ($1.49 to $5.24).

Musicals

These are the theaters catering to musicals.

PALLADIUM Argyle Street, Oxford Circus, W.1 Tel: 437-7373 Underground: Oxford Circus

Of course everyone is familiar with the Palladium. As you probably know, it attracts the greatest stars, and is worth a visit no matter who is performing just to be able to see this famous theater.

HER MAJESTY'S Haymarket, S.W.1 Tel: 930-6606 Underground; Piccadilly Circus

NEW LONDON Drury Lane, W.C.2 Tel: 405-0072 Underground: Aldwych

NEW VICTORIA Vauxhall Bridge Road, Victoria, S.W.1 Tel: 834-0671 Underground: Victoria

PHOENIX Charing Cross Road, W.C.2 Tel: 836-8611 Underground: Tottenham Court Road
PICCADILLY Dennman Street, W.1 Tel: 437-4506 Underground: Piccadilly Circus
PRINCE OF WALES Coventry Street, W.1 Tel: 930-8681 Underground: Piccadilly Circus
QUEENS Shaftesbury Avenue, W.1 Tel: 734-1166 Underground: Piccadilly Circus

MUSIC HALLS

The music halls in London are very much like old vaudeville in days gone by in America. Seldom does one find such a place of entertainment, other than perhaps Las Vegas, where they are generally lavish night clubs. Here in London, they are very serious about their musicals. They are a permanent fixture of night life.

I've listed the most popular. There are many other music halls with varying entertainment and ambiance. Inquire at your hotel or get the magazine *This Month in London,* which lists the programs.

PALLADIUM Argyle Street, W.1 Tel: 437-7373 Underground: Oxford Circus
This is the first and most famous. Almost every international celebrity has trod the boards of the Palladium; in fact, success is often judged by whether or not a performer has played this great theater. Who can forget the tremendous impact of Judy Garland's one-woman show or the fantastic worldwide reviews of Danny Kaye or Tom Jones? The greatest thrill of all is the seasonal royal command performance held for the Queen, when each performer is introduced personally to Her Majesty. The most experienced, the most poised, and blasé performers have been known to tremble at such a great moment and stumble over their greeting to the Queen. There are two performances nightly, at 6:15 and at 8:45 P.M.; matinees Saturdays at 2:40 P.M. Tickets run 70p to £7 ($1.75 to $17.50), depending upon the show being presented.

HATCHETTS 67 Piccadilly, W.1 Tel: 629-2001 Underground: Piccadilly Circus
Another old-style music hall with the same type of entertainment—sing-alongs, boisterous programs, and a gay ambiance. They also have a discotheque for those who wish to do a bit of swinging. There is a special "nosh" menu from £1 to £1.50 ($2.50 to $3.75) and a regular restaurant as well, so this is good for a full evening's entertainment. On Sundays, only the discotheque is open, not the restaurant. Open Sundays and Thursdays from 7 P.M. to 3:30 A.M.; the shows begin at 8:30 and 11 P.M. Open Fridays and Saturdays from 6 P.M.; the shows begin at 7 and 9:30 P.M.

PINDAR OF WAKEFIELD 328 Gray's Inn Road, W.C.1 Tel: 837-7269 Underground: King's Cross

An extremely gay and workable combination of Victorian music hall and typical English pub with the mad mélange of pub fare, loud humorous entertainment, and foaming tankards of ale. To add to the cameraderie, song sheets are handed out so that the audience can join in with the balladeers. After a tankard or two that's not very hard to do, whether you know the song or not. You can imagine the harmony (?). A Friday- or Saturday-night-type place. Performances at 8:30 p.m. It is a good idea to get there early to get a seat.

PLAYERS THEATRE Villiers Street, Strand, W.C.2 Tel: 839-1134 Underground: Charing Cross

A grand old authentic Victorian music hall that will delight you from the moment you step through the door until the regrettable moment you have to leave. Its very authenticity is perhaps that indefinable something that makes it as popular as it is. The costumes are right out of Victorian days as are all the fittings and backdrops, and I suppose you might even say the attitude. It is an ideal place for one or more women to spend an evening, because you can have dinner here and enjoy the entire show at your leisure. The menu features international cuisine and is really quite reasonable, strangely enough, for such a club. Should you not feel like having a full dinner, snacks are available or you may even just enjoy a few drinks while watching a most enjoyable show. The amiable master of ceremonies really keeps things moving and in a very short time makes you feel he is an old friend. The acts are presented in a very warm, friendly, and humorous way and even the audience participates from time to time.

Actually the Players is a private club but you can buy your membership right at the door for £1 ($2.50). The only problem is that you have to wait two days before using it; it might be a good idea to do this soon after you arrive in London, so that you can take advantage of it your first free evening. As a member you pay nothing for a cover charge or admission, but you must pay 50p ($1.25) for any guest you bring with you; Friday and Saturday nights you are allowed as many as five guests, but no more. Performances nightly except Sunday. Shows begin Mondays and Tuesdays at 8 P.M., Wednesday through Saturday at 9 P.M. The restaurant starts serving dinner at 7 P.M. After the show has been completed there is dancing until after midnight.

CINEMAS

London is one place in the world where you can go to films without having to worry about subtitles. They do have international films besides English-speaking ones. The difference between the English and American cinemas is that while we have one screening after the other, they do not. You should check your local paper for the times of the performances. Usually the last performance is at 8 P.M. There are generally queues for good films and it is suggested you get there early. At the box office there is usually a seating chart;

you pay according to the area you wish to sit in. Tickets run 40p to £1 ($1 to $2.50) for the more popular films. Most of the better theaters are around Piccadilly Circus and Leicester Square, with several along Shaftesbury Avenue as well. (Underground: Piccadilly Circus and Leicester Square.) There are also many neighborhood movies throughout London showing first-run films.

CABARETS

What in America is usually called a night club, is called a cabaret in London. This generally means a night-club sort of arrangement where you can have dinner and a complete show of several acts, usually a comic, a master of ceremonies, dancers, vocalists, etc. Those listed below are some of the best in London and are some of the most expensive; however there will be a less expensive category to follow, so stick with us.

A lone woman would not be comfortable going to any of these clubs alone, but two women would have no problem whatsoever. If you are alone and you want to see a bit of night life, the night tours are usually the best bet. The other alternative is to go to the Duet, mentioned earlier in this chapter, where you are bound to meet someone with whom you would like to share an evening—either male or female.

Don't forget the supper clubs, such as 1520 A.D. and the Mediaeval Feestes, mentioned in the restaurant section, which also feature entertainment, though not of a cabaret nature. These, too, are excellent choices for an evening; and all of them make for a very pleasant evening out.

Expensive

THE BLUE ANGEL 14 Berkeley Street, W.1 Tel: 629-1443
Underground: Green Park

In a sense, this is maybe perhaps more of a man's club than a woman's because of the showgirls in their nude costumes and the available girls for dancing. However, women may be interested, as it is Marlene Dietrich's favorite club in London named after the film she is so famous for. It is a small place on the lower level and very elegant. Though it is a private club, there is no club membership. However, you must show your passport at the door in order to qualify as a foreign guest. There is a very short show at 11:30 P.M.; the main show goes on at 1:15 A.M. Fixed-price dinner £3.25 ($8.12). Admission £1 ($2.50). Dancing until 4 A.M. Closed Sundays.

98 LONDON

THE CELEBRITY 15 Clifford Street, W.1 Tel: 493-7636 Underground: Berkeley Square

In Mayfair. The Celebrity not only produces a magnificent extravaganza of a floor show, but their food as well is considered excellent, a rarity in cabarets, where the food is mostly secondary. There are two shows nightly, at 10:45 P.M. and at 1:30 A.M., with dancing in between and after. Cover charge £1.30 ($3.25). Fixed-price dinner, which begins at 6:30 P.M., £3 ($7.50) Monday through Friday, with an additional 50p ($1.25) added on Saturdays.

CHURCHILLS 160 New Bond Street, W.1 Tel: 493-2626 Underground: Bond Street

One of Mayfair's poshest clubs, named of course after Sir Winston Churchill. Churchills has long been the stamping ground of stars such as Judy Garland and Frank Sinatra, to name two of its most illustrious. The shows are backed by some of the most beautiful showgirls in England. Some even manage to detract from the stars themselves with their gorgeous costumes and sensuous movements. Two shows nightly, one at 11 P.M. and one at 1 A.M. The entrance cover charge is £1.50 ($3.75). There is a fixed-price three-course dinner with huge portions for only £3.50 ($8.75). This does not include drinks, but even the drinks are not expensive, considering the usual night-club prices. With its elegance, poshness, and snobbishness, one would expect to be treated in a rather haughty way, but strangely enough, exactly the opposite is true. In fact, Harry Meadows, the proprietor, even gives his guests lovely gifts, scarves for the women, cufflinks for the men. Closed Sundays.

EVE 189 Regent Street, W.1 Tel: 734-0557

Two beautiful floor shows nightly, at 10:30 P.M. and at 1 A.M., with dancing until 3:30 A.M. The shows very often feature celebrities from the Continent but even when they don't, the shows are always beautifully staged and the evening well spent. Dinner begins at 8:30 P.M. with a fixed-price menu at £7 (17.50) that includes one bottle of champagne with your dinner and an after-dinner brandy. An à la carte menu is also available. Immediate membership 50p ($1.25) at the door.

L'HIRONDELLE Swallow Street, W.1 Tel: 734-0362

Just off Regent Street, L'Hirondelle is famous for some of the most magnificent extravaganzas in London. And without all the nonsense of the temporary memberships, cover charge, etc. Dinner and dancing from 7:30 P.M. until dawn. A fixed-price menu with super international cuisine, Monday through Thursday £3.50 ($8.75); Fridays and Saturdays £3.75 ($9.37). Beautiful Parisian-style floor shows, at 10:30 P.M. and 1:30 A.M., generally feature a well-known international star.

STARS AND GARTERS Leicester Square, W.C.2 Underground: Leicester Square

This is one of the other big clubs in London, a good place for women alone. It is all done in the Gay '90s theme with red velvet, pawnbroker-type chandeliers, a band playing old-time music with singers and dancers, all along the same theme. They make a point of trying to bring the guests into the show so that everyone has a good time. The menu, I'm afraid, is a bit limited—they only have snacks; so if you prefer a big meal, you had better have it before you come and then spend the rest of the evening here just for fun. It's a good place for after the theater just for that

Nighttime Entertainment

reason— you can have a snack and relax. There is a 30p ($.75) cover charge and after that the drinks and snacks are not expensive at all.

THE TALK OF THE TOWN Hippodrome Corner of Leicester Square, W.C.2 Tel: 734-5051 Underground: Leicester Square

One of the most popular clubs in all of England very centrally located at Leicester Square. It always has top international entertainers and is generally sold out. There are two extravaganzas nightly, at 9:30 and at 11 P.M. The rest of the time, beginning at about 7:30 P.M., there are three bands to dance to. Of course, you can have dinner there in the restaurant, which is a replica of the old Hippodrome.

There is a set price of £4 ($10) for a complete dinner and a show, really not a bad price at all, considering that you can spend a whole evening here and see some of the world's best performers. On Friday and Saturday nights the price is £4.50 ($11.25) but even that isn't so hard on the budget.

Moderate

There are quite a few cabarets around London where the food is less than palatable and the shows not quite up to par, so as a safer step, for women especially, stick to the few most popular places listed here.

THE CHANTICLEER Roebuck House Palace Street, S.W.1 Tel: 834-5695

The Chanticleer brings to London the warmth and gaiety of Greece. Enjoy the superb Greek food, wine, and ouzo, dance the night away and be entertained by group dancing, music, and song. There is usually a bouzouki player, a Greek trio, and an international act or two. Monday through Thursday only, there is a fixed-price menu at £2.50 ($6.25), including wine and service. There is an à la carte menu and a special dinner menu upon request. Open Mondays and Saturdays for lunch from noon to 3 P.M. and for dinner from 6:30 P.M. to 2 A.M.

THE COPACABANA 177 Regent Street, W.1 Tel: 734-7675

This is the kind of club that does provide dancing partners for men if they wish, but it is still very comfortable for two or more women to go alone without being concerned. You can dine from 8:30 P.M. to 3 A.M. in comfortable air-conditioned luxury and dance to two bands while enjoying a spectacular floor show for an all-in-one price of £3.75 ($9.37). There is also a good à la carte menu. The floor show is spectacular; performances at 9:30 P.M. and 12:30 A.M. The two bands play for your dancing pleasure from 9:30 PM.

GALLIPOLI RESTAURANT 7–8 Bishopsgate, Churchyard, E.C.2 Tel. 588-1922

Here's a show fit for a sultan, set in an exotic Middle East atmosphere. The Gallipoli claims to be Europe's only true authentic Turkish restaurant and its aim is to feed and entertain its guests like sultans. In addition to an expensive menu of authentic Turkish dishes there is also an excellent choice of international cuisine. You may have a three-course dinner, including the dancing and a cabaret show, for £4.50 ($11.25). There are cabaret shows and traditional Turkish belly dancing at 9:30 P.M. and at

1 A.M. Often the fascinating movements of the trained belly dancers are performed on one of the tables! Open Monday through Saturday for lunch from 11 A.M. to 3 P.M. and for dinner and cabaret from 6 P.M. to 3 A.M. for dinner and cabaret. Closed Sundays.

LATIN QUARTER   13–17 Wardour Street, W.1   Tel: GER-6001

In Soho. The shows are very much of the "nudey" type, but are quite good and if the nudity doesn't offend you there is no reason why you shouldn't go. Anyway, there are other acts to offset the nudity, such as good comics, singers, and unusual dancers.

MARBELLA RESTAURANT   3 Long Acre, W.C.2   Tel: 836-7911

Excellent Spanish cuisine in an authentic Spanish setting. Diners enjoy dancing, to the restaurant's resident group, as well as two exciting cabaret spots each night at 9 and 11 P.M. This is one of the few top night entertainment spots that is open Sundays as well as every weekday. It provides a first-class evening with all the jazz and rhythm of Spanish music and dancing, backed by some of the finest cuisine in London. Open Monday through Saturday from 6 P.M. to 2 A.M., Sundays until 11 P.M.

THE SHOWBOAT   Strand Corner House Trafalgar Square, W.C.2   Tel: 930-2781

A huge barn of a place that still manages to be attractive and interesting, the showboat is always bulging at the seams. There is only one long show, from 10:30 to 11:45 P.M., and it is beautifully done. After this you may dine until 1 A.M. Dinner is served from 8:30 to 10:30 P.M. The total cost for dinner and show is £3.50 ($8.75). No membership or cover charges. Open Monday through Saturday.

DISCOTHEQUES

This is perhaps as good a time as any to explain the complicated "private club" situation in London. Most discotheques, jazz clubs, and night clubs are classified as private clubs. Which does not really mean that they truly are private—they are usually more than happy to issue instant membership to any and all comers at the door. This does not mean that every night spot has the same policy—some don't, but being forewarned is to forearmed. The membership ploy is merely a matter of getting around the local closing law, which is supposed to be 11 P.M. Strictly speaking, after that hour it is perfectly legal to have a drink as long as you are eating as well. However, rather than go through all the mumbo-jumbo of the closing hours and—first and foremost—loss of business after 11 o'clock, it is much easier to classify a club as private and issue membership. Look at it simply as a cover charge, which you may pay in better clubs in America in any case. Since the prices of drinks, food, and the shows will be less than what you pay in America, you are still not really spending that much money.

Discotheques in London are frequented pretty much by the A and B age categories, though I must say if you're over 40 it is quite a show in itself to sit and watch, if not get up on the floor and jog a bit yourself. The music is good and loud, the dancing uninhibited, the manner of dress unconventional to way out.

THE MARQUEE 90 Wardour Street, W.1 Tel: 437-2375 Underground: Tottenham Court Road

One of the most popular spots for the latest music on the Continent, the Marquee has managed to stay on top of the discotheque world from its very beginning to decades ago. Many top-name British groups started their careers here, including the Who and the Rolling Stones. All live music with mostly heavy rock and amplified acoustics. No membership is necessary here but there is an admission fee of 40p to 50p ($1 to 1.25), depending upon the show. In addition to the usual drinks, there is a snack bar. Incidentally, this is also a favorite place for other performers visiting London to pop in for a jam session or to meet with their cronies, so keep your eyes peeled. Open from 7:15 go 11 P.M.

THE BAG O'NEILS 9 Kingsley Street, W.1. Underground: Oxford Circus

Near Carnaby Street. A very popular discotheque that also alternates with live bands. The bands play two performances nightly, records in between for dancing. Though it opens at 9 P.M. it's ghostly until much later than that and really doesn't start swinging until about midnight; it closes at 3 A.M. The dance floor is downstairs, and there is another bar upstairs. Very modern décor with huge photos on the wall and a play of lights to intensify the mood. No memberships necessary, only an admission fee of 50p ($1.25) on week nights; Fridays and Saturdays the fee goes up to £1 ($2.50). Drinks are fairly inexpensive at about 25p ($.62) and there are snacks available, also at very moderate prices.

BLAISE'S 121 Queen's Gate, S.W.7 Tel: 589-6228 Underground: Lord Albert Hall

This disco is heavily frequented by the very young, "Dolly" set. A lot of the newly popular groups start here at Blaise's, so the clientele takes special pride in boosting them to their forthcoming fame, which probably accounts for their enthusiasm. The fashion show here, too, is really something to behold. Everybody looks as if they just stepped off the cover of a mod fashion magazine, males as well as females. A special feature at Blaise's is a film show on Sundays, and they are open to suggestions if you have any particular favorites. Thursday is a cheese-and-wine night, and it's served free of charge, so naturally it is very crowded on Thursday nights! Other than that, there is a restaurant for excellent meals that keeps very late hours. Membership costs 25p ($.62) and there is an additional admission fee, for special performances or on very busy nights, of £1 ($2.50). Open until 4 A.M.

THE CHALET SUISSE 74 Charlotte Street, W.1 Underground: Goodge Street

Not at all true to its name—there is nothing Swiss about it. Owned by the same management as the Lorelei, it gets the same international clientele and has the same ambiance as the Lorelei. Temporary memberships

£1 ($2.50). Open Monday through Saturday from 9 P.M. to 2:30 A.M. closed Sundays.

DIE FLEDERMAUS 7 Carlisle Street, W.1 Tel: 734-5741 Underground: Tottenham Court Road

A mecca for Scandinavian and German girls, who seem to gravitate toward this particular discotheque and no other; therefore it also attracts a great number of interested men! Mondays are rather special nights inasmuch as "The Bat" throws a party for its customers on that night, but they do insist on proper dress—no blue jeans or T-shirts allowed, which is a nice switch for a change. The temporary memberships sold at the door cost 50p ($1.25), with an entrance fee of 30p ($.75). The action swings to 3 A.M.

THE LORELEI Falconberg Court Underground: Tottenham Court Road

Between Soho Square and Charing Cross Road. One of the tinier discos, but this only makes for more intimacy and is probably the reason for its largely international clientele, whereas most other discotheques are frequented mostly by Londoners themselves. Temporary membership £1 ($2.50); no admission fee after that. Open Monday through Saturday from 9 P.M. to 2:30 A.M. Closed Sundays.

SADDLE ROOM CLUB 1A Hamilton Mews, Hamilton Place, Park Lane, W.1 Tel: 499-4994 Underground: Hyde Park Corner

In a very posh area just behind Park Lane (home of all the most elegant hotels), the Saddle Room Club is a discotheque with occasional live shows and gets a lot of the Park Laners dropping in for a bit of dancing or drooling. The membership is £5.25 ($13.12), if you plan on doing a lot of "Saddle Rooming"; individual "at-the-door membership" £1.25 ($3.12). And this also includes your first drink. Open from 9 P.M. to 4 A.M. Closed Sundays.

SIX BELLS 197 King's Road, Chelsea, S.W.3

One of the most popular and therefore difficult-to-get-into discos/pubs in Chelsea. During the day it is a pub with the usual English fare at budget prices and a lovely garden to eat, drink, or stroll in. It is particularly popular during the summer. On the main floor the Bird's Nest is where all the disco action takes place. Admission fee 15p ($.37) and 25p ($.62). Drinks are also budget-priced, so this is a good bet for a gay evening. Don't overlook the cellar bar, "Exclusively Yours," for more intimate and quieter atmosphere, if you've got the right escort. Unfortunately, because of the fact that it is a pub and does not have private membership, it must adhere to the standard closing hours, which means 11 P.M., so to take full advantage of the festivities, you'll want to go early.

TIFFANY'S 22–32 Shaftesbury Avenue, W.1 Tel: 437-5012 Underground: Piccadilly Circus or Leicester Square

Near Piccadilly Circus. A huge barn of a place, with the usual kinetic lighting effects that tend to drive the dancers into wild frenzies. Absolutely jammed! Especially on weekends. Open Sunday through Thursday from 7:30 P.M. to 2 A.M., Friday and Saturday from 7:30 P.M. to 3 A.M. Admission Monday through Thursday only 50p ($1.25) before 8 P.M., 80p ($2) between 8 and 11 P.M., and £1 ($2.50) after 11 P.M. Admission Fridays 90p ($2.25) before 9 P.M., £1.20 ($3) after 9 P.M. Admission Saturdays

£1 ($2.50) before 9 P.M., £1.30 ($3.25) after 9 P.M. Admission Sundays £1 ($2.50). I have absolutely no idea why they complicate admission fees and hours so, but that's the way they are, so you must cope the best you can.

TRAFALGAR   200 King's Road, S.W.3

This is right in the heart of Chelsea, a very swinging place to be in London. Instead of the usual bar stools, you sit in the replica of a car or on a wooden horse, not that this makes it any more comfortable, but it does add to the décor. During the day the Trafalgar is a pub and therefore you can get the usual draft beer or ale. Music starts at 7 P.M., but then they keep standard pub hours, which means they close at 11 P.M. weekdays and 10:30 P.M. Sundays.

THE WHISKEY A GO-GO   33-37 Wardour Street, W.1   Tel: 437-7676   Underground: Tottenham Court Road.

In the same area as the Marquee, The Whiskey A Go-Go is another of the most popular discotheques, not only in London but perhaps in the world. It was the first in London back in the 1950s. It's known for keeping up with the "in" music and groups, so it has managed to stay on top in this type of entertainment. Aside from the usual discs with all kinds of music from pop to jazz, there is a special policy of a live band five nights a week. They even have a barbecue bar to satisfy the appetite you are bound to whip up with all the dancing you can't avoid engaging in. This kind of music will provide quite an incentive. Open from 8 P.M. to 3 A.M. This is a membership club charging 53p ($1.32) for females. Admission charges run 25p to 45p ($.62 to $1.12).

JAZZ CLUBS

BATTERSEA PARK   Open Air Concert Pavilion   A-B-C   Underground: Sloane Square, then take Bus 137

On Tuesdays you will find jazz concerts featuring some of the world's greatest, including Mr. Acker Bilk. Admission 25p ($.62), but get there early as the performances begin at 8 P.M. and the queue begins much earlier than that.

RONNIE SCOTT'S   47 Frith Street, W.1   Tel: 437-4752   A-B

Extremely popular with jazz buffs and top international performers. No matter what time of the year you are always bound to find one of the world's top names booked at Ronnie Scott's. Conveniently located in Soho, just a short distance from Piccadilly Circus. This is not a jazz club such as you may have seen in Greenwich Village or similar places in America; it has more of a theater-like atmosphere. The main room is built in tiers so that every table is afforded an excellent view. In this room you can have dinner and spend an entire evening for a very reasonable price. There is a very modern discotheque upstairs for drinking, dancing, and eating if you like and, needless to say, meeting! Downstairs is a very intimate rustic bar where jazz buffs congregate and hope to meet their heroes. Admission fees depend upon the performance of the evening and run £1.25 to £1.80 ($3.12 to $4.50). Open Monday through Saturday from 8:30 P.M. to 3 A.M.; closed Sundays. If you wish to to go the discotheque you can get away with an admission of a mere 75p ($1.87) during the week, or £1 ($2.50) on weekends.

THE 100 CLUB 100 Oxford Street, W.1 Tel: 636-0933 A-B Underground: Tottenham Court Road or Oxford Circus

For traditional and Dixieland jazz, this is the place to be nightly, with the added attractions of a dance floor and Chinese food. The usual "membership at the door" price is 50p ($1.25); the admission price depends on what performers are appearing at the time. Open Sunday through Thursday from 7:30 to 11 P.M., Fridays from 7:30 P.M. to midnight, and Saturdays from 7:30 P.M. to 1 A.M.

TORRINGTON MUSIC 4 Lodge Lane, Finchley, N.12 Tel: 455-7410 A-B Underground: Woodside Park

Top-line jazz stars are featured on two Thursdays a month. Other than that, all types of jazz are showcased here. This is one case where no membership is necessary but there is an admission fee of 60p ($1.50). Open from 8:30 P.M. until the pub closes.

TROUBADOUR COFFEE HOUSE 265 Old Brompton Road, S.W.5 Tel: FRE-7822 A-B

Though this is basically not a jazz spot, it very often does have jazz performers.

The main cup of tea here is folk music and I must say it is a very pleasant evening indeed, as the ambiance is something seldom found in places of this nature. It is always crowded, the people are very friendly and quick to carry on a conversation with their neighbor. The candlelight enhances the atmosphere as well. The décor is early, later, and future "musicana" with every kind of musical instrument hanging from the ceiling. The rest of the décor consists of postcards, old coffeepots, old farm tools, and what have you. It sounds like a junk shop, but really it is quite fun and it does help to set the pace. Eat, drink, and be merry is the theme and the food is geared to the young, budget-minded crowd. A good plate of spaghetti will cost you no more than 30p ($.75), which alone is worth stopping in for.

FEMALE IMPERSONATORS

This may seem like a strange suggestion for a night out, but it really is great fun and a woman need not feel the least bit uncomfortable in going to see any of these acts. Generally they are in the little English pubs in any case so that the atmosphere is of a rather intimate neighborhood crowd rather than a big night club.

The female impersonators in London are really beautiful. Their gowns, wigs, jewels, makeup, walk, etc., are really something to see. Not only in terms of the humor of it all, but what they can do with makeup, clothes, and hairdos is really out of this world!

The greatest of all the impersonators, though he hates to be called such, is Danny LaRue, currently holding sway at the Prince of Wales Theatre, Piccadilly Circus. Danny LaRue is the darling of this particular type of entertainment and has fans such as Ingrid Bergman, the Lunts, Margot Fonteyn, and, believe it or not, even the Royal Family. Danny stands over 6'2", and his gowns are primarily extravaganzas of feathers and beads. He does takeoffs on Elizabeth Taylor, Carol Channing, and Zsa Zsa Gabor, but he tries not to imitate them too closely, because he always prefers to be just "Dan." Danny is expected to be at the Prince of Wales through Autumn of 1975, but should you miss him there, do make sure you track him down because this is one show you won't want to miss. Underground: Piccadilly Circus.

Another such place at a far more budget price is the Union Tavern, Canverwell Mews Road, S.E.5, Tel: 735-2606. This is really a Victorian-type pub but on Wednesdays, Thursdays, and Sundays they feature female impersonators, who really do bring the crowds. So get there early; the show starts at 9 P.M. Inasmuch as the place is a pub, it must keep to the usual pub closing hours, 11 P.M., and 10:30 P.M. Sundays. Underground: Oval.

PUBS

Public houses, or pubs, are an integral part of the British way of life. If you have never been in one before, you must not miss the experience. Beer, incidentally, is different here from beer in most other countries, and there is a much bigger variety. The décor and the ambiance of most pubs are just about the same—wood-paneled walls, wooden chairs and tables,—though they even range into the ultramodern. Pub food is a great specialty and can range from bread and cheese or sausage to a splendid cold buffet; however, fish and chips, steak and kidney pie, and bangers and mash are the usual pub fare. Secretaries in the area, executives, and what have you will pop in for lunch or for a tankard of beer after the office closes. It is not at all difficult to meet people but even if that is not your purpose the ambiance itself is worth any "pub crawling" you may decide to do.

Though a pub may sound like a strictly male domain, this is not true. They are entirely respectable and lone women frequent pubs without the slightest qualms. In fact, it is quite the thing to do in London.

Once you have tried one or two pubs, I have a feeling your interest may be aroused and you'll wish to look into them more thoroughly. There is a Pub Information Center, 333 Vauxhall Bridge Road,

S.W.1, Tel: 828-3261, which can tell you anything you want to know about pubs, including history, exactly which ones to go to, and which ones feature jazz, rock music, or other entertainment. They used to have a pub tour twice a week, which I was told, when I was in London researching this book, was no longer running. However, I have since heard that they have reinstated their tours. I hope so, as they have guides who know everything about the places and take you to only the most interesting ones. The cost is minimal and it is well worth while, so why not call and see if they are running the tours when you are there?

In accordance with London licensing laws, pubs are only open from 11:30 A.M. to 3 P.M. and from 5:30 to 11 P.M., Monday through Saturday; Sundays, they are open from 7 to 10:30 P.M.

THE ANCHOR Bankside, S.E.1 Tel: 407-3003
A fascinating little pub just off the Southwark Bridge and close to the site of the old Shakespeare Globe Theatre and the new Bear Gardens Museum.

COAL HOLE Strand, W.C.2 Tel: 836-7503
A quaint seventeenth-century pub in the heart of theaterland, with many theatrical links.

DIRTY DICKS 202 Bishopsgate, E.C.2 Tel: 283-8471
Cobwebs, dust, and weird ornaments go to make up the bizarre atmosphere of this famous city pub with a history dating back over 200 years.

DUKE OF CUMBERLAND New King's Road, S.W.6 Tel: 736-2777
Victorian-style pub, bearing the name of Queen Victoria's notorious uncle. It was voted Pub of the Year in 1971.

THE ESTATE Mabledon Place, W.C.1 Tel: 307-7739
An unusual pub where the walls are covered with souvenirs of World War II escapees from prison camps. Elbert, R.N., a dummy used in one of the most daring escapes, is on show.

GEORGE INN Borough High Street, S.E.1 Tel: 407-2056
Last remaining galleried coaching inn in London, used as a setting by Dickens in *Little Dorrit*. Built in 1677, the pub is a treasury of old beams, cobblestones, and historic atmosphere.

HOOP AND GRAPES 47 Aldgate High Street, E.C.3 Tel: 709-1375
Thought to be the oldest licensed house in the City of London. Attractions include a bricked-up tunnel to the Tower of London, and a ghost.

JACK STRAW'S CASTLE North End Way, Hampstead Heath, N.W.3 Tel: 435-8885
One of the old regulars here was highwayman Dick Turpin. Charles Dickens also numbered among the clientele. The inn is of a very unusual design.

MAGGIE AND STUMP 18 Old Bailey, E.C.4 Tel: 248-3819
Situated opposite the Old Bailey on the former site of Newgate Prison. The pub windows at one time were rented at high prices for a grandstand view of the public executions held inside the jail.

Nighttime Entertainment

MARKHAM ARMS 138 King's Road, Chelsea, S.W.3 Tel: 589-2021
Copper-luster wall panels reflect the theme of Whistler's Peacock Room. Busy, trendy, and comfortable.

MONTAGUE ARMS 289 Queen's Road, Puckham, S.E.15 Tel: 638-4923
A very popular pub for pop fans. The equipment includes a Moog synthesizer and a light show. A good place for the A age group to meet other people.

NAG'S HEAD 10 James Street, W.C.2 Tel: 836-4678
They start work early at Covent Garden Market and this pub pulls the first client of the day at 6:30 A.M. Very popular with market porters, theatricals, and operagoers.

YE OLDE CHESHIRE CHEESE Fleet Street, E.C.4 Tel: 253-6170
This old city pub, which has good English food, is popular with Fleet Street journalists and reputedly had connections with Dr. Johnson. Closes at 9 P.M. Monday through Friday; closed Saturday evening and all day Sunday.

YE OLDE COCK TAVERN 22 Fleet Street E.C.4 Tel: 353-8570
Charles Dickens's favorite tavern in the heart of literary London.

PIED BULL 1 Liverpool Road, Islington, N.1 Tel: 837-3218
Sir Walter Raleigh once lived here. It is reputed to be one of the first places in England where tobacco was smoked. Just outside is a former public execution place.

PROSPECT OF WHITBY 57 Wapping Wall, E.1 Tel: 481-1317
This riverside pub is steeped in history and very picturesque. It is very popular, particularly on weekends, since it features all kinds of music and jazz.

ROUND TABLE St. Martin's Court, W.C.2 Tel: 836-6436
John C. Keenan, middleweight boxing champion of America, stayed here when he visited England to fight Sayres in 1860.

SPANIARDS INN Spaniards Lane, Hampstead, N.E.3 Tel: 455-3276
Sixteenth-century inn with literary associations (Charles Dickens) and strong links with highwayman Dick Turpin.

TIGER CAVERN 1–2 Tower Hill, E.C.3 Tel: 626-5097
This is on the site of a former pub visited by Russian czar Peter the Great. The original wine cellar contains a secret passage to the Tower of London, said to be used by Queen Elizabeth I. Now the attraction is bistro and go-go girls.

VICTORIA 68 Pages Walk, Bermondsey, S.E.1 Tel: 237-3248
Dockland pub, cozy atmosphere, and voted *Evening Standard* Pub of the Year, 1972.

10
Sightseeing

This is one city in which you never find the time to do all you wish to do or see all there is to see. It is wise to plan your sightseeing itinerary prior to arriving in London. When you arrive, you may obtain free maps at the British Tourist Authority, 64 St. James's St., Piccadilly, Or at any other travel office.

For London sightseeing, the "Go As You Please" plan, which allows you unlimited travel on the London subway or buses is wonderful. This is the ticket you can buy from the British Railway offices in the U.S. for $11 for a four-day pass or $14.50 for a seven-day pass. You can buy them in London from the London Transport offices. The Green Rover one-day special ticket for 60p ($1.50), which allows you to ride any green "country buses" and the Red Bus Rover ticket for 50p ($1.25) which lets you ride the red buses all day, are also wonderful ways to sightsee for very little money. For information on them, check with the London Transport offices at St. James's Park, Oxford Circus, Piccadilly Circus, Victoria Station, Euston, or King's Cross underground stations.

Another, slightly more expensive, ticket that is good for a month, is called the "Open to View" ticket and sells for £2.80 ($7.00). It entitles you to free entrance at over 400 famous sights in England and Scotland. If you plan on visiting Windsor Castle, Hampton Court, Woburn Abbey, and other such historical places you will more than compensate for the price of the ticket. And believe me, there is an awful lot to see! This ticket can be purchased in New York through the British Rail International, Department O.V., 270 Madison Ave., N.Y., N.Y. 10016.

The London Transport Company publishes a very useful pamphlet, "London From a Bus Top," which suggests some sightseeing tours on the regular scheduled bus lines.

It is also wise to buy the book entitled *A–Z*, which contains an excellent street index and maps of the city. It only costs 30p ($.75) and will be one of your best investments.

Special Note

CORDON BLEU COOKING SCHOOL 114 Marylebone Lane, W.1 Tel: 935-3503

If cooking is your "thing" and you have always wanted to attend the Cordon Bleu Cooking School, this just may be your opportunity to do so. The school offers both one-week courses and Wednesday afternoon demonstration classes, so this might very easily fit into your schedule. The intensive one-week courses are held at intervals throughout the year during the term and during holiday time; they have both preliminary and advanced work. Practical work takes place in the morning, demonstrations and entertaining in the afternoon. As part of their training, the students are expected to stay to lunch, for which a nominal charge is made. Hours are from 10:30 A.M. to 4:30 P.M., Monday through Friday. The cost of the course, including lunch, is £38.40 ($96). Wednesday afternoon demonstrations run from 2:30 to 4:30 P.M. and cost £1.65 ($4.11). You don't participate in these cooking demonstrations but they are very well done and if you take notes you should be able to learn a great deal. There are many other courses offered by the school. If you are interested, it is a good idea to write to them directly. Address your letter to Rosemary Hume, Muriel Downes, or Molly Sharland, at the address given above.

TOURS

If time is of the essence, and you want to see as much of London as possible, then the best way is to take an organized tour. I usually recommend at least one full city tour during the daytime and an evening tour. This allows you to see all the major points of interest; then if you have time, you can always go back to the places you found most interesting. This also gives you the opportunity to meet other people in your exact situation, and perhaps find a companion to spend some time with in London.

The tours I suggest here are from two major companies in London:

EVAN EVANS TOURS, LTD. Metropolis House 41 Tottenham Court Road, W.1 Tel: 637-4171

FRAMES & RICKARDS Main office 25/31 Tavistock Place, W.C.1 Tel: 837-6311 or 837-6312

110 LONDON

You can call these numbers day or night for sightseeing information or to make reservations. Their tours depart from four different locations: Frames, Herbrand Street; Seymour Street near Marble Arch; Rickards, 17 Woburn Place; Rickards, Trafalgar Square. When reserving a tour, be sure to specify which place you wish to leave from.

Day Tours

MORNING TOUR OF LONDON'S WEST END Evan Evans Tour No. 1

Monday through Saturday, departs at 9:45 A.M., returns 12:15 P.M. Does not operate on December 25 and 26. Price £1.60 ($4), including all entrance fees. This departs from Tottenham Court Road and Russell Square via the British Museum and London University to Trafalgar Square and Nelson's Column. Then to Parliament Square and the Houses of Parliament (guided visit on Saturdays only) and Big Ben. Nearby is St. Margaret's Church and Westminster Abbey, which you visit with a guide. Then along Whitehall to Buckingham Palace and down The Mall for viewing the Changing of the Guard. Through Knightsbridge and Hyde Park along Park Lane to Grovesnor Square and back to Russell Square.

WEEKDAY MORNING DRIVE Frames & Rickards

Monday through Saturday, except December 25 and 26. Departs at the following hours:

- TOUR 1F from Frames, Herbrand Street, at 9:45 A.M.
- TOUR 1FM from Seymour Street near Marble Arch, at 9:45 A.M.
- TOUR 1R from Rickards, 17 Woburn Place, at 9:45 A.M.
- TOUR 1RT from Rickards, Trafalgar Square, at 10 A.M. All tours return at approximately 12:30 P.M. Price £1.60 ($4). Oxford Street, Marble Arch, Bayswater, Hyde Park, the Serpentine, the Royal Albert Hall, Kensington Museums, Chelsea Barracks, the Tate Gallery, Lambeth Bridge and Palace, St. Thomas's Hospital, Westminster Bridge, Houses of Parliament (visited on Saturdays only), a visit to Westminster Abbey, Whitehall, Downing Street, the Cenotaph, Horse Guards Parade, Trafalgar Square, Admiralty Arch, The Mall, St. James's Palace, Buckingham Palace and the Changing of the Guard, Piccadilly Circus.

SUNDAY MORNING TOUR Evan Evans Tour No. 3

Sundays, except December 25 and 26. Departs at 9:45 A.M. and returns at 12:15 P.M. Price £1.10 ($2.75), including all entrance fees. This is the same as the Morning Tour of the West End, above, but does not include a visit to Westminster Abbey, since services are held there on Sundays.

SUNDAY MORNING DRIVE Frames & Rickards

Sundays, except December 25 and 26. Departs at the following times:

- TOUR 1sF from Frames, Herbrand Street, at 10 A.M.
- TOUR 1sFM from Seymour Street near Marble Arch, at 10 A.M.
- TOUR 1sR from Rickards, 17 Woburn Place, at 9:45 A.M.
- TOUR 1sRT from Rickards, Trafalgar Square, at 10 A.M.

Tour returns at approximately 12:30 P.M. Price £1.10 ($2.75). Bloomsbury, Holborn, Staple Inn, Hatton Garden, Smithfield, St. Sepulchre's, Old Bailey, Cheapside, Bow Bells Church, Guildhall, Mansion House, the

Sightseeing 111

Stock Exchange, the Bank of England, Lloyd's of London, Petticoat Lane, Spitalfields, Bishopsgate, Victoria Embankment, House of Parliament, Westminster Abbey, Lambeth Palace, Whitehall, Downing Street, Cenotaph, Horse Guards, Trafalgar Square, Oxford Street, Hyde Park, Buckingham Palace and the Changing of the Guard, Piccadilly Circus.

AFTERNOON CITY TOUR Evan Evans Tour No. 2

Departs daily at 2:15 P.M., returns at 5:15 P.M. Does not operate on December 25 and 26. Price £1.80 ($4.50), including all entrance fees. Leaving Tottenham Court Road, drive down Kingsway to the Aldwych, passing St. Clement Danes Church and the Law Courts, into Fleet Street, the City of London, and to St. Paul's Cathedral. Drive through the financial center with the Bank of England, the Royal Exchange, Mansion House (home of London's Lord Mayor), the Stock Exchange, and on to visit the Tower of London. Return by way of Doughty Street, passing the house of Charles Dickens, to Russell Square. On Sundays, the Tower is closed and a visit to H.M.S. *Belfast* is substituted.

DAILY AFTERNOON DRIVE Frames & Rickards

Daily except December 25 and 26. Departures at these times:
TOUR 2F from Frames, Herbrand Street, at 2 P.M.
TOUR 2FM from Seymour St. near Marble Arch, at 2 P.M.
TOUR 2R from Rickards, 17 Woburn Place, at 2 P.M.
TOUR 2RT from Rickards, Trafalgar Square, at 2:15 P.M.

All tours return at approximately 4:45 P.M. Price £1.80 ($4.50). Kingsway, a visit to the Old Curiosity Shop, St. Clement Danes Church, the Law Courts, Fleet Street, a visit to St. Paul's Cathedral, the Bank of England, Mansion House, Lombard Street, New London Bridge, Tooley Street, Tower Bridge, a visit to the Tower of London, Victoria Embankment, The Temple, Somerset House, and Trafalgar Square.

WHOLE DAY TOUR OF LONDON Evan Evans Tour No. 4

Monday through Saturday, except December 25 and 26. Departs at 9:35 A.M. and returns at 5:15 P.M. Price £4.20 ($10.50), including all entrance fees and luncheon. Past the British Museum, London University, to Trafalgar Square and past Nelson's Column. Then by the National Gallery, Whitehall, Big Ben and the Houses of Parliament, Westminster Abbey, the Cenotaph, Downing Street, The Mall, and to Buckingham Palace. After lunch, Hyde Park, Oxford Street, the law courts, Fleet Street and the City. Then St. Paul's Cathedral, the Bank of England, the Tower of London, and Tower Bridge.

Night Tours

EVENING CIRCULAR TOUR Evan Evans Tour No. 5

Monday through Saturday, departs at 7:30 P.M. and returns at approximately 9:15 P.M. Price £1.30 ($3.25), including one drink at a historical London pub. This scenic drive goes through Chelsea, where the artists and "swingers" abound, and along the King's Road. Then a drive along the Thames Embankment past Old Scotland Yard and Cleopatra's Needle, and a tour of the West End and colorful Soho.

EVENING DRIVE Frames & Rickards Tour 3F

Departing every Friday from Frames, Herbrand Street, at 7:15 P.M. Price £1.15 ($2.87). A lovely drive through night-time London, including a stop at an old pub.

EVENING TOUR AND "TALK OF THE TOWN" Evan Evans Tour No. 6

Departs at 7:30 p.m. Monday through Saturday, except December 24, 25, 26, and 31. Price Monday through Thursday £7..50 ($18.75); Friday and Saturday £8.20 ($20.50); all-inclusive. A guided tour of the sights, followed by an exciting evening's entertainment at Talk of The Town, one of London's leading establishments, with a drink, a three-course dinner, spectacular cabaret, and dancing. Gentlemen must wear a jacket and tie. Return transportation is not included, so you can stay as long as you like. Taxis are easy to get here.)

EVENING DRIVE AND "TALK OF THE TOWN" Frames & Rickards Tour 3cF

Departs every Friday from Frames, Herbrand Street, at 7:15 p.m. Price £7.60 ($19), all-inclusive. An evening drive, then entertainment at Talk of The Town, with dinner, dancing, and a floor show. No return transport, so stay as long as you wish to.

EVENING TOUR AND "SHOWBOAT" Evan Evans Tour No. 8

Departs 7:30 p.m. Monday through Saturday, except December 24, 25, 26, and 31. Price £6.50 ($16.25), all-inclusive. A tour of the sights, and an evening at the Showboat, with a colorful floor show, dinner with a half-carafe of wine, and dancing. Here, too, men should wear a jacket and tie. Stay as long as you like, since return transport is not included.

EVENING DRIVE AND "SHOWBOAT" Frames & Rickards Tour No. 3aF

Departs every Friday except during December from Frames, Herbrand Street, at 7:15 p.m. Price £6 ($15), all-inclusive. An evening drive, followed by entertainment at the Showboat, including dancing, cabaret, and dinner. Again, return transport is not included so you can remain as long as you like.

ELIZABETHAN BANQUET Evan Evans Tour No. 26

Tuesday and Saturday (except December 25 and January 1), and December 31. Departs at 6:50 p.m. and returns at approximately 11:30 p.m. Price £6.50 ($16.25), all-inclusive. Travel northward on the Great North Road through Kentish Town, Highgate to the 15th-century Palace of Hatfield. This is a wonderful opportunity to participate in a splendid banquet in grand Elizabethan style on the grounds of Hatfield House, where Henry VIII detained his three children, Mary, Elizabeth, and Edward, and where Princess Elizabeth was held until she was crowned queen after the death of "Bloody Mary." During the evening you will be entertained in traditional style with minstrels and ballad singers, all in full Elizabethan regalia. The menu is specially printed to serve as a memento of your visit and the dinner. The dinner itself is four courses, Elizabethan style, with wine and mead!

Thames River Trips

Regular motor launch services operate along the whole stretch of the river from April to September. There are daily services from Westminster Pier to Kew Gardens, Hampton Court, and the Riverside at Richmond. From Charing Cross Pier you can go to Tower Bridge and Greenwich, and from Kingston you can get to Windsor and Oxford. From Paddington and Waterloo Railway Stations there are combined rail/river trips to Windsor, Staines, Chertsey, Oxford, Henley, and elsewhere. For more information about these and other river trips, contact the British Tourist Authority, the London Tourist Board, or Thames Passenger Services Federation, York Villa, Church Street, Twickenham, Middlesex, Tel: 892-5255.

Canal Trips

The London canals are very interesting, though few tourists know anything about them. There are Venetian-style trips on these canals that you can take.

REGENT'S PARK CANAL, "Jason's Trip"
This is a cruise of 1 hour and 20 minutes in the traditionally painted canal narrow boat *Jason,* through the most picturesque part of the canal. Moored at Canaletto Gallery, opposite 60 Bloomfield Road, W.9. Price 25p ($.62). Departs Saturdays and Sundays at 2 and 3:30 P.M. daily after Whitsun. For bookings and further information, Tel: 286-3428.

ZOO WATERBUS Underground: Warwick Avenue
From Little Venice to the Zoo. Monday through Saturday, runs every hour on the hour from 10 A.M. to 5 P.M.; Sundays runs from 2 to 6 P.M., Returning every hour on the hour. Price, including admission to zoo: 60p ($1.50); return: 15p ($.37).

JENNIE WREN Underground: Camden Town
A cruise of 1½ hours in the traditionally designed and painted canal narrow boat *Jennie Wren* from Camden Town, through the zoo and Regent's Park, to Maida Vale, around the island at Little Venice, and returning along the canal. Moored at the Garden Jetty, 250 Camden High Street, London, N.W.1. Runs Saturdays and Sundays at 2 and 3:30 P.M. Price 30p ($.74). For bookings and other information, Tel: 485-6210.

ON YOUR OWN

The Traditional Sights

CHANGING OF THE GUARD at Buckingham Palace S.W.1
Underground: Strand, Westminster, or Trafalgar Square Bus: 3, 11, 12, 24, 29, 39, 53, 88, 159
Ever since Britain became a monarchy the ceremony of mounting and dismounting guards at royal palaces has been standard British army procedure drill. The most famous of these is, of course, the Changing of the Guard at Buckingham Palace. When the new guard is being mounted from Wellington Barracks, they leave to march to the courtyard of Buckingham Palace at just about 11:30 A.M. If the new guard is being mounted from Chelsea Barracks, they start marching to the palace at around 11:10 A.M. In both cases the Guards march behind a military band from one of the Foot Guard regiments. At Buckingham Palace, the old guard is drawn up in the courtyard ready to hand over the guard duties and when

the ceremonial transfer has taken place, the band, which plays during the inspection and changeover ceremonies, again heads up the marches and leads the old guard back to their barracks. The uniforms worn by the Brigade of Guards are not merely for the purpose of pomp and ceremony. They are the same uniforms worn by the guards as far back as 1642 when the Red Tunics were meant to camouflage blood-stains from the wounds sustained in the wars the Britons had fought throughout their history. This unique and picturesque ceremony takes place daily at 11:30 A.M. in the forecourt of Buckingham Palace. Its precision and pageantry form one of London's outstanding tourist sights. It is advisable to get there early.

HOUSEHOLD CAVALRY Whitehall, S.W.1 Underground: Charing Cross, Trafalgar Square, and Strand (a short walk from any of these) Bus: 76

After seeing the Changing of the Guard at Buckingham Palace, on another day go see the Changing of the Guard performed by the Household Cavalry at the Horse Guards Parade, Whitehall, very close to Buckingham Palace on the other side of St. James's Park. Many tourists are not aware of this beautiful show, which I find even more exciting than the Buckingham performance. Here the cavalry guards are resplendent in shining silver breastplates and waving plumes as they prance out on their magnificent black horses. A not-to-be-missed pageant. It takes place on weekdays at 11:30 A.M., Sundays at 10 A.M.

BUCKINGHAM PALACE the Mall, S.W.1

Buckingham Palace is the official London home of English Kings and Queens. When the Queen is in residence the Royal Standard is flown at the masthead. It is not open to the public. The palace was originally built for the Duke of Buckingham and later became the home of King George III. From the small country manor house of the Duke the building was added on to and remodeled continually. During the war it was bombed and again rebuilt. Today it contains over 600 rooms. After the guard-changing ceremony you can visit the Queen's Gallery in Buckingham Palace. Here paintings by the world's masters from the Queen's private collection are on view Tuesday through Saturday from 11 A.M. to 5 P.M. and Sundays from 2 to 5 P.M. On Wednesdays and Thursdays between 2 and 4 P.M., the Royal Mews, where the royal ceremonial carriages are housed, is open to visitors. Admission to both 15p ($.36).

THE TOWER OF LONDON Tower Hill, E.C.3 Underground: Tower Hill Bus: 14 (to Monument)

This foreboding tower/fortress/palace/prison is one of the most interesting sights in London. Virtually every brick and stone tell a story of its past—some gay, some humorous, but most gory and bloodcurdling. The Tower of London is not just one tower, as the name implies, but a complex of many towers and buildings. It stands on the north bank of the Thames, which made it convenient to bring prisoners here by boat. The stone dock and stairs still remain. Queen Elizabeth, when still a princess, was brought up those steps to the Tower of London for imprisonment. There is so much to see and so much history to learn that it would be a shame to come here for just a cursory look; try to arrange to spend several hours. Building was started by William the Conquerer and the central White Tower dates from Norman times, though almost every succeeding period of English architecture is represented within the walls. Until James I, the Tower was a Royal residence; it has also been used as a fortress. Many historical names are on the list of famous people who were imprisoned in the Bloody Tower, among them Sir Walter Raleigh, Judge Jeffreys, and Princess Elizabeth. It was in the Bloody Tower that the Little Princes, Edward V and the Duke of York, were supposedly murdered by their uncle Richard III in 1483. Tower Green is a pleasant little parklike area, surrounded by stone-cottage-like cells. Famous prisoners were kept in these prior to their final walk across the green to the scaffold—which claimed the lives of Anne Boleyn, Catherine Howard, Lady Jane Grey (the nine-day Queen), her husband Dudley, and Sir Thomas More. Above Tower Green at Tower Hill is to be found the headsman's block where heads rolled. Queen Elizabeth herself, after spending a nightmare period in the Bloody Tower, expecting daily to take her last walk to the headsman's block, had such vivid memories of her fear that she chose the very same punishment for her lover, the Earl of Essex, when she discovered that he had plotted a rebellion against her. A stone slab today is all that is left of the spot where the guillotine once stood. All over the green you will see large black ravens who are said to actually be registered as official Tower residents and are fed on horsemeat by the keepers because it is said that if the ravens ever leave the Tower, a curse will cause it to collapse. The best way to see the entire area is to take a guided tour. There is an office to the right just after you step through the main gate, where you can make arrangements to join one. There is so much history here that it would be a pity to miss out on any of it and there is no better way to hear all of it than via one of these tours. You will see Salt Tower where the prisoners scratched messages in the walls with anything they could find. The Wakefield Tower houses the two famous collections of England's Crown Jewels, including the magnificent Imperial State Crown. The world's most famous, made for Queen Victoria's coronation in 1838, it contains the famous Black Prince Ruby, worn by Henry V to celebrate the English defeat of the French in 1415, plus over 3,000 other jewels, primarily diamonds. The present Queen Elizabeth still wears this crown when she opens Parliament—though how she is able to hold her head up I certainly do not know! Incidentally, that huge glasslike bauble incrested on the Royal Sceptre is not glass at all. It is a mere 516 carat diamond! Your eyes are sure to bug out of your head at the sight of the precious stones used to embellish the huge swords, crowns, scepters, and robes of the British monarchs at their coronation. They are well guarded by the Yeoman Wardens in their brightly colored Tudor uniforms. In the late 17th century, Colonel Blood almost succeeded in stealing these precious jewels. In the same White Tower there is an armory where you can view the historic English weapons and armor used for centuries by British soldiers. There is also a rather blood-chilling display of instruments of torture and execution. The guards you see everywhere in the peculiar costumes are known as "Beefeaters" after whom the popular gin was named. As impractical and theatrical, almost comical, as they may seem, the costumes are authentic, from the Tudor period. From March through October, open from 9:30 A.M. to 5 P.M.; admission 20p ($.48). From November through February, open from 9:30 A.M. to 4 P.M.; admission

10p ($.24). Closed Sundays and public holidays, except from March through October when it is open on those days from 2 to 5 P.M. Admission to the jewel collection 10p ($.25).

WESTMINSTER ABBEY Broad Sanctuary, S.W.1 Underground: St. James's Park or Westminster (circle and district lines) Buses: 11, 24, 29, 39, 76, 77, 88, 127, 134, 503 (Red Arrow)

Founded by Edward the Confessor in 1065, his cousin William I (William the Conqueror) was the first to be crowned there in 1066. You can see the chair on which each sovereign sat ever since that time, with the exceptions of Edward V and Edward VIII. With its superb English Gothic architecture, the square Twin Towers are most impressive indeed, but the Abbey is far more than one of the finest ecclesiastical structures in the world, it is really a living book of the history of England for the 900 years since the Norman conquests.

Next to the tomb of Edward the Confessor, in a place of honor, stands the coronation chair with the historical, ancient Scottish relic, the Stone of Scone, under the seat. There was quite a bit of publicity about this same stone when it was stolen just prior to Queen Elizabeth's coronation, but it was retrieved in time. The Sword and Shield of Edward III also is displayed near the coronation chair.

The beautiful Henry VII chapel, dating from the 16th century, with some of the finest fan vaulting in the world, contains not only the tomb of King Henry himself but also those of Elizabeth I, Mary Tudor ("Bloody Mary"), and Cromwell. Over the tomb of King Henry there is a lovely Vivarini painting and on the other end a stained-glass window depicting the Battle of Britain, in honor of the RAF.

The Abbey does not contain tombs merely of monarchs, but pays tribute to famous writers and poets as well in the Poets' Corner, just to the right of the entrance to the Royal Chapel. Here there are memorials to such as Chaucer, Shakespeare, Shelley, Byron, Tennyson, Dickens, Kipling, Hardy, the Brontë sisters, Thackeray, and Longfellow.

In the North Transept you will find Statesman's Aisle where such as Darwin, Disraeli, and Newton are either entombed or honored by monuments.

Just inside the Great West Door is the simple poppy-framed Grave of the Unknown Warrior of the First World War. And nearby can be found the memorial stone to Sir Winston Churchill laid in 1965.

Don't miss the Norman Undercroft, in the Cloisters, where you will find the Exhibition of Abbey Treasures, including the famous effigies in wood and wax of Kings and queens, many of them in contemporary costume, such as that of Charles II. There are also effigies of William Pitt, Earl of Chatham, and Lord Nelson, together with numerous historic documents and seals, the specially made Coronation Chair of Mary II (wife of William of Orange) and other interesting exhibits concerned with the history of the Abbey; the Capeline worn by Charles II, the Ring that Elizabeth I gave to the Earl of Essex. Open daily except Sunday from 9:30 A.M. to 5 P.M. Admission 10p ($.24).

The 13th-century Chapter House can also be visited. You will be given special shoes so as not to mar the beautiful 700-year-old floor. This is where Parliament used to meet and much of the history of England was decided. March through September, open from 10:30 A.M. to 6 P.M.; closed Sundays. October through February, open from 10:30 A.M. to 3:30 P.M. Admission 2½p ($.06).

While Westminster Abbey is a unique treasure house of English history, it is first and foremost a living church. Three services are held here each weekday and five on Sundays. It is worth visiting at these times for the pageantry of the mass.

During the summer months the Abbey is bound to be very crowded and it is difficult to see all you would like. Try to visit it early in the morning, at midday, or in early evening. Best of all is Wednesdays between 6 and 10 P.M. The Abbey is open daily all year round from 8 A.M.; Wednesdays it closes at 10 P.M., Sundays after the evening congregational service, and every other day of the week at 6 P.M. The Royal Chapels are open Mondays and Thursdays from 9:30 A.M. to 4:30 P.M., Tuesdays and Fridays from 10 A.M. to 4:30 P.M., Wednesdays from 9:30 A.M. to 4:30 P.M. and from 6 to 10 P.M. (admission free Wednesday evenings), Saturdays from 9:30 A.M. to 2P.M. and from 3:45 to 5 P.M. The Chapels are closed Sundays. Admission 20p ($.50).

There are guided Super-Tours Monday through Friday at 10:45 A.M. and 2:30 P.M., conducted by Abbey Vergers or by specially selected and authorized guides. Parties are limited to 25. Saturdays there is only one tour, at 10:45 A.M. Fee £1 ($2.50) including a souvenir leaflet with plans and notes, and free admission to the Royal Chapels, the Exhibition of Treasures, the Chapter House, and (if available) parts of the Abbey not normally open to the public. If you wish to join one of these tours, apply at the information desk in the nave of the Abbey.

HOUSES OF PARLIAMENT Westminster, S.W.1 Underground: Westminster Bus: 3, 11, 12, 24, 29, 39, 53, 59, 59A, 88, 159, 503

Just across the street from Westminster Abbey, this is a likely stop to make next. Originally built in 1840, it was bombed and burnt on May 10, 1941. The New Chamber, designed by Sir Giles Gilbert Scott, is a free interpretation of late-Gothic style. The famous Churchill Arch to the House of Commons was constructed from the rubble of the German blitzing in 1941.

Both the House of Commons and the House of Lords hold sway in what was once the Royal Palace of Westminster, the official palace until Henry VIII deserted it in preference Whitehall.

There are really two reasons to visit the English Houses of Parliament. One is the actual beauty of the buildings themselves. You cannot help but be impressed with the 320-foot tower encasing the largest clock in the world, Big Ben. When the House of Commons was bombed in 1941 the tower withstood the attack and stood proudly throughout, striking its chimes just as before. This became a symbol of Britain's courage and determination to hold their ground. The chimes are affectionately used as the signature of Britain's news broadcasts. A guided tour is the best bet through these magnificent buildings. Not only will it prevent you from becoming lost, but you will get all the details of the historical import of the various rooms. The tour will take you through the Royal Galleries, the Robing Room, and the Prince's Chamber.

The other reason for visiting the Houses of Parliament is to hear some

118 LONDON

of the debates from the Strangers' Gallery, which always promises to be extremely interesting and lively. The House of Commons is the most interesting because the debates are the least inhibited. The members get very excited and don't hesitate to shout in order to make a point. The House of Lords is a bit more proper, with members being more polite. To obtain a seat in the Strangers' Gallery of the House of Commons, join the public queue outside St. Stephen's Entrance. Queue is admitted Monday through Thursday after 4:15 P.M., Fridays after 11:30 A.M. If you wish you can also make advance arrangements to attend a debate by applying to your embassy or the High Commissioner's Office in London. This is the best way to be assured of a seat since if you are standing in the queue it is quite possible that seats will be taken before your turn is reached. To obtain a seat in the Strangers' Gallery of the House of Lords, join the public queue at the St. Stephen's Entrance, too. Queue is admitted Tuesday through Thursday, after 2:00 P.M.

If you visit the Houses of Parliament when they are not in session—Saturdays; Mondays, Tuesdays, and Thursdays in August; and Thursdays in September—you will be admitted from 10 A.M. to 4:30 P.M.

Be sure to visit Westminster Hall, which dates back to 1097 and is the oldest public building in London. The Hall is absolutely huge and was originally supposed to be one of the Palace bedrooms. It was here that the famous trial of Charles I and Guy Fawkes took place. When the House of Commons is not sitting, open Mondays, Thursdays, and Saturdays from 10 A.M. to 1:30 P.M. When neither house is sitting, open Monday through Friday until 4 P.M., Saturdays until 5 P.M.

MADAME TUSSAUD'S Marylebone Road at the Baker St. Station, N.W.1 Underground: Baker Street Bus: 13, 27, 30, 74, 159

Madame Tussaud began her strange hobby of modeling during the French Revolution. I say strange because she seemed to be preoccupied with the heads that rolled at the guillotine. She is said to have personally taken the death masks from the guillotined heads of Louis XVI and Marie-Antoinette—which are still to be found in the museum today. She and her husband opened a wax-works museum in 1770 in Paris, and 30 years later she moved the whole thing, lock stock, and barrel, to England. Here she enjoyed great success until her death in 1850. The waxworks remains one of the most interesting—and gory—sights in London. Many of the figures to be seen today were actually done by Madame Tussaud, though of course the administrators keep the exhibition up to date by adding new figures all the time. The exhibitions are so lifelike there are times when you are sure Sir Winston is about to speak to you, or perhaps Benjamin Franklin, George Washington, or even our own John F. Kennedy. I am sure many of the male visitors wish that Brigitte Bardot were as alive as she looks! For visitors with strong stomachs, there is the chamber of Horrors where Jack the Ripper is enshrined, along with Dr. Crippen the poisoner, Marat the murderer who specialized in aristocrats, Lee Harvey Oswald, and many other familiar figures. There is the bathtub in which George Smith drowned three of his wives, the guillotine blade that saw so much action during the French Revolution, a gallows, and an iron cage where prisoners were starved to death in Milazzo, Sicily. On the main floor you can see the entire Battle of Trafalgar and actually step aboard

Nelson's flagship, re-created to the tune of $120,000. Going below, you come upon the lifelike figure of Nelson himself lying on his deathbed. The Battle of Britain, fought in 1940, in which the RAF proudly defeated the Luftwaffe, is also on display. The newest addition to the waxworks is the neighboring planetarium. A kind of *son et lumière* takes place here as the copper dome becomes a theater of the sky, projecting astronomical configurations and space events. The performances are exciting and fully narrated. They take place every hour on the hour weekdays from 11 A.M. to 6 P.M., Sundays from 1 to 6 P.M. Royal Ticket, including admission to the waxworks, the battles, and the planetarium, 85p ($2.12). The Wax Museum itself is open daily from 10 A.M. to 7 P.M.

KENSINGTON PALACE and THE LONDON MUSEUM Kensington Gardens, W.8 Underground: Queen's Way and Bayswater (north side of Gardens), High Street, Kensington (south side of Gardens) Bus: 9, 12, 88 (12 and 88 run along north side of Kensington Gardens, 9 runs along south side).

The Kensington Palace is the home of the Royal State Apartments and the London Museum, and is the residence of Princess Margaret and her family. The Palace was originally the home of William III in 1689, but was last used as the royal residence when George II died in 1760. Both Queen Victoria and Queen Mary were born at the Palace and the Royal Apartments still contain many of their personal things, with early Georgian and Victorian works, paintings from the Royal Collections, royal costumes, furniture and *objets d'art*. You can visit Queen Victoria's bedroom where she was told in 1837, after the death of William IV, that she was the new Queen. On that day she began the longest reign in British history. Her toys and dollhouse still remain in the little room next to her bedroom. The late Queen Mary was born in this same bedroom. The robes she and her husband King George V wore at their coronation in 1911 can be seen here today.

Another Mary, Mary II, consort of William III, also lived at the Palace and her things are on view in Queen Mary's Gallery.

You just may be lucky enough to see Princess Margaret or some of her family since they are in and out of the Palace all the time. Her quarters are, of course, off-limits; the public entrance to the palace is near the Orangery. Incidentally, her wedding dress is on view in the King's Drawing Room in the Palace.

After viewing the Royal State Apartments, wander over to the London Museum for a most complete and exciting reenactment of the history of London from prehistoric days up to modern times, illustrated mainly by archeological material, topographical views and models, costumes and products of London crafts. Special collections are devoted to coronation regalia and royal costumes of the theater and children's toys. There are neolithic and iron-age relics that were unearthed at Heathrow Airport on display, in Room 1. Room 2 depicts the life of the Britons under Roman rule. In Rooms 9 and 10 you will find models of medieval London, including the London Bridge, quaint old shops and homes of that period. Room 12 is the shrine of coronation attire. Room 14 depicts the Great Fire of 1666 when most of the city was destroyed. Room 18 contains costumes of the 18th century. Take as much time as possible in wandering through the museum, since it is such a good opportunity to learn English

120 LONDON

history, from its very beginnings up to the present. Allow enough time to stroll in the Palace Gardens. The Royal State Apartments and the museum are open Monday through Saturday from 10 A.M. to 6 P.M., Sundays from 2 to 6 P.M. In October and February they close at 5 P.M., and from November through January at 4. Closed Good Friday, Christmas Eve, Christmas day, and Boxing day. Admission free.

ST. PAUL'S CATHEDRAL E.C.4 Underground: St. Paul's Bus: 6 , 9, 11, 15, 22, 53, 615

The largest and most famous church in the city, built by Sir Christopher Wren. Standing on Ludgate Hill, this beautiful cathedral unfortunately is surrounded by unattractive buildings. St. Paul's has a history of adversity. Churches on this site have been destroyed by Norsemen, burnt down several times, and hit during the blitzing of London. The present St. Paul's itself was built on the wreckage of an earlier Cathedral that was destroyed in the Great Fire of 1666.

The interior is not as beautiful as some and a bit austere to my eyes, but it does have a great historical interest. The Duke of Wellington is buried here, as are Lord Nelson and the architect himself, Wren. The funeral carriage of the "Iron Duke" is one of the interesting things to see. The American Memorial Chapel pays loving tribute to the thousands of American service men who gave their lives for Britain during World War II.

A huge cross tops the cathedral, resting on a golden ball. Encircling the interior of the dome is a whispering gallery, so named because even the slightest whisper can be heard clear around to the other side.

Open daily from October through March, from 8 A.M. to 5 P.M; from April through September, from 8 A.M. to 7 P.M. Inspection is not possible during service times. The crypt and galleries and the upper dome are open Monday through Saturday from 10:45 A.M. to 3:30 P.M. Admission to the crypt 20p ($.50); all galleries 15p ($.37).

WHITEHALL S.W.1 Underground: Strand, Trafalgar Square, or Westminster Bus: 3, 11, 12, 24, 39, 53, 59, 88, 159

This immense complex of buildings extends from Trafalgar Square to Parliament Square and comprises the seat of British government. The grounds of the whole area at one time belonged to Whitehall Palace before it burned down in a great fire in 1698. All that remains is the banqueting house built by Inigo Jones, from 1619 to 1622, for James I. The banqueting house formed part of the once splendid Whitehall Palace of the Tudor and Stuart Monarchs, and it was from here that Charles I went to meet his executioners in 1649. This was the only important part of the Palace to escape the fire of 1698. The beautifully painted ceiling is by Rubens. Open Tuesday through Saturday from 10 A.M. to 5 P.M., Sundays from 2 to 5 P.M. Admission 5p ($.12).

Those are the most popular and well-known things to see. If you have more time, here are some others you'll enjoy.

LANCASTER HOUSE Stable Yard, St. James's, S.W.1 Underground: Green Park

Just opposite St. James's Palace, this is considered the finest surviving example in London of a great town mansion of the early Victorian period,

Sightseeing 121

restored and redecorated by the Department of the Environment. And it is quite interesting to imagine how people lived in those days in London. The State Apartments are used for important international conferences and official functions today, so they may be closed on short notice. However, they are usually open on Saturdays, Sundays, and bank holidays from Easter through mid-December, from 2 to 6 P.M. Admission 15p ($.37).

DICKENS'S HOUSE 48 Doughty Street, Bloomsbury, W.C.1 Underground: Russell Square, Holborn, Chancery Lane Bus: 17, 19, 38

Charles Dickens lived here from 1837 to 1839. The house remains as it was in his time, with his library, manuscripts, the desk at which he wrote, and a kitchen—which has been transformed into a model of the Dingley Del kitchen from *Pickwick Papers*, which was written here. The house is very modest and with none of the trappings one might have expected for this most famous of all British authors. Dickens took great pleasure in the low life of London, and it was here that he got his inspiration for many of his works, including *Oliver Twist*, which was also written here. Open Monday through Saturday from 10 A.M. to 12:30 P.M. and from 2 to 5 P.M. Admission 15p ($.37)

OLD BAILEY Newgate St., E.C.4 Underground: St. Paul's Bus: 6, 9, 11, 15, 22

This is Central Criminal Court, of which much has been heard in the recounting of famous British trials. It is rather interesting to attend a trial to watch the very conservative and proper barristers present their cases in their white wigs and black robes. The public gallery is open Monday through Friday from 10:15 A.M. to 1:45 P.M. Line up at the door in Newgate St. Admission free.

DOWNING STREET off Whitehall, S.W.1 Underground: Westminster

A short street of little houses belonging to very important personages. No. 10, for instance, is the official residence of the Prime Minister and was presented by George II to Sir Robert Walpole in 1731. The Chancellor of the Exchequer and the government Chief Whip live at Nos. 11 and 12. You have to content yourself with merely strolling the street, however, since none of the houses is open to the public. It is not unusual to see any of these gentlemen popping in and out of their houses, but there are always guards to keep you from getting too close.

BEAR GARDENS MUSEUM Bear Gardens Alley, S.E.1

During medieval times the southern bank of the River Thames around Southwark was notorious for its whorehouses, in those days called "stewes." At the Bear Gardens Museum, the history of these "stewes" is traced from Roman up to Elizabethan times. Packed with fascinating material displayed in period rooms, the exhibition is extremely interesting. Open Tuesday through Friday from 10 A.M. to 7 P.M., Saturdays and Sundays from 1 to 7 P.M. Admission 10p ($.25).

GUILDHALL King's St., Cheapside, E.C.2 Underground: Bank, Mansion House, or Moorgate Buses: 6, 9, 15.

The civic hall of the Corporation of London, rebuilt in the 15th century, where civic activity and proud ceremonials have been centered for almost 1,000 years. Local governments have developed in the City of London from the ancient Court of Husting to the modern Common Council. The laws and customs of Guildhall have equal force with the common law of the land. The first mayor was installed here in 1191 or 1192 and the Lord Mayor and Sheriff are still elected and admitted to office each year within its walls. But the hall has been the scene of far more than local elections and civic government. It has witnessed the trials of traitors and clamors for reform, remonstrances to kings and Parliament, protests and joyful acclaims, and the brilliant reception of royal personages, presidents, and emperors. Lord Mayor's banquets and international hospitality, conferences and the ceremonial conferment of the freedom of the city on statesmen, heroes, and patriots are traditional events. The Guildhall suffered serious damage in the Great Fire of 1666 and again in the 1940 blitzing of London. But each time it has been rebuilt. Restoration has been in the same Gothic architecture of the original, including a medieval entranceway. Stained-glass windows commemorate the Lord Mayors and Mayors elected here and there are monuments to Winston Churchill, Lord Nelson, and the Duke of Wellington, not to mention a 15th-century crypt. Hand-receivers for a 20-minute radio tour of the building are available to visitors upon application to the beadle (the officer in charge). Open Monday through Saturday from 10 A.M. to 5 P.M., Sundays from 2 to 5 p.m. Admission free.

TRAFALGAR SQUARE Underground: Trafalgar Square, Strand Bus: 3, 6, 9, 11, 12, 13, 15, 24, 29, 53, 88, 159, 505

One of London's best-known landmarks. From the top of a 185-foot-high column the figure of Nelson looks down on busy Trafalgar Square, with its famous fountains, traffic, crowds, and pigeons. Visitors can obtain an excellent view from the steps of the National Gallery. From here you can look southward to Whitehall and the offices of government. To the southwest is Admiralty Arch and the Mall and to the east is the Strand and St. Martin-in-the-Fields, parish church of Buckingham Palace. At Christmas and New Year's the square is decorated with a huge tree presented by the city of Oslo.

GRAY'S INN W.C.1 Underground: Chancery Lane

One of the four remaining Inns of Court. The buildings have all been restored and there are outstanding gardens plus a 17th-century gatehouse. Francis Bacon was one of the most famous tenants to have stayed here. From May through July and in October the gardens are open Monday through Friday from noon to 2 P.M.; in August and September, from 9:30 A.M. to 5 P.M. Closed Sundays and bank holidays.

LINCOLN'S INN Chancery Lane, W.C.2 Underground: Chancery Lane, Holborn Buses: 6, 8, 12, 77, 77B.

The records of the present Inn of Court go back to 1422. The rolls of the inn contain such famous names as Sir Thomas More, John Donne, William Penn, Horace Walpole, Cardinal Newman, Disraeli, Gladstone. The gatehouse was originally erected in 1518 and Oliver Cromwell is said to have lodged there as a law student. The Old Hall was built in 1491 and extended in 1624. The Chapel is built in Gothic style and attributed to Inigo Jones. New Square is a charming and well preserved quadrangle of the late 17th century, where Dickens at the age of 14, served as a clerk in the solicitor's office. The halls, library, and Chapel are open Monday through Friday from 10 A.M. to 4:30 P.M. and the gardens Monday through Friday from noon to 2:30 P.M.

THE TEMPLE Fleet Street, E.C.4   Underground: Temple   Bus: 6, 9, 13, 77, 77B.

The Temple is an area that takes its name from the medieval order of the Knights Templar. The 16th-century Middle Temple Hall has one of the most splendid double hammer-beamed roofs in England. The long serving table is said to have been made from the timber of Drake's ship, the *Golden Hind.* The Hall was opened by Elizabeth I in 1576. Shakespeare's own company is believed to have performed *Twelfth Night* in the Hall on February 2, 1602. The hall is open Monday through Saturday from 10 A.M. to noon and from 3 to 4:30 P.M., if not in use. After seeing the Temple Hall wander over to Temple Church, which serves both the Inner and Middle Temple. It has a circular nave and is one of only five medieval round churches surviving in England. The church contains many fine 12th- and 13th-century military effigies. Open daily in the winter from 10:15 A.M. to 4:30 P.M., in the summer from 10:15 A.M. to 5 P.M. The Inner Temple Hall was destroyed by bombing in 1941 and was rebuilt by Sir Hubert Worthington. The vaulted chamber called the Buttery is at the west end, with a crypt below surviving from the 15th century. Open Monday through Friday from 10 to 11:30 A.M. and from 2:30 to 4 P.M.

H.M.S. *DISCOVERY* Victoria Embankment, just below the Waterloo Bridge, W.C.2

The *Discovery* is the research ship used by Captain Robert Scott on his abortive Antarctic expedition. All his trouble was for naught, since the South Pole was reached by the Norwegian Amundsen before Scott could make it. He and his crew died after that in a raging blizzard. Scott's cabin, the bridge, and the upper deck are all open to view, and there are many exhibitions of interest regarding the trips to the Antarctic. Open daily from 1 to 4:30 P.M. Admission free.

London's Streets

PICCADILLY W.1

Piccadilly is always associated with motor showrooms, airline offices, banks, art galleries, Fortnum and Mason, and the Burlington Arcade. Piccadilly Circus gives it worldwide fame and the Ritz at Green Park adds an extra distinction. The origin of the name is uncertain but is thought by some to come from "piccadilly," the wild flower that used to bloom on the edge of London.

REGENT STREET W.1

This street was designed by the famous architect John Nash, who envisaged it as a superb professional way, lined with elegant buildings and extending from the Prince Regent's house in Pall Mall to his projected house in Regent Park. The Regent Park house was never built, but the result was one of London's most famous streets.

BOND STREET W.1

It caters to those who want the best, and are prepared to pay for it. One glance at the sleek chauffeur-driven cars and the well-dressed shoppers confirms that. Now perhaps the most fashionable shopping street of all,

Bond Street was once a muddy country lane frequented by highwaymen and other villains. Bond Street is divided into Old and New. The former built in 1686.

CARNABY STREET
Carnaby Street was where the young-clothes craze began in the mid-1960s and continued. The commercial magic of the name has spread into the neighboring streets, and the area is alive with noise and color. Most of the clothes are inexpensive and not too many of them should be taken seriously.

KNIGHTSBRIDGE S.W.1
Harrods Department Store is located here. The street is said to have gotten its name from two knights who fought in this part of London on their way to the Crusades. It is now a chic and attractive shopping center.

SOHO W.1
A center for entertainment of all types and just about every nationality in restaurants. Here you'll find nude strip teasers, sexy peep shows, and even some good cabarets, but notably good restaurants, particularly inexpensive ones.

COVENT GARDEN Bow Street, W.C.2
Covent Garden is the mecca for legitimate theaters and movie theaters, and lies northeast of Trafalgar Square.

SHAFTESBURY AVENUE W.1, W.C.2
A long street of primarily legitimate theaters, it runs just off of Piccadilly Circus.

MAYFAIR—KINGS ROAD
A potpourri of just about every kind of boutique, for lower class, way-out fashions and very expensive and elegant garb.

London on Foot

I have always felt the best way to see any city is on foot. You learn so much more about the city, its people, and its history by merely walking around it. Following are some suggested walks for the most important areas of London.

MUSEUMLAND
This walk starts at busy Marble Arch. Go due west through Hyde Park, parallel with Bayswater Road, as far as the pleasant water gardens at the north end of the Serpentine. Cross the gardens, then walk south down a tree-lined avenue (you are now in Kensington Gardens) to the elaborate and fussy Albert Memorial, erected between 1864 and 1876 as a monument to Queen Victoria's beloved Prince Consort. The huge brick-colored building across the road is the Albert Hall (1867–71), used at different times for promenade concerts and wrestling matches, among other functions. Cross Kensington Road to Queen's Gate, along which you turn left into Prince Consort Road. Here you see the back of the Albert Hall and part of Imperial College and the Royal College of Music. Turn right into Exhibition Road. Two hundred yards along this you reach the Science Museum, one of the great museums that owe their existence to the profits of the Great Exhibition of 1851. Beyond the Science Museum, which is especially recommended for those with children in tow, are the Natural

History Museum, the Geological Museum, and most famous of all, the Victoria and Albert Museum. Walking time to the museums, about one hour. Be sure to allow at least two hours for each of the museums you want to visit. If you wish to skip the museums, walk along Brompton Road into the smart shopping area of Knightsbridge (Harrods is there).

PICCADILLY TO THE ZOO

From Piccadilly Circus, walk southwest along Piccadilly. Look in at the unique gourmet store of Fortnum and Mason, then cross the road past the Royal Academy and go up Burlington Arcade, where there are dozens of tiny shops looking more like galleries in a museum of fine arts. At the end of the arcade, turn left and then right, into what is probably the most elegant street of shops in London, Bond Street. The shops here are of all sorts, and specialize in the luxurious and expensive. Cross over Oxford Street and walk toward Marylebone High Street. Among visitors, this is one of London's most neglected areas, but it has as much interest and vitality as parts of Soho. Bookshops, intimate restaurants, pubs where you can enjoy a modest lunch for 30p ($.75) or less, boutiques and unusual antique shops all add color to the street. Look out especially for the old-fashioned fresh fish shop a few yards along Paddington Street, on your left. A little farther on, turn left into Devonshire Street. A hundred yards along this, you cross Harley Street, traditionally associated with doctors, surgeons, and dentists. Turn left into Portland Place at the end of Devonshire Street, then fork right into Park Crescent. Cross Marylebone Road, walk up the privately owned Park Square East, and into Regent's Park. From this entrance to the park, which was originally part of Henry VIII's hunting forest and was later made into a park by the Prince Regent and John Nash, it is a 15-minute walk to the zoo. Walking time about 1¼ hours.

SOUTH BANK

There's very little of London that doesn't merit exploration on foot. But one part that is often overlooked is the walk along the South Bank of the Thames, between Westminster Bridge and Waterloo Bridge. You get an excellent impression of the London skyline and many of the most famous landmarks. Such a walk can be combined with a visit to the Royal Festival Hall, or the Queen Elizabeth Hall, or even, if you know someone who is a member, to the National Film Theatre or its excellent restaurant. To escape the crowds, you should take a "City Stroll, an official London Tourist Board walk. This starts at the Guildhall, and goes to the huge building development at the Barbican, through Roman and Medieval London. Details and a map can be had from all Tourist Information Centres.

TRAFALGAR SQUARE, BIG BEN, AND BUCKINGHAM PALACE

Walk south from Piccadilly Circus down the Haymarket, which was a busy thoroughfare as long ago as 1720. The Georgian façade of the Haymarket Theatre makes this into one of the most attractive theaters in London. Turn left at the end of the Haymarket, and you come to Trafalgar Square, with Nelson on his 185-foot column, the lions, and the Fountains. It is bordered on the side by the National Gallery and, nearby, the church of St. Martin-in-the-Fields. On the opposite side is Admiralty Arch, the entrance to the Mall leading to Buckingham Palace. Walk southward down into Whitehall, with its stern ministerial façades. Walk through Horse Guards, easily identifiable by its smart scarlet-coated sentries, then turn left and left again into Downing Street, where at Nos. 10 and 11 respectively are located the official homes of the Prime Minister and the Chancellor of the Exchequer. At the end of Downing Street, turn right, back into Whitehall, and thus into Parliament Square, with the Houses of Parliament and Westminster Abbey. Turn right at the Abbey, walk along Birdcage Walk, then turn into St. James's Park, at the end of which you reach Buckingham Palace. Walk up the Mall, turn left past Clarence House into St. James's Place, then through Ambassador's Court into St. James's Street. Near the top of this turn right along Jermyn Street, well known for cheeses, shirts, and shoes. At the end of Jermyn Street you are back within a few yards of Piccadilly. Walking time about 1½ hours.

LUDGATE CIRCUS TO THE TOWER

Ludgate Circus, at the eastern end of Fleet Street, is on the edge of the old City of London, and affords the best view of St. Paul's Cathedral. Walk up the hill toward St. Paul's but turn left before you reach it into Old Bailey, location of the Central Criminal Court. At the end of the street, turn right into Newgate Street, named after the notorious "gaol" on whose site the Criminal Court now stands. Turn right again into Warwick Lane, and you will be following the line of the Roman Wall around the city, traces of which can be seen in the gardens on your right. Turn left into St. Paul's Churchyard, and thus to St. Paul itself, the greatest of Wren's creations. Walk round St. Paul's into Cheapside and Poultry, turning left at King Street to the Guildhall, used for municipal occasions and state banquets. Turn left toward Moorgate, then right into Princess Street to Bank. Opposite you is the Mansion House, official home of the Lord Mayor, and, on the left, the Royal Exchange. turn left up Threadneedle Street, with the Bank of England and the Stock Exchange on your left. Opposite this, turn down a little lane past the Royal Exchange Buildings into Cornhill, then left to Leadenhall Market with its intricate Victorian ironwork and, during business hours, its colorful displays of produce. Walk through Eastcheap to the Monument commemorating the Great Fire of 1666, then down Monument Street to Billingsgate Fish Market—just follow your nose. Walk left down Lower Thames Street, turn up Bywards Street, then back into Eastcheap and thus to the Tower of London. Walking time about 1½ hours.

THE RIVER WALK

This walk begins at the steps of the impressive statue of Queen Boadicea on Westminster Bridge, which lead down to Westminster Pier, the busy starting point for the launches making trips up and down the Thames. Looking across the river at this point you will see the imposing façade of County Hall, administrative hub of the Greater London Council, and the huge Shell Centre. Continuing along the pleasant tree-lined Embankment with its quaint dolphin lampposts, you will now see the magnificent sweep of the Thames and the distant view of the dome of St. Paul's. A short distance beyond Hungerford Bridge is Cleopatra's Needle, and from here you will be able to see the modern complex of the Royal Festival Hall, the Hayward Gallery, and the National Film Theatre, over the South Bank. Soon to be added is the new National Theatre. The Victoria Embankment Gardens, across the road to the left, have colorful displays of flowers, an open-air café and a bandstand where bands play throughout the summer. They are overlooked by the famous Savoy Hotel. Just past the graceful arches of Waterloo Bridge is H.M.S. *Discovery,* Captain Scott's beautifully maintained polar research ship. The fine building to the left is Somerset House, part of which is occupied by King's College. Just a short distance away are the Temple gardens, and nearly the end of the walk. Cross the road at the traffic lights, walk up Temple Avenue to Fleet Street and the Cheshire Cheese, in Wine Office Court, a pub with strong historic and literary associations. Walking time about 1¼ hours.

THE BRITISH MUSEUM TO DR. JOHNSON'S HOUSE

From the British Museum, most famous of London's museums, walk down Museum Street, with its Georgian façades. Drop into the Museum Tavern, which was Oscar Wilde's "local" for a drink or a quick meal, then turn right onto Bloomsbury Way. This leads to Holborn, via Sicilian Avenue, rich in Italian restaurants and good for shopping. Go down Kingsway to Africa House, then turn left into Lincoln's Inn Fields. Go around the square, where you will notice the Soane Museum and the Royal College of Surgeons, and then continue to your left into the Inns of Court, and thence to Chancery Lane. Opposite the end of this are Prince Henry's Rooms, reputed to have been the lodgings of Henry, the elder son of James I. Walk down Fleet Street, the axis of the newspaper world, as far as Bolt Court, a tiny alley to your left. Along here is Gough Square. where Dr. Johnson, one of England's best-loved literary figures, once lived. The house, which he occupied between 1748 and 1758, is open to the public. Walking time about 1¼ hours.

CHARING CROSS ROAD, SOHO, AND CARNABY STREET

Start this walk at the southern end of Charing Cross Road, famous for its new and secondhand bookshops. It is worth a detour along Shaftesbury Avenue to see Gerrard Street, with its strong Chinese flavor (it runs parallel to Shaftesbury Avenue). Walk up Charing Cross Road, turn left at Sutton Row into Soho Square, where you can rest your feet and look at a statue of Charles II, in whose reign the square was laid out. Walk down Greek Street, and you enter the tinselly, garish world of Soho proper. After a first impression of intimate restaurants and strip clubs, turn right into Old Compton Street, which is chiefly remarkable for its wine shops and delicatessens. At the end of this, turn left into Wardour Street and then right into Brewer Street. During office hours, explore the lively fruit and vegetable market in Rupert Street, which is lined with clubs and garish bookshops, and which crosses Brewer Street at right angles. Near the end of Brewer Street, which has some remarkable food shops, and also the huge baker and confectionery where Sir Winston Churchill's birthday cakes used to be made, turn right into Upper John Street. Turn left at the end of this and you come to bright and breezy Carnaby Street, would-be hub of London's young fashion scene. Walking time about 1 hour.

MUSEUMS AND GALLERIES

There are too many museums in London to mention all of them so we will limit ourselves to just those that are the most important and most interesting. Visiting museums sometimes seems a bit dull but I feel that it is the best way to learn the history and the traditions of a country. I don't suggest, of course, that you run from one to the other the entire time you are in London, but surely a few of them should be visited.

THE BRITISH MUSEUM Great Russell Street, W.C.1 Underground: Russell Square, Holborn, or Tottenham Court Road Buses: 14, 24, 29, 68, 73, 77

A gloomy-looking edifice in Bloomsbury, the British Museum houses a National Library and a Museum of History, Archaeology, Art, and Ethnography. There is so much to see, and time is necessary. We will just hit on the highlights here. The hall of Egyptian Sculpture contains the Rosetta Stone, whose discovery led to the deciphering of hieroglyphics. There is a booklet available that details the method of deciphering. The Grenville and King's Library offers thousands of manuscripts, deeds, Bibles, etc. The most important are the Magna Carta, Shakespeare's first folio of plays and his mortgage deed to the Black Friars Gatehouse, the log book of Nelson's *Victory,* and the journals of Captain Scott, detailing his attempt to discover the Antarctic. In the King Edward VII Galleries can be found the exciting Sutton Hoo Funeral Deposit, said to be the most exciting treasure to have been taken from British soil, It consists of armor, weapons, gold jewelry, silverware, and other accessories to make the journey of the spirit of the entombed more comfortable. Though no body was found, it was believed to be the tomb of a king of East Anglia who died in the 7th century. The top floor features the Egyptian Gallery. Women will enjoy its excellent exhibition of ancient cosmetics, tools, leather work, cooking utensils, and rare art. The rest of the priceless exhibitions on display you will simply have to see for yourself. Open Monday through Saturday from 10 A.M. to 5 P.M., Sundays from 2:30 to 6 P.M. Closed Good Friday, Christmas Day, Christmas Eve, and Boxing Day. Admission free.

BRITISH THEATRE MUSEUM Leighton House 12 Holland Park Road, W.14 Underground: Kensington High Street Bus: 9

An exhibition of specially selected items chosen from the museum's unique collection of material relating to the British theater—playbills, costumes, pictures, that go back over 400 years of English theater. The exhibition is set in what was once the home of Lord Leighton, an artist himself, who designed the Oriental-inspired house. Open Tuesdays, Thursdays, and Saturdays from 11 A.M. to 5 P.M. Admission free.

COMMONWEALTH INSTITUTE Kensington High Street, W.8 Underground: Kensington High Street, Buses: 9, 73

London's newest museum, opened by Queen Elizabeth in 1962, illustrates life in every country in the Commonwealth from Australia to Zambia and Malaysia. There are art exhibitions of painters from these countries and daily film shows of approximately 45-minute duration that show various aspects of life, work, and accomplishments in these countries. Open Monday through Saturday from 10 A.M. to 5:30 P.M., Sundays from 2:30 to 6 P.M. Admission free.

COURTAULD INSTITUTE GALLERIES Woburn Square, W.C.1 Underground: Russell or Euston Square.

This is one of the most beautiful art galleries in the world, containing the most important collection in the country of Impressionist and Post-impressionist paintings together with other works of art. The lighting is extraordinary and the interior is lovely. There are eight excellent paintings by Cézanne, a self-portrait by Van Gogh, and works by Toulouse-Lautrec, Gauguin, Modigliani, Monet, and many others. There is a good selection of more classical works as well: Botticelli, Veronese, and others. Open Monday through Saturday from 10 A.M. to 5 P.M., Sundays from 2 to 5 P.M. Admission Free.

THE GUILDHALL MUSEUM Gillett House 55 Basinghall Street, E.C.2 Underground: Bank or Moorgate Bus: 6, 9, 11, 15

The museum houses antiquities of the City of London all the way back to Roman times, including the marble head of Mithras discovered in a 2nd-century Roman temple. There is also a museum of leather craft, tracing the history of leather from the Bronze Age to the Victorian Age. Open Monday through Saturday from 10 A.M. to 5 P.M. Closed Good Friday, Easter Saturday, bank holidays, and Christmas Day. Admission free.

JEWISH MUSEUM Woburn House Upper Woburn Place, W.C.1 Underground: Euston or Euston Square Bus: 14

A fine collection of Jewish antiquities, illustrating the public and private worship of the Jews down through the ages. Open Monday through Thursday from 2:30 to 5 P.M., Friday and Sunday from 10:30 A.M. to 12:45 P.M. Closed bank holidays, Saturdays, and Jewish Holy Days. Admission free.

NATIONAL GALLERY Trafalgar Square, W.C.2 Underground: Trafalgar

A magnificent Neoclassical building stretching along the northwest side of Trafalgar Square. The Gallery houses an unrivaled collection of the chief European schools of painting from the 13th century to 1900. Gallery 5 has been specially lit to enhance several excellent paintings by Leonardo da Vinci. Gallery 7 holds an excellent collection of 16th-century Venetian canvases by Tintoretto and Titian, and the famous *Darius Family Kneeling before Alexander the Great* by Veronese. I particularly love the Venetian school because of the marvelous bright colors and detailing. The British are well represented here by Gainsborough, Constable, Hogarth, Turner, and Reynolds. The Spanish, too, have a good representation with portraits by Goya and Velasquez, and El Greco's *Agony in the Garden*. For the Flemish school, there is a unique viewing arrangement: You view the paintings through what amounts to a peephole. It certainly does rivet one's attention to an individual painting. The French collection is vast and includes both Impressionists and Post-impressionists such as Renoir, Manet, Degas, Cézanne, Monet. Open Monday through Saturday from 10 A.M. to 6 P.M., Sundays from 2 to 6 P.M. Admission. free.

NATIONAL PORTRAIT GALLERY St. Martin's Place, W.C.2

Directly behind the National Gallery. Here you will find portraits of famous men and women in British history from the age of the Tudors to the present day. It is a good second stop after the National Gallery.

Open Monday through Friday from 10 A.M. to 5 P.M., Saturdays from 10 A.M. to 6 P.M., Sundays from 2 to 6 P.M. Closed Good Friday, Christmas Eve, Christmas Day, and Boxing Day. Admission 10p ($.25)

THE PUBLIC RECORDS OFFICE Chancery Lane, W.C.2 Underground: Temple or Chancery Lane

A small museum, it has a wealth of documents rarely seen anywhere else in the world, including Elizabeth II's "Ode to Govern Great Britain," an authentic Shakespeare signature plus his last will and testament, and letters from Catherine the Great, Napoleon, Marie-Antoinette, and George Washington. Handwriting experts enjoy this museum for its marvelous array of autographs. Open Monday through Friday from 1 to 4 P.M. Admission free.

TATE GALLERY Milbank, S.W.1 Underground: Westminster

Standing alongside the Thames, in Westminster, the Tate is a bit smaller and less haughty in appearance than most of the large museums. Its claim to fame is one of the best collections of British paintings from the 16th century up to the present day, including an excellent collection of modern art. Some art lovers find it confusing to see the entire gallery at one visit, mixing their views of the modern and traditional collections. It is much easier to view one school at one time. If it is not possible to come back again limit yourself to perhaps the traditional first and then the modern school. Sculptors, too, are represented here, including Rodin, Epstein, Marini, and Maillol. As at the National Gallery there is a good representation of Reynolds and Gainsborough (there is a *Blue Boy* here, though not the famous one that he is especially noted for).

There are five galleries devoted to one painter alone, William Turner, who bequeathed his collection to the Tate and the National Gallery. The selection here is vast and the scenes run the gamut from the *Shipwreck* to his beautiful sunset and sunrise canvases with vivid colors. From the modern school you will find Chagall, Dali, various periods of Picasso, and Modigliani, as well as others. Even Pop Art can be found at the Tate. Should you get hungry, there is a cafeteria downstairs with budget prices. Open Monday through Saturday from 10 A.M. to 6 P.M., Sundays from 2 to 6 P.M. During special exhibitions, open Tuesdays and Thursdays from 10 A.M. to 8 P.M. Closed Good Friday, Christmas Eve, Christmas Day, and Boxing Day. Admission free.

WALLACE COLLECTION Manchester Square, W.1 Underground: Bond Street or Baker Street

In this magnificent townhouse, the late Lady Wallace has put together an interesting collection of beautiful paintings from the 17th to 19th centuries, as well as a collection of Oriental and European arms—a strange combination. The arms collection includes beautiful Persian scimitars, swords, and varying styles of suits of armor. The art collection features Rembrandt's self-portrait, Fragonard, Watteau, Gainsborough, and Boucher. There's also some lovely 18th-century Sèvres porcelain and beautiful French furniture. Open Monday through Saturday from 10 A.M. to 5 P.M., Sundays from 2 to 5 P.M. Admission free.

WELLINGTON MUSEUM Apsley House 149 Piccadilly, W.1 Underground: Hyde Park Corner

The original townhouse of the Duke of Wellington (the "Iron Duke"), the man who defeated Napoleon at Waterloo. There are countless souvenirs of Wellington's battles and honors, a marble statue of Napoleon, and an excellent art collection. Most interesting from a woman's point of view is the china and porcelain collection, and the actual furnishings of Wellington's days in the house. Open Monday through Friday from 10 A.M. to 6 P.M., Sundays from 2 to 6 P.M. Admission 10p ($.25).

VICTORIA AND ALBERT MUSEUM Cromwell Road, S.W.7 Underground: South Kensington

Perhaps one of the most important in all of London, this museum was so named because Queen Victoria herself insisted upon it. There are so many wings and rooms to be visited I won't even attempt to describe it in detail and will highlight just a few of the important exhibitions for you. One in particular is Room 43. The entire room resembles a domed, gilded church, with displays of early medieval art, from early Christian wood carvings to the Byzantine Keroli Casket. In Rooms 11 through 20 you can view beautiful Renaissance art from Italy. Room 38 features tapestries, the most famous of which are perhaps the Devonshire collection of hunting scenes. Room 55 offers a gallery of portrait miniatures, including that of Anne of Cleves, done by Hans Holbein for Henry VIII. Scattered throughout are the furnished period rooms with all the paneling, fireplaces, furniture, etc. of days gone by. Open Monday through Saturday from 10 A.M. to 6 P.M., Sundays from 2:30 to 6 P.M. Admission free.

PARKS

A born Londoner would probably insist that, rather than trying to imitate nature, the London parks surpass nature itself. The Royal Parks are as essential a part of the London scene as red buses. They are precious green breathing spaces—on land that would be worth many millions of pounds to a property developer—where you can hear birds' songs uninterrupted by the sound of traffic, where you can picnic, play tennis, go rowing, swimming, or riding, listen to music, or watch open-air plays. In fact you can do almost anything except pick the flowers.

The main parks in central London are Hyde Park, Kensington Gardens, Regent's Park, Green Park, and St. James's Park; along with Richmond Park, Greenwich Park, and others outside the center, they are known as the Royal Parks.

HYDE PARK

This was the first opened to the public in the time of Charles I and was originally a hunting forest belonging to Henry VIII. Queen Caroline, wife of George II, was responsible for the construction of the Serpentine, always a busy scene on a summer day with its bathers and rowers. At the southeast corner of the park is Hyde Park corner—not the place for nervous drivers—and Apsley House, once the home of the Duke of Wellington and now a museum dedicated to his memory. At the northeast corner is Speakers' Corner, just across from the Marble Arch, where soapbox orators can be heard letting off steam seven days a week. Rotten Row, just south of the Serpentine, is London's most fashionable spot for horseback riding. There is a lovely restaurant in the park just off the bridge overlooking the Serpentine.

KENSINGTON GARDENS

They adjoin Hyde Park on its western side. It is perhaps easier here than in any other park to leave the sound of traffic and imagine you are deep in the country. In the gardens is the statue of Peter Pan, the popular and very English fairy-tale figure created by Sir James Barrie. The London Museum is also to be found here. Right on the southern edge is the Albert Memorial and across the road the Albert Hall. Of all the parks, it is in Kensington Gardens that the "nannies" flourish best, a corps of neat, uniformed children's nurses pushing their small charges along the tree-lined avenues toward the famous Round Pond to sail model boats.

REGENT'S PARK

This is the biggest of the central London Parks, and is always closely associated both with the magnificent Regency terraces on its edge and the zoo that lies at its northern boundary (though not strictly within the park). Two roughly circular roads run through the park. The small inner one embraces Queen Mary's Rose Garden, one of the finest of its type in Britain. There is also a Japanese Garden close by. There are many facilities for outdoor games in Regent's Park, especially tennis. The Regent's Park Canal runs along the north edge and you can board a passenger-carrying canal boat that gives an extra dimension to London Transport. There is also an open-air theater, especially well known for its Shakespearean productions.

GREEN PARK

Very centrally placed, only five minutes' walk from Piccadilly Circus, it really is green, and is much more remarkable for its trees and lawns than for its flowers, which are few. Before the middle of the 17th century, it was a popular place for settling quarrels with dueling pistols or swords. It became a favorite place of Charles II, who loved to walk through it and who was chiefly responsible for its development as a public park. The well-known "Broad Walk" starts at Queen Victoria's Memorial outside Buckingham Palace and continues through the Park to Piccadilly.

ST. JAMES'S PARK

Close to Buckingham Palace, this is the oldest of the London parks, on land originally acquired by Henry VIII in 1532. James I set up a menagerie here and Charles II had the park laid out with a long stretch of water to make it look as much like Versailles as possible. George IV redesigned it to make it look English and replaced the canal with the present lake. This has many unusual waterfowl, including several pelicans. The famous Mall is part of the park, which is really like an ornamental garden, a green oasis among the tall buildings. The Horse Guard Parade borders onto the east end of the park and St. James's Palace. Clarence House, where members of the British royal family live when they are in London, is just opposite the park across the Mall.

11
Excursions Out of London

I know how exciting London can be and how involved one can get in all the fabulous shopping, the magnificent restaurants, and exciting night life it has to offer. However, it would be a pity indeed if you did not take the time to see some of the interesting sights within one day's excursion out of London. You may think that by doing so you miss too much of London itself but, believe me, these sights are as much a part of London and England as Big Ben, the Houses of Parliament, and Buckingham Palace.

I guarantee you will not be disappointed or feel any of these excursions are a waste of time. I often wish, when I write about things of this nature, that I could take every reader by the hand and say, "Now today we're going to Windsor Castle," and personally show them around every little nook and cranny. Since I can't do that I'll settle for putting my impressions down and hope that they are intriguing enough to make you want to go on your own.

There are so many things to see that it can get a bit confusing trying to decide where to go, so if you will allow me I'll suggest the most important sights first.

It's not necessary to take a guided coach tour to any of these places, though of course it is preferable because of the excellent information you receive. But it does cost a bit more than if you do it on your own. If the budget permits, this is my suggestion. If not, you can get to any one of these places on your own.

If you wish to go on your own, drop into the office of the British Tourist Authority (BTA) and they will be happy to give you all the information necessary for your excursion. The Green Line Coaches are especially good for this kind of touring.

TOURS

I've listed here some of the coach guided tours you might enjoy most. These come from the two London tour agencies:

EVAN EVANS TOURS LTD. Metropolis House, 41 Tottenham Court Road, W.1. Tel: 637-4171

FRAMES & RICKARDS Main office 25/31 Tavistock Place Tel: 837-6311 or 837-6312.

WINDSOR AND HAMPTON COURT Evan Evans Tour No. 12

Daily except December 25 and 26. Departs at 1 P.M. and returns at 6 P.M. Price £1.80 ($4.50) for adults, £1.20 ($2.75) for children. Via Eton College, over the Thames River to Windsor and the Royal Castle. You will see the royal apartments, except when the Queen is in residence, when you pay a visit to the St. George's Chapel, a Gothic church of magnificent splendor and beauty where past kings lie buried. Leaving Windsor, you drive via the Long Walk through Runnymede, where King John put his seal to the Magna Carta, to Hampton Court Palace, where you visit the gardens and the palace exterior. Then a drive through Bushey Park to the statue of Diana and the lake, then back to London.

WINDSOR AND HAMPTON COURT Frames & Rickards

TOUR 5F from Frames, Herbrand Street, Wednesdays, Fridays, Saturdays, and Sundays at 1 P.M.

TOUR 5FM from Seymour Street near Marble Arch Wednesdays, Fridays, Saturdays, and Sundays at 1 P.M.

TOUR 5R from Rickards, 17 Woburn Place, Mondays, Tuesdays, Thursdays, and Sundays at 1 P.M.

TOUR 5RP from Paddington Rail Station, Mondays, Tuesdays, Thursdays, and Sundays at 1:15 P.M.

TOUR 5RL from 66 Lancaster Gate (Charles Dickens Hotel), Mondays, Tuesdays, Thursdays, and Sundays at 1:30 P.M.

All tours return at approximately 6 P.M. Tours don't run on December 25 and 26. Price £1.80 ($4.50).

Via Notting Hill Gate, through Chiswick to Windsor Castle, which you visit. Windsor Great Park, Runnymede, Egham, Staines, a visit to the Gardens at Hampton Court Palace, Bushey Park, Richmond, Shepherds Bush, and Bayswater.

WINDSOR, STOKE POGES, AND HAMPTON COURT Evan Evans Tour No. 23

Departs at 10 A.M. Mondays, Wednesdays, Fridays, and Saturdays, except December 25 and 26. Price £3.50 ($8.75). Same as the Evans Windsor tour, above, but with a longer stay at Windsor Castle, and a visit to Stoke Poges, a lovely village with the church of St. Giles, where Thomas Gray is buried.

WINDSOR, STOKE POGES, AND HAMPTON COURT Frames & Rickards Tour 6F

Departs from Frames, Herbrand Street, on Tuesdays, Thursdays, and Saturdays, except December 25 and 26. Leaves 10 A.M.; returns at 5:15 P.M. A visit to Stokes Poges, and, after lunch, a visit to Windsor Castle, then on the Hampton Court Palace and Gardens.

Excursions Out of London

OXFORD AND CAMBRIDGE Evan Evans Tour No. 20
Departs Wednesdays and Fridays at 8:30 A.M., returning at 7:30 P.M. Price £4.20 ($10.50), including entrance fees, lunch, and tea. A visit to the two great Universities, each with its own beautiful old buildings and lovely setting. First to Oxford, and Magdalen College and Magdalen Tower, and the town's cathedral, the smallest in England. Then on to Cambridge, on the River Cam, and its King's College and Sir Christopher Wren's chapel at Pembroke College. Then back to London.

CAMBRIDGE UNIVERSITY AND WOBURN ABBEY Frames & Rickards Tour No. 12F from Frames, Herbrand Street.
Departs on Wednesdays and Sundays at 8:30 A.M., returning at 7:30 P.M. Price £5 ($12.50), including morning coffee, lunch, tea, and all admission fees. A drive to Cambridge, and a visit to some of the beautiful colleges. Then on to Bedford on the river Ouse, and a visit and tour of Woburn Abbey, a magnificent place with galleries and State Apartments filled with interesting treasures. It's been the home of the Dukes of Bedford for over 300 years.

CANTERBURY CATHEDRAL AND DICKENS LAND Frames & Rickards Tour No. 14F
Departs from Frames, Herbrand Street, Saturdays, at 9 A.M., returning about 6:45 P.M. Price £4.20 ($10.50), including lunch, tea, and admission fees. A drive through the picturesque "Cray" district, past the old Pilgrim's Way, across the North Down to Canterbury. A visit is made to the eleventh century cathedral and the shrine of St. Thomas à Becket, murdered there in 1170. After lunch, you return via Rochester and the Eastgate House mentioned in Dickens's *Edwin Drood,* have tea in Rochester, and see the Leather Bottle Inn in Cobham, and Cobham Park.

CANTERBURY AND ROCHESTER Evan Evans Tour No. 21
Departs at 8:45 A.M., returns at 7:15 P.M., Tuesdays, Thursdays, and Sundays. Price £4 ($10), including lunch, tea, and all entrance fees. Drive over Waterloo Bridge through the English countryside to Canterbury. A visit to the Cathedral, the Pilgrim's resthouse, Canterbury Castle, and St. Martin's Church, the oldest in England. After lunch, a drive back to Rochester and its beautiful Norman-style cathedral, tea at Rochester, then back through the little towns to London. On Sundays arrival in Canterbury will be at 10:30 A.M., so you may attend the Cathedral service at 11 A.M.

WINCHESTER, SALISBURY, AND STONEHENGE Frames & Rickards Tour No. 15F
Departs from Frames, Herbrand Street Tuesdays and Fridays at 8 A.M., returns at 7:30 P.M. Price £2.80 ($7), including morning coffee, lunch, tea, and all admission fees. From London you drive to Guilford, where you stop for coffee and visit the Cathedral, consecrated in 1961. Then a drive over open country to Winchester for lunch and a visit to the 11th-century Cathedral. Then to Salisbury, where you have tea, and a visit to the Salisbury Cathedral, which has one of the four existing copies of the Magna Carta. Then on to Stonehenge, the magic circle of 50-ton megaliths from the Bronze Age, created by a civilization more than 3,000 years ago. Then a drive back to London via Andover.

136 LONDON

WINDSOR

Windsor means Windsor Castle, home of the English monarchs, where Queen Elizabeth and her family still maintain residence; it means Eton College, where many of the monarchs have been educated; and it means a quaint, picturesque Victorian village.

You can reach Windsor by train from Waterloo or Paddington Stations, or by bus coach from Victoria Coach Station, or the Green Line 704 or 705 from Hyde Park Corner or Green Line 718 via Hampton Court.

WINDSOR CASTLE

William the Conqueror managed to complete the building of the castle before he died in 1087, and it has from that time on become the scene of great English history. Queen Victoria became known as the "widow of Windsor" after her husband Albert died in 1861 and she spent her grieving years here at the castle. Charles I was incarcerated here before going to the guillotine, and King John spent many angry, anxious days at Windsor prior to being forced to sign the Magna Carta in 1215. Queen Bess lived through many of her trials and tribulations at Windsor. With Queen Elizabeth II and her family today using Windsor as their home, it is the largest inhabited castle in the world. When Queen Elizabeth is in residence her royal standard flies and unfortunately that means that the State Apartments cannot be visited at that time. Otherwise they are open to the public from November through February, Monday through Saturday from 11 A.M. to 3 P.M.; March and April, Monday through Saturday from 11 A.M. to 4 P.M.; from May through September, Monday through Saturday from 11 A.M. to 5 P.M.; October, Monday through Saturday from 11 A.M. to 4 P.M. On Sundays from April through October, open from 1:30 P.M. Admission 15p ($.37). For several weeks at the time of the Ascot Races the Queen is generally here, as she is for about five or six weeks at Eastertime, so judge accordingly if you want to see the apartments.

The apartments themselves are quite beautiful and contain all manner of *objets d'art*, exquisite furniture, and even armor. Many of the great masters are represented here as in the King's Drawing Room, which is virtually a Rubens museum. The Grand Reception Room is resplendent in Gobelin tapestries, some of the world's most exquisite.

Queen Mary's Doll House is a magnificent recreation of a miniature royal mansion of the 1920s, completely livable, dwarfed size. Absolutely nothing has been left out. Even the bottles in the wine cellar contain the actual vintage wine of that particular period! It really has to be seen to be believed. There is also a collection of dolls presented to various members of the royal family by other monarchs and nations. Luckily, the doll house remains open even during the period when the state apartments themselves are closed so at least you can see that much if you arrive at a bad time. Admission 5p ($.12). The Old Master Drawings is a collection owned by the royal family, on display in the castle, particularly of works by Leonardo da Vinci. The drawings can be viewed during the same hours as the state apartments. Admission 5p ($.12).

St. George's Chapel was founded by Edward IV in the 14th century on the same site as the original Chapel of the Order of the Garter (Edward II, 1348). The tombs of Queen Mary and George V rest in the nave. In the Edward IV Choir is a flat tomb within which lies the vault of Charles I (who lost his head to the guillotine), Henry VIII, and Jane Seymour, Henry's third wife. Open Monday through Saturday from 11 A.M. to 3:45 P.M.; Friday from 1 to 3:45 P.M.; Sundays from 2:30 to 3:45 P.M. Daily services are open to the public. Admission 15p ($.37).

The Albert Memorial Chapel was built in Albert's memory by his wife. Open from April through October, Monday through Saturday from 10 A.M. to 1 P.M. and from 2 to 4:45 P.M.; from November through March, from 10 A.M. to 1 P.M. and from 2 to 4 P.M. Closed Sundays. Admission free.

ETON COLLEGE

Credit for the building of this most famous "public" school (in England "public" actually means private) goes to King Henry VI. The students still wear the Edwardian-style uniform with black tails, top hat, and stiff collar. Eton has been the alma mater of many of England's most famous men as well as its monarchs. It is said that the doors will now be open to boys of all classes and income brackets. You can visit the schoolyard and cloisters Monday through Saturday from 2 to 5 P.M., in the summer until 8 P.M.; Sundays from 11:30 A.M. to 5 P.M. Admission free.

THE TOWN OF WINDSOR

Windsor is a most picturesque and charming town with cobblestone streets, little brick buildings, and tiny antique shops such as you often see in old English prints, with the rounded bay windows and tiny panes of glass. It is the kind of town one should try to spend at least one day and night in. Take as much time as you like to see Windsor Castle and Eton and then spend the rest of the time wandering around the town staying in one of its lovely little hotels, enjoying a good meal and going back to London the day after. Nell Gwynne, the Cockney mistress of King Charles, actually occupied one of the old shops on Church Street, which abounds with little tearooms. Should you decide to stay overnight, a good bet is the Old House Hotel, right next to the Eton Bridge, on Thames Street. (Tel: 61345; single £3.50 ($8.75); double £7 ($17.50). Built in 1676 by Sir Christopher Wren, one of England's busiest and most important architects, the hotel has quite a history in itself. In the old wing the rooms are rather small but all are quaint. Most have fireplaces, all have telephone, wall-to-wall carpeting, private bath, and traditional furniture. The restaurant is said to serve some of the best food in England. There is also the Bamboo Terrace room with an outside garden, a cocktail garden and a drawing room for cocktails with a natural fireplace.

While in Windsor you can visit the Windsor Safari Park at St. Leonard's. There are lion and cheetah reserves, dolphin displays, leopards, zebras, ostriches, chimps, etc. It is open daily from 10 A.M. until dusk. Admission 30p ($.75).

Nearby, too, is the Ascot Race Course, famous for the Royal Ascot meeting in June that includes the Ascot Gold Cup. Ascot is always attended by the Royal family and everyone who is anyone in England tries to make it. The fashion parade is unbelievable. The King George VI and the Queen Elizabeth Stakes are held in July and the Queen Elizabeth II Stakes in September. To inquire about prices, seats, etc. Tel: Ascot 2-2211.

HAMPTON COURT

A short ride west of London on the Thames stands one of the finest Tudor palaces in all of England. The 16th-century palace belonged originally to Cardinal Wolsey who later made a gift of it to King Henry VIII. Though a generous gift it was, generosity was not the motivation behind the gift. King Henry did not take kindly to the fact that this palace was far grander than his own living quarters and the cardinal was crafty enough to offer it to the king rather than, I would imagine, lose his head (as had so many others who annoyed dear Henry).

Once the king took over ownership of the palace he began a great spurt of renovating and rebuilding, which included the Anne Boleyn Gateway as a tribute to the beautiful young girl he loved, married, and eventually beheaded. Here can be seen the magnificent astronomical clock created by Nicholas Oursian in 1540 which tells the date, the time, the high-water mark at London Bridge, and even the phases of the moon. From the court in which this clock stands, you can see another one of Henry's additions, the Great Hall, famous for its hammer-beam ceiling.

You can visit the huge original kitchens where banquets for hundreds of people were prepared.

In later years, Queen Mary commissioned Christopher Wren to build a new addition to the palace, because she could not stand the dreariness of the Tudor styles. The result was the beautiful fountain court, the east wing that faces the garden. The difference between the two palaces is quite striking.

You can visit the royal apartments with all their fittings: tapestries, china, porcelain, paintings, antiques. By our standards, some of the rooms and furnishings may seem a bit austere, but for those days, everything was most elegant, indeed. Just for the fun of it, try to find your way out of the shrubbery maze—but be sure to tell someone where you've gone, or you may not be found for quite some time.

Ghost lovers take note! The ghost of Catherine Howard is said to rant and rave all over the palace, on full moon nights, begging Henry not to behead her. The State Apartments are open from May through December, Monday through Saturday from 9:30 A.M. to

5:30 P.M., Sundays from 11 A.M. to 5:30 P.M.; November through February, Monday through Saturday from 9:30 A.M. to 3:30 P.M., Sundays from 2 to 3:30 P.M.; March, April, and October, Monday through Saturday from 9:30 A.M. to 4:30 P.M., Sundays from 2 to 4:30 P.M. Closed Good Friday, Christmas Eve, Christmas Day, and Boxing Day. Admission, April through September, 20p ($.50); October through March, 10p ($.25). All the gardens are open to the public free every day until dusk but no later than 9 P.M.

You can get to Hampton Court by train from Waterloo; by coach Green Line 716, 716a, 718 from Marble Arch, Hyde Park Corner, or Baker Street; or by river on launches from Westminster Pier (fare one way is 38p [$.95]).

If you want to take in Windsor and Hampton Court all in one day, it can very easily be accomplished on a "do-it-yourself" basis. Go to Windsor by motor coach first in the morning, spend as much time as you wish browsing around, and then take a Green Line coach just opposite the gate of the castle to Hampton Court. Fare is only 25p ($.62) and it is an hour's drive. From Hampton Court you can either take a coach back to London or one of the later launches on the Thames, which will give you a much broader view of the entire area. Refreshments are available upon the launch for your return trip, so it can be done very comfortably indeed.

CAMBRIDGE

In Cambridgeshire, 54 miles from London, Cambridge is one of the great university cities of the world. You can reach Cambridge by train from Liverpool Street or King's Cross Station. The trip takes from an hour and a quarter to an hour and three-quarters. Or you can go by coach from Victoria Coach Station, which takes 2¾ hours.

From 1284 (when Peterhouse was founded) the next few hundred years saw the building of more than 20 colleges, abounding in spires and turrets, cloisters and courtyards, and all the rich flowering of Norman and Gothic architecture. The finest examples are King's College Chapel, Trinity College with its great court and fountain, and the gateway at St. John's.

Several colleges, like Queen's, Trinity, and St. John's, lie on the Backs, a tranquil half-mile stretch of the river Thames. Their yellow walls can best be seen from a leisurely flat-bottomed punt, which can be hired by the hour just as Darwin, Cromwell, Newton, and

Wordsworth must have done in their days at the University. One of the most important sights to see is King's College Chapel, one of the most architecturally perfect edifices in the world today and known for its beautiful stained-glass windows dating back to 1515, though the West window is of the Victorian era. The windows illustrate biblical stories. Another special feature of the Chapel is its fantastic fan vaulting. Open during the year on school holidays, Monday through Saturday from 9 A.M. to 5 P.M., Sunday from 10:30 A.M. to 5 P.M. in the summer, open Monday through Saturday from 9 A.M. to 6 P.M., Sundays from 10:30 A.M. to 6 P.M. During the school term, open Monday through Saturday from 9 A.M. to 4 P.M., Sundays from 2 to 3 P.M. and from 5 to 6 P.M. Closed December 26 through January 1.

The Chapel is a good central point from which to visit the other colleges such as Trinity College on Trinity Street, the largest of the colleges at Cambridge, with a magnificent courtyard. It was founded in 1546 by Henry VIII.

PETERHOUSE COLLEGE Trumpington Street
Founded in 1284 by the Bishop of Ely, it is the oldest college at Cambridge. Unfortunately a fire in the 15th century destroyed the original buildings.

EMANUEL COLLEGE St. Andrews Street
Founded in 1584 by the Chancellor of the Exchequer to Elizabeth I, it is of interest for the lovely gardens and the chapel designed in 1677 by the very busy and popular Sir Christopher Wren.

ST. JOHN'S COLLEGE St. John's Street
Founded by the mother of Henry VII in 1511 on the site of an old hospital. The Tudor Coat of Arms still adorns the huge gateway for the first sight you will have of St. John's College. Don't miss the famous "Bridge of Sighs" spanning the Cam River, a replica of the bridge by the same name in Venice. It links the old and new areas of the college.

QUEEN'S COLLEGE Queen's Lane
Founded in 1448 by the wife of King Henry VII and wife of Edward VI. The 16th-century Presidents Lodge and the Cloisters are the interesting sights to be seen here at Queen's College.

There are many other colleges as well but none with any spectacular points of interest other than the fact that they all date back several centuries. After seeing the first ones mentioned, take the time instead to visit the town, which is also rather interesting. St. Benedict's Church, with its Saxon tower, the Church of the Holy Sepulchre, oldest of the four round Crusader Churches in England. The Church of St. Mary the Great, just opposite King's College Chapel, dating back to 1478, the University Botanic Gardens and Fitswilliam Museum on Trumpington Street, said to be the finest in all of England, founded in 1816 by the Viscount Fitzwilliam when he presented his art and rare books collection to the University with sufficient money to build a museum. It houses excellent art collections, archeological relics, porcelain, etc. Open Monday through Saturday from 10 A.M. to 5 P.M., Sundays from 2:15 to 5 P.M. Closed Good Friday and Christmas.

Lunching in Cambridge

TURK'S HEAD GRILLE   14 Timothy Street
Right in the center of town. A beautifully picturesque half-timbered building that is supposed to be one of the oldest in Cambridge and abounds with history, particularly stories of some of the famous alumni of the various colleges. All old beams, creaking staircases, balconies and lovely old furniture, with bright shining brass and soft subtle pewter accessories. The menu is rather extensive and also offers the traditional English fare, but there are steak bars as well, all for under £1 ($2.50). Open for lunch from noon to 3 P.M. and for dinner from 6 to 11:30 P.M.

ARTS RESTAURANT   6 St. Edwards Passage
In the center of town. Particularly popular because it seems to be the meeting place of stage stars performing at the next-door arts theater. Also popular because of the roof garden, which allows you to enjoy a beautiful view of Cambridge with your lunch. Lunch from noon until 2 P.M., dinner in the roof garden from 6:30 to 8:30 P.M. and in the arts restaurant from 6 to 8 P.M. Again, very inexpensive, with a very good lunch for under £1 ($2.50).

OXFORD

In Oxfordshire, 57 miles from London. The world-famous university was founded on the banks of the Thames and Cherwell Rivers more than 10 centuries ago. There are fine examples of every architectural era dating from the 13th century when Merton, St. Edmund Hall, University, and Balliol colleges were founded. Actually the town of Oxford is a town of colleges, as they are scattered around just as homes would be in any other town. You can get there by train from Paddington Station; this takes about 1¼ hours. Or you may go by coach from Victoria Coach Station; about 2¼ to 2¾ hours.

There are two main streets, The Broad and The High and they alone are something to see, flanked by the University Church of St. Mary, the Sheldonian Theatre, and the Bodleian Library, one of the oldest and most important in the world. To lend an austere note to the beauty of these two streets, the broad street still carries a cross that marks the spot where Bishop Cranmer, in 1556, and Bishops

Ridley and Latimer, in 1555, were burned at the stake by order of "Bloody Queen Mary."

Oxford consists of 28 colleges including five for women alone. Unless you are going to spend quite a bit of time here you are obviously not going to be able to see all of them. But here are some that you must see if you are going to take the time to come to Oxford at all.

Christ Church College   St. Aldate's Street
Begun in 1575 by Cardinal Wolsey. King Henry VIII decided to take over in 1546 and completed what is now affectionately called "the House." It forms the largest quadrangle of any of the colleges in Oxford. If you should happen to be in Oxford at 9:05 on any evening you will hear the magnificent 18,000-pound bell of "Great Tom" signaling the closing of the college gates. Originally the townspeople had to listen to 101 clanging thuds which was to signify the number of students at the college at that time. Luckily, the clanging of the bell does not keep up with the registration of today's students! At the college you will see the 10th-century Great Hall, which is well known for its hammer-beam ceilings and its art collection, including Gainsborough and Reynolds. You see many portraits of England's prime ministers and other ruling members since Oxford was a traditional alma mater for aspiring politicians and other greats.

A lovely lily pond, which seems so out of place almost in this college town, sits in the middle of Tom Quad and also a tranquil spot for meditation. The 12th-century Cathedral, famous for its vaulted Choir and Norman pillars, should also be seen. The college is open from 8 A.M. until twilight and the Great Hall is open from 10 A.M. to noon and from 2 to 4 P.M.

Magdalen College
(Be sure to pronounce it "maud-len" or no one will know what you are looking for) was founded in 1458 by William of Wayneflete, who was then Bishop of Winchester, and later became Chancellor of England. This is the site of the famous 15th-century bell tower where, on May Day at dawn the Magdalen chorusers sing in Latin—a beautiful moment if you happen to be there at that time. There is also a 15th-century chapel with a 17th-century screen that is quite interesting to see. Everyone from Cardinal Wolsey to Oscar Wilde attended Magdalen College and often took Addison's Walk, so named in honor of the 18th-century poet, and a favorite of the local students. Christ Church College. This may have the largest quad but Magdalen College most certainly has the largest grounds and even a deer park. Magdalen is open Monday through Saturday from 2 to 5 P.M., Sundays from 10 to 5 P.M.

University College   The High
Dates back to 1249 and is therefore the oldest college at Oxford. There is still a bit of controversy about the original founder and it has never been decided whether Alfred the Great or a church official of Durham was the gentleman responsible for it. It was totally renovated during the 17th century, with new touches added on through the years as they became necessary. The great poet Shelley was an alumnus of University College and there is a memorial plaque in his memory standing there

today. Strangely enough, while at the college he was soundly chastised and nearly kicked out of the school because he helped to write a pamphlet on atheism. The colleges can be visited during school holidays from 10 A.M. to noon and from 2 to 6 P.M. during school days, from 2 to 4 P.M.

Merton College
The second oldest college in Oxford, founded in 1264, stands on Merton Street, one of the only medieval cobbled streets left in Oxford. Merton's main claim to fame is its library, supposedly the oldest in England, dating back to 1371. And one of its treasures is its Astrolabe, a strange instrument used to measure the position of the sun and stars, supposed to have been owned by Chaucer. Open from 10 A.M. to noon and from 2 to 4 P.M.

New College
This is not so new when you consider it was built in 1379 by William of Wykeham, Bishop of Winchester. The 14th-century quadrangle was the first to be built in Oxford and set the pace for all those to follow. Visit the ante-chapel (the entrance is on New College Lane) to see its treasure, Sir Jacob Epstein's sculpture of "Lazarus." New College is open to visitors weekdays during the term from 2 to 5 P.M., when school is not in session it can be visited from 11 A.M. to 6 P.M.; open weekends from noon to 6 P.M.

Lunching in Oxford

TACKLEY HOTEL   106 High Street
Right in the city center. You can dine in an historical old academic hall in an old-world atmosphere with a personality all its own. The food is exquisite, though usually of the traditional English type. Many selections for under £1 ($2.50) The dessert trolley is a delight with all its mouth-watering goodies beckoning for your attention. Open Tuesday through Sunday.

HEATH AND HEATHER   3 King Edward Street
This is perfect if you are on a diet or want a light salad of some kind. As a vegetarian restaurant, it specializes in just that sort of thing. All the salad fixings are fresh and the choice is rather large. The average salad course is about 30p ($.74). They also have delicious homemade soups, again all with natural vegetarian ingredients, at about 8p ($.20) per bowl. A good place, too, for a coffee break in the morning or afternoon. Open daily from 10 A.M. to 5:30 P.M.; closed Thursday afternoon and all day Sunday.

LA CANTINA di CAPRI   34 Queen Street
Extremely good Italian cuisine, with a few English dishes thrown in for good measure. The fixed-price lunch runs from 55p to 70p ($1.37 to 1.75). I am a real lasagne buff and in my opinion theirs ranks with the best.

GOLDEN CITY   1-2 Ship Street
An excellent Chinese Restaurant, just at the top of The High, just off Corn Market. Apparently because students aren't usually laden with loot, prices are kept within their budget. From Monday through Friday, there is a special three-course luncheon for 40p ($1) and it really is delicious! At all other times the menu is à la carte, but even then it is still very inexpensive. Open seven days a week from noon to 11:30 P.M.

BLENHEIM PALACE

The ancestral home of the Churchills; in Woodstock, just 8 miles out of Oxford. Sir Winston was born here. There is a fine collection of "Churchilliana" for Churchill fans to browse through. Blenheim was originally built for John Churchill, who was then the first Duke of Marlborough, a favorite of the then reigning Queen Anne. After a particularly good show of military strategy by the Duke, Queen Anne decided he should be rewarded and the palace was the reward. It has been inhabited by all succeeding Dukes of Marlborough since it was presented to the first Duke in 1704. It is currently inhabited by the 10th Duke of Marlborough and it is not unusual to see him strolling his beautiful grounds.

The palace itself is huge and far more elegant than many Royal Palaces of its kind. My first view of it, through the trees at Bladen cemetery, was absolutely breathtaking!

The palace is open to the public, allowing you to drool over the magnificent paintings, tapestries, antiques, porcelain, family portraits, and all the "not-to-be-seen-elsewhere" finery that one expects only in a palace of this nature. Surrounding the palace is a beautiful park in which you will find the Blenheim Model Railway, which is supposed to be the second longest in Britain. You can ride it on weekends during the season. From March 20 to July 22, the palace is open Monday through Thursday; from July 24 to September 23, open daily except Fridays; from September 27 to October 28, open Monday through Thursday. Open on all these dates from 1 to 6 P.M. Admission 30p ($.75). There are tours available at the reception desk to explain all of the treasures of the palace.

Two local bus services run between Oxford and Blenheim: City of Oxford Motor Services, 395 Cowley Road, Tel: 77161 and South Midland Motor Services, 118 High Street, Tel: 44138 Both companies operate tours.

Or you can take bus No. 44 from the Gloucester Green Bus Station.

SULGRAVE MANOR

Sulgrave is a natural progression from Oxford or Blenheim, just between Oxford and Stratford-on-Avon. Sulgrave Manor is of particular interest to Americans. It is the ancestral home of our own George Washington. Washington's ancestral roots are very deep in the history of County Durham, where the senior branch of the family lived from 1183 until 1399. I'll skip all the history in between in order to bring us up to date. Lawrence Washington, mayor of Northampton, bought Sulgrave Manor from King Henry VIII in 1539. He then rebuilt the Manor House, where the family was to reside for the following 70 to 80 years. Four generations later, in 1656, George Washington's great-grandfather and his brother emigrated to America, where George himself was born in 1732. Although Washington Old Hall (Sulgrave Manor) dates from the 12th century, it was largely rebuilt in the 17th century.

The manor is situated in Washington Village on a small, pleasantly wooded hill next to the parish church. At the entrance to the grounds is one of the many gifts to the Old Hall, a pair of 18th-century gates presented by Chapter 11 of the Colonial Dames of America.

Inside the house many of the items on display are connected with George Washington, others are simply associated with the district. The building forms a capital "H" shape with the Great Hall at its midst. In medieval times this would have been the communal dining room. The fireplace here, the Yorkshire chairs, and the heavy oak dining table date from the 17th century. The entrance to the kitchen from the Great Hall is through arches at the west end of the room. These have survived from the original 12th-century house.

The huge open fireplace has a complex system of roasting jack and spits. Displayed around the house are pictures and mementoes related to George Washington. There is an 18th-century uniform of his personal bodyguard, the Washington grays, two busts, one by the French sculptor Houdon, who stayed with Washington at Mount Vernon in 1785; a unique portrait of the president painted on parchment by John Trumbull of Salem, Massachusetts, in 1780; a fan presented to Martha Washington by Lafayette; and many other objects in the display case in the downstairs lobby. At one end of the Great Hall you will see the original coat of arms of the Washington family, with three stars and two stripes. It has been said this could very easily have provided the inspiration for the American flag.

From April through September, open daily except Wednesdays, from 10:30 A.M. to 1 P.M. and from 2 to 5:30 P.M.; from October through March it closes at 4 P.M. Admission 15p ($.37).

CANTERBURY

In the county of Kent, 56 miles from London. The tourist today can follow the route of Chaucer's pilgrims five centuries ago through the West Gate, to the shrine of Archbishop Thomas à Becket, murdered at prayer in the Cathedral by four knights in 1170. After the slaying the king walked barefoot to the tomb of his friend and committed himself to a public flogging in penance. The shrine was later destroyed by Henry VIII in 1538 as part of his determination to suppress all religious control and devotion. The site of that shrine may still be seen in Trinity Chapel near the High Altar in the Cathedral. There are some magnificent stained-glass windows illustrating some of the many miracles that Becket was supposed to have been responsible for. Here, too, are buried the Black Prince who died in 1376 and Henry IV who died in 1413 and his wife, Joan of Navarre. The 14th-century Gothic nave of the Cathedral with its fan-vaulted ceiling is absolutely huge! Leaving the Cathedral, step around behind the chapel to see "Becket's Crown" housing St. Augustine's chair, signifying the authority of the Archbishop of Canterbury.

The town of Canterbury itself is also very interesting. You can stand on King's Bridge in the High Street and look over the riverside houses of the Huguenot weavers, who came to Canterbury from northern France and the Low Countries to escape religious persecution. There are many other historical notes attached to Canterbury. Julius Caesar lived nearby for a while and Bloody Mary had a great number of its inhabitants burned at the stake. You can make your pilgrimage to Canterbury by train from Victoria, Charing Cross, Waterloo, or London Bridge Stations (time: 1½ hours), or by coach from Victoria Coach Station (time: 2 to 3 hours).

HATFIELD HOUSE

In Hatfield, Hertfordshire, just about 18 miles north of London, the seat of the Marquess of Salisbury. This is a noble Jacobean mansion built in 1611 and set in a fine park. Henry VIII detained his three children, Mary, Elizabeth, and Edward here, and Princess Elizabeth was kept here until she was crowned Queen Elizabeth I in 1558, after the death of Mary Tudor (Bloody Mary). It was here that Elizabeth I heard of her succession to the throne and called her first council of State. There is quite a good collection of fine portraits, state papers, and relics of Queen Elizabeth I to be seen inside, as well as the Solar Room with its views of the magnificent roof. You can also climb the old staircase to the tower with the window where it is said that Mary Tudor, under house arrest, tried to catch the eye of Henry VIII as he passed by, hoping that he would relent. From Easter Sunday through the end of April, open Monday through Saturday from noon to 5 P.M.; from May 1 to the first Sunday in October, Tuesday through Saturday from noon to 5 P.M. On late spring and summer bank holidays, open Sundays from 2:30 to 5:30 P.M. and Mondays from noon to 5 P.M. Admission 30p ($.75).

Get to Hatfield by coach on Green Line 716, 716A from Hyde Park Corner, or by train from King's Cross.

SYON HOUSE

In Brentford, Middlesex, 9 miles from London; the estate of His Grace the Duke of Northumberland. A monastery had been founded here in 1415. Twenty years later King Henry VIII abolished the monastery, and a beautiful Tudor mansion was built. The king kept his fifth wife, Catherine Howard, locked up here until she was to be beheaded. This became the home of the first Duke of Northumberland in 1766. Much renovation was done to the original house and the current redecoration of the interior, which is strictly 18th-century, is generally regarded as Robert Adam's masterpiece. The state rooms with their period furniture, paintings, tapestries, and other collections are just beautiful. The mansion is situated on the north bank of the Thames, opposite Kew Gardens on the road to Hampton Court and flanked on either side by the Gardening Centre. From March 30 to July 28, open Monday through Friday from 1 to 5 P.M.; from July 30 to October 1, Monday through Thursday, from 1 to 5 P.M. Admission 25p ($.62). A guide is optional at no extra charge.

You can get there by underground to Hammersmith, then Bus 267 to Brent Lea entrance; or by district line to Gunnersbury, then Bus 117 or 267 to Brent Lea entrance, or by train from Waterloo to Kew Bridge, then same buses as above; or by coach, the Green Line 701 and 702, to Brent Lea entrance.

The Gardening Centre

These 55 acres on the Syon estate are a must for anyone who enjoys a garden, flowers, or plants. This horticultural spectacle presents all the elements of gradening from display to sale of plants and garden equipment. The Centre includes a 6-acre rose garden and also many varieties of shrubs, herbaceous plants, etc., which may be bought or ordered at the Centre's selling area. The focal point is the great Conservatory, built in the early 19th century and the first of its size and kind in the world. There is also a permanent open-air display of British sculpture. The nicest part of it is that the attendants are more than happy to answer any questions you might have about raising your own plants. They can cheerfully tell you how to make the most of your garden, what is wrong with ailing plants, and so on. The garden is open daily. From May through August, open from 10 A.M. to 9 P.M.; in September from 10 A.M. to 5:30 P.M.; from October through February from 10 A.M. to 5 P.M.; in March and April from 10 A.M. to 5:30 P.M. Admission 35p ($.87). There are meals and refreshments available.

WADDESDON MANOR

Near Aylesbury, Buckinghamshire, a magnificent home built for Ferdinand de Rothschild in French Renaissance style between 1880 and 1889. The mansion contains a magnificent collection of French 18th-century works of art and English 18th-century portraits, a magnificent library, park, and aviary. Huge and yet intimate in style, there is a feeling about Waddesdon Manor different from many other English manors. In the garden, there is a lovely pool with a series of beautiful mounted statues in the center. There is also a restaurant for snacks. The house is open from March through October, Wednesday through Sunday, from 2 to 6 P.M.; bank holidays from 11 A.M. to 6 P.M. The grounds are open Sundays from 11:30 A.M. Admission to the house, grounds, and aviary, 30p ($.75). Fridays an additional 20p is charged. Grounds and aviary only 10p ($.25).

Get to Waddesdon Manor by train from Marylebone, Baker Street, or Paddington to Aylesbury, then Red Rover Bus to Waddesdon Village.

WOBURN ABBEY

Magnificent 18th-century Georgian mansion at Woburn, Bedfordshire, that offers as a focal point what could be loosely termed an amusement park. Though soundly jeered by his peers, the present Duke of Bedford has turned his stately home into one of the most commercial projects around these days. It is easy to understand that aristocrats look down their noses on such commerical enterprises, but taxes being what they are in England, I think that the Duke deserves quite a pat on the back for all he has managed to accomplish here. Without his need for tax funds, we would not be privileged to see this magnificent home or its displays of art. The Abbey has been the home of the Dukes of Bedford for almost three centuries and has been lived in continuously. One of the beauties of visiting this mansion is that everywhere you see antiques being used by the family. The state apartments are so elegant as to be breathtaking! The rich array of tapestry, antique furniture, the art collection, porcelain, china, and silver is almost too much to believe. You can go through the dining rooms and see a table set for a formal dinner in the most beautiful china and silver imaginable. And everywhere there are Rembrandts, Gainsboroughs, Van Dycks, and other famous paintings, supposedly valued at £7 million. It is not at all unusual to see the Duke and Duchess of Bedford strolling through the rooms as you take your tour through the mansion. They are extremely kind and congenial. They also have guests for dinner, but for this you have to ckeck with your travel agent, since they are not regularly scheduled.

As you go through the mansion, you see the bed where Queen Victoria slept and even the nightgown she wore. Much later, Marilyn Monroe slept in the same bed.

One room houses only the various souvenirs of the "Flying Duchess"—so named because of her penchant for flying. She was the wife of the Eleventh Duke and unfortunately disappeared on a solo flight in 1937, at the grand old age of 72. No trace of her or her airplane has ever been found.

As you enter the Abbey there is a marvelous grotto of shells that is quite well known. To the left there is a souvenir shop with cards, shells, and all the usual things.

The mansion itself is only one of the features of this complex, however, as it is surrounded by the largest game reserve outside of Africa: 3,000 acres on which run live lions, cheetahs, giraffes, baboons, and a unique herd of white rhino. There are over 11 varieties of deer alone. As if that isn't enough, there is also a garden center, a railway, a pets' corner, amusement parks, lakes in which you can actually fish, various rides, restaurants, and snack bars. There is even an antique market featuring three streets of little shops selling various antiques and *objets d'art*.

I would say that Woburn Abbey is a must on any tourist list. The Abbey is open throughout the year. From March through mid-

September, the park is open Monday through Saturday from 10:30 A.M. to 6 P.M. and the Abbey is open from 11:30 A.M. to 5:30 P.M.; Sundays the park is open from 10 A.M. to 6:30 P.M. and the Abbey from 11:30 A.M. to 7 P.M. From November through February, the park is open Monday through Saturday from noon to 3:30 P.M. and the Abbey from 1 to 4 P.M.; Sundays the park is open from noon to 4 P.M. and the Abbey from 1 to P.M.

You can reach Woburn Abbey by coach on regular excursions from London from Victoria Coach Station. Tel: 730-0202.

12
Sports

RIDING

THE ESTELLE RIDING STABLES 63 Bathurst Mews, W.2   Tel: 723-2813   Underground: Paddington
Open daily from 10 A.M. to 4 P.M. Fee £2 ($5) per hour; private lessons £2.50 ($6.25) per hour. Riding in Hyde Park.

LILO BLUM'S RIDING ESTABLISHMENT 32A Grosvenor Crescent Mews, S.W.1   Tel: 225-6846   Underground: Hyde Park Corner
Open daily from 7 A.M. until dusk. Fee £2.50 ($6.25) per hour; private lessons £3 ($7.50) per hour. Riding in Hyde Park.

A little bit out of London to the west near Richmond Park and Wimbledon there are a couple more stables. These are not as accessible as the above, though quite a bit cheaper. The best way to find out how to get to them is to call them for directions.

COOMBE HILL STABLES Queen's Lane West, Kingston-upon-Thames   Tel: 949-4171
Open daily except Mondays from 9:15 A.M. to 3 P.M. Fee £1.20 ($3) per hour. Riding in Richmond Park and Wimbledon Common.

DULWICH RIDING SCHOOL COMMON S.E.21   Tel: 693-2944
Open daily from 8 A.M. to 7:30 P.M. Fee £1 ($2.50) per hour; private lessons £1.50 ($3.75) per hour. Instructions at the school only; no riding out.

FRITH MANOR SCHOOL Lullington Garth, Woodside Park, Finchley, N.12   Tel: 346-6703
Open daily except Mondays from 9 A.M. to 1 P.M., from 2 to 5:30 P.M., and from 6:30 to 9 P.M. Fee £1.50 ($3.75) per hour; private lessons £2.50 ($6.25) per hour.

HILCOTE RIDING STABLES 24B High Street, Wimbledon, S.W.19 Tel: 946-2520
Open daily, except Mondays from 10 A.M. to 3:30 P.M., later in the summer. Fee £1.30 ($3.25) per hour; lessons £2 ($5) per hour; weekend riding £1.75 ($4.37) per hour. Riding in Wimbledon Common and Richmond Park.

SWIMMING

THE BERKELEY HOTEL Knightsbridge, S.W.1 Tel: 235-6000 Underground: Knightsbridge
Residents only. Membership can be arranged, but there is a waiting list.
DOLPHIN SQUARE Chichester Street, S.W.1 Tel: 828-1681 Underground: Pimlico
Open Monday through Friday from 7:30 to 9:30 A.M. and from noon to 9:30 P.M.; Saturdays and Sundays from 9 A.M. to 5:30 P.M. Fee for nonresidents 52p ($1.30).
GREAT SMITH STREET BATHS entrance on Anne Street (beside Westminster Abbey) Tel: 232-4549 Underground: Westminster
Open Monday through Saturday from 9 A.M. to 6 P.M. Fee 10p ($.25)
GROSVENOR HOUSE HOTEL Park Lane, W.1 Tel: 499-6363 Underground: Marble Arch or Hyde Park Corner
Residents and guests only but membership can be arranged.
OASIS 32 Endell Street, High Holborn, W.C.2 Tel: 936-9555 Underground: Covent Garden
Open Monday through Friday from 9 A.M. to 6:45 P.M., Saturdays from 9 A.M. to 4:45 P.M.; Sundays from 9 to 11:45 A.M. Fee weekdays 10p ($.25); weekends 15p ($.39).
SEYMOUR HALL Seymour Place, W.1 Tel: 723-8018 Underground: Edgware Road
Open Monday through Friday from 9 A.M. to 6:30 P.M., Saturdays from 9 A.M. to 4:30 P.M., Sundays from 9:30 A.M. to noon. Fee 10p ($.25).

13
Beauty Comes First

HAIRDRESSERS

The average cost for basic services are:

	Expensive	Moderate	Budget
Shampoo and set	£2 ($5) and up	£1.25 to £1.95 ($3.12 to $4.87)	90p to £1.20 ($2.25 to $3)
Cut	£2 ($5) and up	£1 to £3.50 ($2.50 to $8.75)	55p to 90p ($1.37 to $2.25)

ALEXE 17 Queen Street, Mayfair, W.1   Tel: 499-5808
  Specializes in shaping, styling, and coloring.
ALLAN Piccadilly Hotel   Piccadilly, W.1   Tel: 437-5544
ELIZABETH ARDEN 25 Old Bond Street, W.1   Tel: 629-8211
  Sophisticated styles and make-ups to match.
BARKERS Kensington High Street, W.8   Tel: 937-5432
  Shampoo and set from 90p ($2.25); cut from 65p ($1.62). Last appointment Thursdays at 6 P.M.
BEAUTY CLINIC 118 Baker Street, W.1   Tel: 935-3405
  Facials. Last appointment Thursdays at 6 P.M.
ANDRE BERNARD 10 Bond Street, W.1   Tel: 937-8860
  Specializes in cutting for both young and older styles.
BOURNE and HOLLINGSWORTH Oxford Street, W.1   Tel: 636-1515
  Shampoo and set 85p ($2.12) or £1.25 ($3.12); cutting from 80p ($2). Last appointment Thursdays at 7 P.M.
BRUNO AND JOHN 2 Hinde Street, W.1   Tel: 486-5053
  Shampoo and set £1.43 ($3.57).

LONDON

CHEVEUX 15 Abingdon Road, W.8 Tel: 937-8860
Specializes in "trendy" styles. Last appointment Thursdays at 6 P.M.

CRIMPERS 80A Baker Street, W.1 Tel: 486-4522
Another good place for the "trendy" styles. A popular place with the young London "dollies." Last appointment Thursdays at 6 P.M.

CUT 'N' DRY The City Golf Club Bridge Lane (off Fleet Street), E.C.4 Tel: 353-3831
Closed Saturdays. Open every night.

DERRY AND TOMS Kensington High Street, W.8 Tel: 937-3774
Facials. Open Saturdays. Last appointment Thursdays at 6 P.M.

ESCALADE 187–191 Brompton Road, S.W.3 Tel: 581-0691
Open Saturdays. Last appointment daily at 6 P.M.

D. H. EVANS 318 Oxford Street, W.1 Tel: 629-8800
Facials. Shampoo and set for short hair £1 ($2.50); for long hair £1.35 ($3.37); cutting from 55p ($1.37). Last appointment Thursdays at 5:45 P.M.

EVANSKY 17 North Audley Street, W.1 Tel: 629-3930 Specializes in cutting and coloring.

FENWICK Bond Street, W.1 Tel: 629-9161
Shampoo and set £1.64 ($4.10). Last appointment Thursdays at 6 P.M.

ROBERT FIELDING 215 Regent Street, W.1 Tel: 734-3231
Shampoo and set £1.65 ($4.12).
63 King's Road, S.W.3 Tel: 730-6245.
Shampoo and set from £1.45 ($3.63) and cutting from £2.20 ($5.50).

GALATAEA 1C Palace Gate, W.8 Tel: 584-6944
Facials. Last appointment Thursdays at 5:45 P.M.

GIGI COIFFURE 27A Gloucester Road, S.W.7. Tel. 589-0337
Shampoo and set 93p ($2.32); cutting from 64p ($1.60); restyle £1 ($2.50).

GINGER GROUP 47-49 Brompton Road, S.W.3 Tel: 584-4714
3 Lower Sloane Street, S.W.1. Tel: 730-7195
317 King's Road, S.W.3. Tel: 352-0710
Shampoo and set £1.50 ($3.75).

MARC GOUTIER 17 Queen Street, Mayfair, W.1 Tel: 499-5808
Last appointment Thursdays and Fridays at 6 P.M.

HAIRLINE 68 Gloucester Road, S.W.7 Tel: 584-7193
Shampoo and set from £1.45 ($3.62); trim from 90p ($2.25); cut £1.20 ($3). Last appointment Thursdays and Fridays at 6 P.M.

HARLEY MUSE 83 Duke Street, W.1 Tel: 629-1271
Modern approach to styling and cutting.

HARRODS HAIR AND BEAUTY SALON Harrods Department Store. Brompton Road, Knightsbridge, S.W.1 Tel: 584-8881
Facials. Shampoo and set £1.85 ($4.62); restyling £2.50 ($6.25). In the Crescent Room, shampoo and set £1.25 ($3.12). All cutting £1 ($2.50); cut, wash, and blow dry £2.50 ($6.25). Open Saturdays. Last appointment Wednesdays, 6 P.M.

JINGLES 125 Baker Street, W.1 Tel: 935-3929; 125 Wilton Road, S.W.8 Tel: 834-0032
Shampoo and set £1.76 ($4.40); Cut, shampoo set/blow dry £3.63 ($9.07). Last appointment Thursdays and Fridays at 6:45 P.M.

Beauty Comes First 155

JOHN, MARC and PAUL. 31 Bruton Street, W.1 Tel: 470-7436
Young, imaginative, and careful stylists.

MICHAEL JOHN 23A Albemarle Street, W.1 Tel: 629-6969
High-fashion hairdressing and Kenneth J. Lane jewelry available at the reception desk.

PETER JONES DEPARTMENT STORE Sloane Square, S.W.1 Tel: 730-3434.
Facials, too. Last appointment Wednesdays at 5:15 P.M.

JOSEPH SALON 33B King's Road, S.W.3 Tel: 730-7664
Shampoo and set from £1.50 ($3.75); cut from £3.30 ($8.25). Last appointment Thursdays at 6:30 P.M.

LEONARD AND TWIGGY 76–78 Sloane Avenue, S.W.3 Tel: 584-8875
Shampoo and set from £2.31 ($5.77); cut from £2.31 ($5.77). They prefer to cut on your first visit.

JOHN LEWIS Oxford Street, W.1 Tel: 629-8517
Facials. Open Saturdays. Last appointment at 5:45 P.M.

LOCKS 281 Fullham Road, S.W.10 Tel: 351-1123
Shampoo and set £1.25 ($3.12); cut and blow dry from £2.75 ($6.87).

HARVEY NICHOLS Department Store Knightsbridge, S.W.1 Tel: 235-7207.
Facials. Shampoo and set £1.45 ($3.63); cutting from 90p ($2.25). Last appointment Wednesdays at 5:45 P.M.

NODUMKY 17 Connaught Place, W.2 Tel: 723-6636
Shampoo and set (or blow dry) from £1.50 ($3.75); cutting from £1.50 ($3.75).

PENTA HOTEL Cromwell Road, S.W.7 Tel: 373-7755
Shampoo and set from £1.25 ($3.12); cut from £1 to £2.50 ($2.50 to $6.25); manicure 75p ($1.87).

REBELLE 31 Brook Street, W.1 Tel: 499-8167
Styling for difficult hair.

REGENT PALACE HOTEL Piccadilly Circus, W.1 Tel: 437-8989
Shampoo and set £1.50 ($3.75).

RICHE 14 Hay Hill, W.1 Tel: 493-3368
Facials, too. Last appointment Thursdays at 6 P.M.

MR. ROBERT HAIRDRESSING and SAUNA Gloucester Hotel Harrington Gardens, S.W.7 Tel: 373-6030, extension 189/190
Shampoo and set £2.20 ($5.50), cut £2.20.

HELENA RUBENSTEIN 3 Grafton Street, W.1 Tel: 499-9050
Sophisticated hairstyles.

ANNIE RUSSELL 398 King's Road, S.W.1 Tel: 352-5693
Shampoo and set £1.70 ($4.25); cut from 90p ($2.25). Last appointment Thursdays at 6 P.M.

VIDAL SASSOON 171 New Brown Street, W.1 Tel: 629-9665
44 Sloane Street, S.W.1 Tel: 235-7791
Grosvenor House, Park Street, W.1 Tel: 629-2463
Avant-garde styling in a modern atmosphere. Sassoon is perhaps the most famous of all British hair stylists. Prices are determined by whether or

156 LONDON

not you are having the work done by a stylist, manager, artistic director, or by the European artistic director. Cut £2 to £4 ($5 to $10); set £1.90 ($4.75), £3.50 ($8.75). Open Thursdays and Fridays from 9 A.M. to 4:30 P.M., Saturdays from 9 to 11:30 A.M. The South Molton Street Branch is open all day Saturdays until 5:50 P.M., Thursday and Friday nights until 6 P.M.

SELFRIDGES DEPARTMENT STORE Oxford Street, W.1 Tel: 629-1234
Shampoo and set £1.25 ($3.12); cut from 80p ($2); cutting and restyling, blow dry £2.45 ($6.12).

SISSORS 46A King's Road, S.W.3 Tel: 589-9471
11A Kensington Church Street, W.8 Tel: 937-6354
Shampoo and blow dry £1.50 to £2 ($3.75 to $5). They specialize in cutting and natural styling and coloring. Especially good at young styles for long hair. This is a popular place with the "dolly" set.

STEINER Platform 1, Victoria Station, S.W.1 Tel: 828-3747
Shampoo and set from 95p ($2.38).
Royal Garden Hotel Kensington High Street, W.8 Tel: 937-1228
Imperial Hotel Russell Square, W.C.1 Tel: 278-6363
Shampoo and set from £1.50 ($3.75). Open Saturdays. Last appointment at 7 P.M.

SWEENY'S 48 Beauchamp Place, S.W.3 Tel: 589-3066
Cut and blow dry for short hair £4.50 ($11.25); for long hair, £5.50 ($13.75).

VANILLA 11A Kensington Church Street, W.8 Tel: 937-6354
Open Saturdays until 5:30 P.M. Last appointment daily at 6:30 P.M.

JOEL VELLA 11 St. Christopher's Place, W.1 Tel: 935-7070
Shampoo and blow dry £2.47 ($6.17).

WHITELEYS Queensway, W.2 Tel: 229-1234
Shampoo and set £1.04 ($2.60); cut from 55p ($1.37).

XAVIER 3 William Street, S.W.1 Tel: 235-6141
Well known stylists for sophisticated and chic hairdressing.

HAIRDRESSERS WITH TRICHOLOGISTS

Trichologists deal with hair and scalp problems. Those we have listed here are all members of the Institution of Trichologists.

BRUNO AND JOHN 2 Hinde Street, W.1 Tel: 486-5053
Consultation £1.05 ($2.62). Treatment takes 45 minutes to one hour; from £1.25 ($3.12).

GINGER GROUP 47–49 Brompton Road, S.W.3 Tel: 584-4714
Free consultation. Treatment £2.10 ($5.25).

LEONARD 6 Upper Grosvenor Street, W.1 Tel: 629-5757; 76–78 Sloane Ave, S.W.3 Tel: 584-8923
Consultation free. One treatment £2.10 ($5.25).

RICHE 14 Hay Hill, W.1   Tel: 493-3368
Treatment takes an hour and costs £2.80 ($7).
STEINER 66 Grosvenor Street, W.1   Tel: 629-5245; Platform 1, Victoria Station, S.W.1   Tel: 828-3747
Consultation with Mr. Oscar Steiner; £3.46 ($8.65).
JOEL VELLA 11 St. Christopher's Place W.1   Tel: 935-7070.
Consultation free. One-hour treatment £3.63 ($9.07).

SALONS FOR BEAUTY TREATMENTS

ELIZABETH ARDEN 20 New Bond Street, W.1   Tel: 629-8211
A full range of treatments using their own cosmetics and a special physiotherapy department for slimming and toning. Open Monday through Friday from 9 A.M. to 6 P.M.

CYCLAX 58 South Molton Street, W.1   Tel: 629-0054
The salon has a wide range of beauty treatments including a facial costing £2 ($5) and a "cleanse and makeup" at £1.25 ($3.12). Open Monday through Friday from 9:30 A.M. to 5:30 P.M., Wednesdays to 7:30 P.M. Closed Saturdays.

EYELURE "LET'S FACE IT" 8 Grosvenor Street, W.1   Tel: 629-7874
An entire beauty service that includes a "trial area" with test samples for all their cosmetics. You can have a single lesson or a crash course in the art of eye makeup and there's even a wig-hire service. Open Monday through Friday from 9:30 A.M. to 5:30 P.M.

FACE PLACE 26 Cale Street, S.W.3   Tel: 589-4226
This was the first salon to have a "trial area" for testing cosmetics. They have a large selection of brands and give you independent advice on the type and brand you should use as you try them out. Open Monday through Friday from 10 A.M. to 6 P.M.

MAX FACTOR 16 Old Bond Street, W.1   Tel: 493-6720
A pleasant salon offering treatments and advice on the use of their cosmetics. Open from 9:30 A.M. to 5:30 P.M.

GALA OF LONDON 48 Burlington Arcade, W.1   Tel: 493-4965
Facials and beauty treatments can be arranged during lunch hours and often after 5:30 if you book in advance. Open Monday through Friday from 9:30 A.M. to 5:30 P.M.

BARBARA GOULD 2 Bond Street., W.1   Tel: 493-7171
There's a free trial area to test cosmetics on the ground floor and two salons downstairs where a facial runs from £1.25 ($3.12). Open Monday through Friday from 9 A.M. to 5:30 P.M., Saturday to 1 P.M.

DOROTHY GRAY HAIR AND BEAUTY SALON 45 Conduit Street, W.1   Tel: 734-7885
They have a comprehensive beauty service including an "early bird" scheme Monday through Thursday whereby all appointments before 10:30 A.M. merit a discount. Open Monday through Friday from 9 A.M. to 6 P.M., Saturdays until 1 P.M.

INNOXA 170 New Bond Street, W.1   Tel: 493-6949
Fullscale beauty treatments. Open from 9 A.M. to 5:30 P.M.; Thursdays and Fridays until 7:30 P.M.

LANCOME 14 Grosvenor Street., W.1 Tel: 493-6811
An excellent range of French cosmetics and the salon's cosmetologists will advise on their use. Usual beauty service. Open Monday through Friday from 9:30 A.M. to 5 P.M. Closed Saturdays.

HELENA RUBENSTEIN 3 Grafton Street, W.1 Tel: 499-9050
A comprehensive range of beauty treatments and preparations for the care of your skin. Open from 9 A.M. to 5:30 P.M., Thursdays until 7 P.M. Closed Saturdays.

YARDLEY 33 Old Bond Street, W.1 Tel: 629-9341
There is a "try before you buy" beauty playroom, with full treatment available in private rooms. Specialists on delicate skin. Open Monday through Friday from 9 A.M. to 5:30 P.M.

BEAUTY CLINICS FOR SPECIAL PROBLEMS

Most beauty salons specialize in facials, cleansing, new makeups, and the usual sort of treatments good for normal skin. However, the following beauty clinics deal with other beauty problems that cannot be improved or hidden by makeup. There is a wide variety of services, so read each one carefully.

VIOLET ADAIR AT GALATAEA 1C Palace Gate, W.8 Tel: 584-6944
Instant suntan £2.50 ($6.25) per treatment.

THE ALLAN CLINIC 3 Vincent Court, Seymour Place, W.2 Tel: 262-9306
Colonic lavage £6 ($15); vitamin B_{12} injections £5 ($12.50) for a course of 6.

MICHELINE ARCIER 4 Albert Gate Court, 124 Knightsbridge, S.W.1 Tel: 589-3225
One-and-a-half-hour initial examination by Madame Arcier £13 ($32.50); one hour aromatherapy treatment £5.98 ($14.95); 6 treatments £31.20 ($78).

ELIZABETH ARDEN 20 New Bond Street, W.1 Tel: 629-8211
Slimming and spot-reducing treatments (30 minutes) £2.50 ($6.25); course of 6 treatments £12.50 ($31.25).

OLIVE BEAUCHAMP (downstairs at CHEVEUX) 15 Abingdon Road, W.8 Tel: 937-8659
Facials using homemade face packs containing honey or cucumber. 1½-hour treatment £4 ($10). Saturday and evening appointments by arrangement.

BEAUTY CLINIC 118 Baker Street, W.1 Tel: 935-3405
They deal with skin trouble, figure problems, and unwanted or unruly hair. While you are there, have a facial, a manicure, and a pedicure.

JOY BYRNE 37 Albemarle Street, Mayfair, W.1 Tel: 493-2633
Comprehensive skin-care and beauty service and a hairdressing salon.

Beauty Comes First 159

Slimming courses include a one-week "rapid-reducing-course," ideal for the tourist and a "top to toe" grooming for that special night out; takes four hours and costs £3.15 ($7.87). Open Monday through Thursday from 8:30 A.M. to 5 P.M., Fridays from 8:30 A.M. to 6:30 P.M., Saturdays from 8:30 A.M. to 1 P.M.

COUNTESS CSAKY Tel: 629-3732

Rejuvenating facials (1½ hours) £8.80 ($22); hands and arms £2.20 ($5.50).

FINA DE PARIS 147 Edbury Street, S.W.1 Tel: 730-8685

Treatment for scars. Five herbal peeling treatments £25 ($62.50); wax baths £3.30 ($8.25).

ELIZABETH FLAIR 303 Finchley Road., N.W.3 Tel: 435-6780

One-hour acne treatment £3.15 ($7.88); treatments £16 ($40).

GIGI 27A Gloucester Toad, S.W.7 Tel: 589-0337

Figure correction by steam bath, massage, or vibration. Ultraviolet suntan treatment, facials, hairdressing, ear-piercing, and chiropody. Open 6 days a week.

JULIE HACKER 124 Knightsbridge, S.W.1 Tel: 589-7581

Acne treatment £3.30 ($8.25); course of 6 treatments £16.50 ($41.25).

MARIA HORNES 16 Davies Street, W.1 Tel: 629-2823

One-hour facial with honey mask £3 ($7.50); peeling treatments £19 to £32 ($47.50 to $80).

BLANCHE KRAMER, HELENA HARNIK AND AGNES BALINT 25 Welbeck Street, W.1 Tel: 935-1657

Specialize in electrolysis, acne, and the removal of warts, moles, broken veins, and freckles. Open Tuesday through Friday from 10 A.M. to 6 P.M., Mondays from 10 A.M. to 7 P.M.

MME. LEONI 4 Manchester Street, W.1 Tel: 935-1824

Individual sauna cabinet baths followed by shower and manipulated body massage £6 ($15) for 1½ hours.

MME. LUBATTI 14 Montagu Mansions, Baker Street, W.1 Tel: 935-2171

Face treatment, including neck and spinal massage, £2.10 ($5.25).

DR. PAYOT'S SALON 139A New Bond Street, W.1 Tel: 493-5516

Special acne treatments, using Payot preparations, 1½ hours, £4.50 ($11.25); technical facial with spinal massage, 1½ hours, from £3.50 ($8.75).

REGENCY BEAUTY CENTRE 5 Mill Street, W.1 Tel: 493-5626

Remedial beauty treatments, manicures, ear-piercing, and hairdressing. Open Monday through Friday. Open Tuesdays, Wednesdays, and Fridays from 10 A.M. to 6 P.M., Mondays and Thursdays until 8 P.M.

TAO CLINIC 153 Brompton Road, S.W.3 Tel: 589-4847

Remedial treatment for the face. A free consultation service and slimming courses. Open Monday through Friday from 10 A.M. to 6 P.M., Wednesdays from 10 A.M. to 7 P.M., Saturdays from 9 A.M. to 4:30 P.M.

TOWN AND COUNTRY HEALTH SALON 2 Yeoman's Row, Brompton Road, S.W.3 Tel: 584-7702

All kinds of special treatment for the face, figure, and hair, a health food bar, and a boutique. For a sociable slimming-down, join the club.

AROMATHERAPY

This is a unique treatment based on old Chinese and Japanese techniques of massage utilizing natural oils and herbal essence. It effects both a physical and emotional improvement.

MICHELINE ARCHIER 61A Brompton Road, S.W.3 Tel: 584-0999
Again specializing in aromatherapy to suit individual needs. The "essential oils" are also sold at the salon. Closed Saturdays.

MARION AYRES SALON The International School of Natural Beauty Therapy 45–47 George Street, Portman Square Tel: 935-4765
All health and beauty treatment is based on homeotherapy. Facilities include a Finnish log sauna. They are also very good at helping with camouflage makeup. Open Monday through Friday from 1 to 7 P.M.

DANIELE RYMAN The Park Lane Hotel Piccadilly, W.1 Tel: 499-6321, extension 285
Aromatherapy treatments as practiced by the late Madame Maury. Consultation from £3.85 ($9.62); treatment from £5.77 ($14.42).

CELL THERAPY

This is the treatment discovered by Dr. Paul Niehans, which has come to be known as the "youth serum." It was used with great results by many famous celebrities, such as Gloria Swanson, W. Somerset Maugham, and Charlie Chaplin. The serum is made of the organs of young sheep. It is said to correct many physical problems such a obesity, sexual impotence or frigidity, and kidney and liver diseases; it also rejuvenates the organs to such an extent that all the old cells are replaced by new ones, thereby giving them new life. Of course, this shows in the way you feel, look, and act—hence the name "youth serum." Originally this treatment was only given by injection and one had to stay in a clinic. Now, however, there is a doctor in London who has perfected a new method utilizing suppositories instead. This means that you can administer the treatment yourself easily. For more information, or to make an appointment to discuss the nature of your problem, call Dr. Peter Stephen at the Cell Therapy Centre, 52 Welbeck Street, Tel: 486-5938. If you plan on being in London less than ten days, it is suggested that you write to Dr. Stephen prior to your visit so that he can tell you what tests to have taken; he can have them analyzed prior to your arrival, giving you the results of the test and the treatment while you are in London.

COSMETICS

In London you can buy all the main brands of cosmetics whether they be American, French, Italian, or whatever. A good buy, too, are the less expensive brands that I have found to be exceptionally good: Miners, Outdoor Girl, and Rommel—which are generally found at Woolworth's—plus Woolworth's own brand, Baby Doll Cosmetics.

BEAUTY WITHOUT CRUELTY 49 Upper Montague Street, W.1 Tel: 262-1375
If you hate the idea of animal fats being used as bases in your makeup, you may like to try these cosmetics made purely of herbs, flowers, and natural essences. They will also advise on skin problems. Open Monday through Friday from 10 A.M. to 5 P.M., Wednesdays until 7 P.M.

COSMETICS A LA CARTE, LTD 16 Motcomb Street, S.W.1 Tel: 235-0596
I've just discovered one of the most exciting new innovations in the cosmetics field. Three young women, a cosmetic chemist, a color formulator, and a beautician, have joined forces in this sweet little shop where they can formulate any kind of cosmetic for you in any shade! Bring in a piece of fabric, send them a lock of your hair, or whatever, and they will prepare something to match it identically. You can even tell them the consistency you want, from dry to extra-rich. I have found this to be a special boon since no lipstick was ever creamy enough for me, and I was delighted to be able to get exactly what I wanted. Formulating new lipstick costs £2.50 ($6.25), but all repeat orders are only £1.75 ($4.37). They keep your formula on hand and can repeat it at any time. If you don't have time to stop in and see Christine, Lynn, and Janet, don't hesitate to drop them a line with your color sample. I'm positive you'll be very satisfied. They also give one-hour makeup lessons for £4.50 ($11.25).

EAR-PIERCING SPECIALISTS

MRS. O'MAHONY Gilbert House, Westmoreland Terrace, S.W.1 Tel: 828-4167.
An expert ear-piercer. Fees from £1.50 ($3.75), depending on the type of earring.

CYRIL WILKINSON 62 Grosvenor Street, W.1 Tel: 629-0437
They have pierced the ears of many eminent people. Fees from £3.30 ($8.25).

EYE CARE AND CONTACT LENSES

CONTACT LENS CLINIC 8 Wilton Crescent, S.W.1 Tel: 235-4888
They offer advice and help on lenses and their use.

EYE CARE INFORMATION BUREAU 55 Park Lane, W.1 Tel: 499-0609
They offer advice on eye care and can tell you where to obtain treatment.

FOOT CARE

CHELSEA FOOT CLINIC 250 King's Road, S.W.3 Tel: 352-0749
Remedial treatment for all problems.

DR. SCHOLL FOOT CARE 254 Regent Street, W.1 Tel: 734-3583; 59 Brompton Road, S.W.3 Tel: 589-1887; 44 Cheapside, E.C.2 Tel: 248-4327
Complete foot- and leg-care service, which really comes in handy when you're running around the city sightseeing.

HAND- AND NAIL-CARE SPECIALISTS

If your hands or nails are beyond the scope of your regular manicurist, these specialists will treat dermatitis, allergies, etc.

MME. ANGELA CURTIN 70 Duke Street, W.1 Tel: 493-5619
Initial consultation £3.75 ($9.37); subsequent treatments £2.25 ($5.62).

THE HAND AND NAIL CULTURE INSTITUTE 35 Old Bond Street Tel: 493–7561
Manicures, wax and clay packs are a specialty. They give advice and treatment for all kinds of nail infections and disorders, and provide treatment by mail to carry out in your home. First one-hour appointment £1.95 ($4.87); course of 7 £7 ($17.50).

HARRODS BEAUTY SALON (Harrods Department Store) Knightsbridge, S.W.1 Tel: 584-8881
Revlon manicure lasting one-half hour 82p ($2.05) or 93p ($2.32) with Ultima II polish; wax manicure (hand wrapped in warm wax to draw out impurities), £2 ($5); hand massage 43p ($1.07).

MAVALA INTERNATIONAL MANICURE SCHOOL 54 Knightsbridge, S.W.1 Tel: 235-4729
Free consultation on any nail-care problems. Three-quarter-hour manicure with student, using Mavala products 30p ($.75).

PERFUMES

We all have our favorites and most stores carry all ranges of all the better known perfumes. However, sometimes you will have better luck in the actual salon of the particular perfume house so I have listed some of these here. Another reason I enjoy these salons is that many of them have additional perfume gifts, which you may either keep or give as gifts.

FLORIS 89 Jermyn Street, W.1   Tel: 930-2885
 Besides their exquisite perfumes, this old, established firm also specializes in ceramic potpourri jars, scented pomanders, and perfumed candles.

GALERIES LAFAYETTE 188–196 Regent Street, W.1   Tel: 734-6740.
 This branch of the famous French store carries one of the largest ranges of haut parfums in London.

LANVIN PERFUMES 53 Dorset Street, W.1   Tel: 935-8238

LENTHERIC 17 Old Bond Street, W.1   Tel: 493-1733
 They carry their own range of perfumes and the Morny Bath Salts.

SAUNAS

ABC SAUNA Whiteleys, Queensway, W.2   Tel: 229-6452
 Sauna £1.05 ($2.62); sauna and massage £3.05 ($7.62).

VIOLET ADAIR AT GALATAEA 1C Palace Gate, W.8   Tel: 584-6944
 Sauna £1.05 ($2.62); sauna and massage £3.15 ($7.87).

MARION AYERS CLINIC 8 New Quebec Street, W.1   Tel: 723-9487
 Sauna and half-hour manual massage £3 ($7.50).

CHEVEUX 15 Abingdon Road, W.1   Tel: 937-8659
 Sauna £1.50 ($3.75).

CLARENDON COURT HOTEL SAUNA Maida Vale, Edgware Road, W.9   Tel: 286-7227
 Sauna £1.30 ($3.25); sauna and massage £3.50 ($8.75).

ESCALADE 187-191 Brompton Road, S.W.3   Tel: 589-9203
 Sauna £1.65 ($4.12), for as long as you like.

GILLES 175 Sloane Street, S.W.1   Tel: 235-2534
 Sauna £2.10 ($5.25).

DOROTHY GRAY 45 Conduit Street, W.1   Tel: 734-7885
 Sauna £1.50 ($3.75); sauna and full manual massage £3.60 ($9).

HARRODS BEAUTY SALON Knightsbridge, S.W.1   Tel: 584-8881
 One half-hour sauna £1.65 ($4.12). Sauna and half-hour massage £3.30 ($8.25).

HEALTH AND BEAUTY 31 Fife Road, Kingston-upon-Thames, Surrey   Tel: 549-3609
 Sauna £1.10 ($2.75); sauna and one half-hour massage £2.40 ($6).

LONDON HEALTH AND FITNESS CENTRE 140 Marylebone Road, N.W.1   Tel: 935-4002
 Sauna £1.50 ($3.75); sauna and massage £5 ($12.50); massage only £4 ($10).

ORLANDO 14 Dover Street, W.1   Tel: 493-6378
 Sauna £1.35 ($3.37) for as long as you like. Sauna plus half-hour massage £2.95 ($7.37).

MR. ROBERT HAIRDRESSING AND SAUNA The Gloucester Hotel Harrington Gardens, S.W.3   Tel: 373-6030, extension 189 or 190
 Sauna £1.75 ($4.37).

WIGGERIES

ALEXE 17 Queen Street, Mayfair, W.1   Tel: 499-5808
They stock a large selection of hand made wigs and specialize in hair and wig styling.

JOSEPH SALON 33B King's Road, S.W.3   Tel: 730-7664
Excellent selection of wigs and hairpieces which can be set and conditioned there.

JOHN LONDON 7 Station Approach, Baker Street Station, M.W.1   Tel: 935-3612
You can rent wigs or hairpieces for 24 hours or a weekend.

ST. MICHAEL 11 St. Christopher's Place, Wigmore Street, W.1   Tel: 935-7070
Skilled cutting and modern styling for both your own hair and your wig. Good supply of wigs.

TEEDA 63 South Molton Street, W.1   Tel: 499-7282
Large stock of wigs and hairpieces in many styles. Experts in permanently waving either your own hair or your wig.

THE WIGGERY 16 Knightsbridge Green, S.W.1   Tel: 589-3780
A large stock of wigs. Can also make wigs to fit specifications and from the client's own hair. An excellent after-care service.

BEAUTY FARMS

This is a good idea if you wish to combine a vacation with a rejuvenating session. You could spend a week at any of the following beauty farms and then another week in London or wherever you wish to go. You'll certainly feel and look a lot better for it. The directors will tell you how to get there or make arrangements to pick you up. All of the following are just a short distance out of London and very convenient. I have personally seen every single one of them and they are all very well managed. Henlow Grange, Forest Mere, and Grayshott Hall are extremely popular with stage and screen celebrities, many of whom come here to slim down before their shows. They also get quite a few aristocrats.

Beauty farms are run on the American pattern and concentrate on all kinds of beauty treatments including slimming.

HENLOW GRANGE Henlow, Bedfordshire   Tel: Chicksands 7141
Accommodation for 36 people; double and single rooms, a few with private bathrooms. There is a wide selection of body treatments available, including Panthermal, which combines steam, ozone, and oxygen; hydrotherapy under-water massage; sauna and hand massage; G5 and seaweed baths; volcanic mud baths; cold stocking treatment for legs; electrical

treatments; the latest gas and steam cabinet treatment from Germany; and facials, skin peeling, manicures, pedicures, scalp treatments, and hairdressing. They also have a heated indoor pool and an exercise room. Daily exercise classes. Controlled diets. Cost of a single room is from £53 ($132.50) per week.

SHENLEY LODGE HEALTH RESORT Ridge Hill, Shenley, Hertfordshire Tel: Potters Bar 4242

Accommodation for about 12 people. The emphasis here is on slimming and reeducating people to eat sensibly on a controlled, high-protein diet. Mr. Chapman gives daily exercise classes in the gym, and these can be followed by sauna and manual massage given by experienced masseuses. A selection of beauty treatments is also available, including facials, manicure, pedicure, and hairdressing. Cost of a single room is from £7.50 ($18.75) per day.

HEALTH HYDROS

These are country houses run on naturopath lines. They specialize in treating health problems—and slimming—using homeopathic remedies.

CHAMPNEYS NATURE CURE RESORT Champneys, near Tring, Hertfordshire Tel: Berkhamsted 3351

Accommodation for 110 people; double and single rooms, detached and semidetached chalets, some with lavatories. Naturopath treatments under the supervision of Mr. Peter Lief. Yoga lessons twice a week. Single room from £49 ($122.50) per week.

ENTON HALL Near Godalming, Surrey Tel: Wormley 2233

Accommodation for 72 people; double and single rooms; garden rooms with showers and private lavatories; detached chalets. Naturopath treatments under the supervision of the founder, Mr. Atkinson Reddell. Single room from £37 ($92.50) per week.

FOREST MERE Liphook, Hampshire Tel: Liphook 2051

Accommodation for about 72 people; double and single rooms, all with own lavatories, some with showers; modern chalets. Naturopath treatments under the supervision of Mr. Timothy Gray. Single room from £66.50 ($166.25) per week.

GRAYSHOTT HALL HEALTH CENTRE Grayshott, near Hindhead, Surrey Tel: Hindhead 4331

Accommodation for about 70 to 80 people; double and single rooms and suites, all with own lavatory and with bath or shower; new wing, all rooms with lavatory. Naturopath treatments, hydrotherapy, ultraviolet therapy. Single room from £52.50 ($131.25) per week.

METROPOLE HEALTH HYDRO Hotel Metropole Brighton Tel: Brighton 775432

Accommodation for 50 to 60 people; luxurious double rooms, suites, all with private bathrooms. Naturopath treatments under the supervision of Mr. Ian Scott. Room £69 ($172.50) per person per week.

RAGDALE HALL Ragdale, Melton Mowbray, Leicester Tel: Rotherby 831

Accommodation for about 18 people; some rooms with private bath/shower. New hydro with emphasis on reeducating patients to eat sensibly on a balanced diet. Set in 13 acres of grounds, with croquet, putting, riding, and heated swimming pool. Staff of trained beauticians. Cost for one week £65 to £70 ($162.50 to $175).

SHRUBLAND HALL HEALTH CLINIC Coddenham, near Ipswich, Suffolk Tel: Ipswich 830404

Accommodation for 40 people; double and single rooms, each with hot and cold water. Not many private bathrooms; four well-equipped chalets. Naturopath treatments are supervised by Mr. J. H. Chown. Single room from £36 ($90) per week.

THIRLMERE HEALTH HYDRO Hastings Road, Bexhill-on-Sea, Sussex Tel: Bexhill 2401

Accommodation for 30 to 40 patients, double and single rooms, some with private lavatories. This small, well-equipped hydro is run by a doctor and is conveniently situated in the residential area of Bexhill, close to the sea. They specialize in diets and have an arrangement with a spa in Austria to give their mud baths. Single room from £48 ($120) per week.

TYRINGHAM NATUROPATHIC CLINIC near Newport Pagnell, Buckinghamshire Tel: Newport Pagnell 610450

Accommodation for 69 patients; double and single rooms, some with their own shower or bath and lavatory, and a number of rooms with 3 to 6 beds in cubicles. The clinic is housed in a Georgian mansion in large and beautiful gardens. Treatments under the supervision of Mr. Rose-Neil. Registered as a nursing home. Single room from £43 ($107.50) per week, according to season.

14
Shopping

For a visitor to London, a shopping trip—nice and simple in most other cities—can be a baffling experience. Whether you want a new dress, a second-hand car, an art masterpiece, or a wig, there is a shop in London somewhere with an answer to your prayers—but where? We will try to answer these questions for you in the following pages and make it as easy as possible.

Keep in mind whenever shopping that it is most important to keep the receipts so that you can produce them at customs if necessary. If you are taking your purchase home with you, you are allowed $100 duty-free and everything over that will have a duty levied against it. To avoid the duty, you can try one of several things: 1) The Over-the-Counter Scheme: in this case you take your goods with you plus a tax-exemption form. If the shop deducts VAT, you should produce the goods and hand the forms over to the customs at your departure. If the tax is not deducted in the shop, claim it at the customs desk. 2) The Retail Export Scheme: taxes are deducted from the goods in the shop and sent direct to your home. You may, however, be asked to pay postage and packing costs. 3) The Personal Export Scheme: this operates only if you are traveling home by sea. The tax is deducted in the shop, where you sign a form. The taxes are then sent off to the shipper. The only thing that you have to do after that is to indicate the parcels to the customs office on passing through the control for your return voyage. The goods are then stored. Many major London stores operate this scheme. 4) Duty Free Gift: you can mail anything you like back home, duty-free, as long as it is under $10 and not more than one parcel is sent to one address per day. This is usually the easiest way to do your shopping because it saves you the trouble of taking it with you and having to find place in an already bulging suitcase, it arrives just about the same time you do, and there is no customs formality to go through when you arrive back in your country.

In general, London stores stay open from 9 A.M. to 5:30 P.M., Monday through Saturday, and are closed Sundays. Shops on the West End of London stay open until 7:30 P.M. Thursdays. On Knightsbridge, Sloane Square, and King's Road, late shopping night is Wednesday—until 7:30 P.M. A few shops are not open on Saturday afternoons, among them: Heal's, Tottenham Court Road; Peter Jones, Sloane Square; John Lewis, Oxford Street; Moss Brothers, Bedford Street, Covent Garden; The Needle Woman Shop, Regent Street; John Barnes, Finchley Road; and Fortnum and Mason's, Piccadilly.

Every country is known for certain things, so gifts of this nature are much more interesting than just any other gift. Britain, too, has its own share of such gifts, including the traditional woolens, cashmere sweaters, tweeds, Wedgwood and other china, rare books, antiques, paintings, and miniature horsemen. You'll also like pomander balls, which are filled with sachet and hung in the closet, pomander locket-type necklaces, silver, cutlery, and old maps of Europe that can be framed beautifully.

DESIGN CENTRE 28 Haymarket, S.W.1 Tel: 832-8000
The headquarters of the government-backed Design Council, which has a comprehensive pictorial card index listing some of the best in British quality goods, their price, and where to buy them. A first-class place to go for gift ideas, if you want British made products.

Sales

Bargain hunting is a somewhat bizarre and energetic pastime much loved by English housewives, and you are more than welcome to join in the fun. In early January and early July each year, the big London stores sell their stock out at reduced prices. Some of these reductions can be quite spectacular. Recently a £1,000.95 ($2,502.37) mink coat was marked down to £400 ($1,000). There are loads of bargains to be had at rock-bottom prices, although you may have to be prepared to join in a regular free-for-all to get what you want. The sales generally last a week. Days and times of opening are usually published in the London newspapers, the *Evening Standard* and the *Evening News*.

DEPARTMENT STORES

There is nothing more exciting than wandering around little streets and alleyways to find an unusual shop with a unique gift. We don't all have that much time, though, so a better bet is to visit the major department stores and select what you need or want quickly and easily. This also gives you a good idea of what the country has to offer.

These are just a few of the most important department stores. There are at least 20 others specializing in various arrays of international goods.

FORTNUM AND MASON   181 Piccadilly, W.1   Underground: Piccadilly Circus

This has got to be the world's most posh, most elegant, most opulent department store, primarily because of its gourmet food section. Would you believe crystal chandeliers, clerks dressed in striped trousers and tails, and groceries wrapped as though they were ready to be presented to the Queen! Even if you can't afford to buy anything you really should stop in just to see it because it is the only place in the world of its kind. You'll rub elbows with aristocracy, celebrities, or maybe just their chauffeurs. If you can afford it this is an ideal place to send a gift from. They have many selections to offer, all packaged in beautiful flasks, porcelain jars, stone jars, china bowls, baskets, and the like. Though one generally thinks of Fortnum and Mason's gourmet department, that isn't all it has to offer. It is a department store in the traditional sense of the word, and its other floors carry clothing, china, silver, antiques, and so on.

HARRODS   87–135 Brompton Road, Knightsbridge, S.W.1   Underground: Knightsbridge

One of London's most famous department stores carrying anything you could possibly want, including food, though not as elegant as Fortnum and Mason.

MARKS AND SPENCER   458 Oxford Street, W.1 (near the Marble Arch)   Underground: Marble Arch; 173 Oxford Street, W.1 (in Soho)   Underground: Oxford Circus; and 258 Edgware Road, W.2   Underground: Edgware Road

Marks and Spencer stores are famous for the budget-priced but excellent quality goods. They look very much like our own American Penney's, and I would say the quality is perhaps very much the same. They are exceptionally good on knitwear. Their prices compared with equal quality in other stores are exceptionally low. They also have a good children's wear department, and a food department, if you want to pick up some goodies to keep in your room.

HARVEY NICHOLS   109–125 Knightsbridge, S.W.1   Underground: Knightsbridge

This is the most famous shop in this section of the road and has been since 1817. A luxurious department store specializing in fashion and household goods.

SELFRIDGES 398–429 Oxford Street, W.1 Underground: Marble Arch

One of the largest department stores in all of Europe, Selfridges can offer you anything you want, whether it is a British-made product or an import from any other country. Prices are in the reasonable range, service is excellent. On the top floor you'll find a tax-free export shop where you can buy all British products and ship them out of the country tax-free.

BOUTIQUES

For the most bizarre shop fronts in London, and some of the most revolutionary clothes, for both men and women, visit King's Road, Chelsea, where Biba's Boutiques, antique shops, coffee bars, and inexpensive restaurants jostle colorfully for position along the road. Carnaby Street, between Regent Street and Soho, is one of the busiest shopping streets in London, where you can buy informal and trendy clothes at mass-production prices. For more exclusive, and more expensive, clothes, Bond Street is the place to go, while only a few minutes' walk away Oxford Street has dozens of bright and breezy boutiques where prices are kept to a minimum. Many of the big department stores along Regent Street and Oxford Street have "Young Shops."

LEATHER GOODS

For shoes there is quite a good variety of shops and prices. **Bally,** the famous shoemaker, has shops on Oxford, Tottenham Court Road, and Piccadilly. So do **Dolcis, Sacha, Ravel,** and **Peter Lord.** Each has branches elsewhere, too. **Ferragamo** on Old Bond Street is famous for beautiful shoes and accessories. On Brompton Road, **Louis Jourdan, Rayne,** and **Dellman** hold sway. **Shoosissima** in Beauchamp Place sells a fine range of excellent Italian shoes, bags, and belts.

Rawhide on Oxford Street east specializes in leather and suede —expensive but good. **Salisbury** on Tottenham Court Road features a good selection of leather bags and gifts.

David Russell on Oxford Street west is worth looking into. World-famous **Gucci** can be found on New Bond Street, with **Chavila** down the street for leather fashions. **Susan** specializes in good handbags and other leather goods. **Swaine Adeney Brigg & Sons** in Piccadilly is a good spot for all leather gadgets. **The Suede and Leather People** on Kensington High Street has a wide variety

Shopping 171

of fashions. **Suedecraft** and **Cornoba** in Beauchamp Place are two good shops for men's and women's leather fashions.

FOR HIM

Burtons and **Hornes,** opposite each other on Tottenham Court Road, **The Village Gate, Gary Elliott, Jr. James, Take Six,** the **Squire Shop,** and the **Jeans Shop,** on Oxford Street east are all good men's shops. The **Scotch House** on Regent Street specializes in authentic Scottish gifts, **Aquascutum** and **Burberry** are two other favorites, as is **Austin Reed. Gieves** in Old Bond Street has traditionally outfitted some of England's best-known figures. If you want to have some lovely shirts made for your man, go to **Airey and Wheeler** in Piccadilly. **Turnbull and Esser** in Jermyn Street is the place for shirts, dressing gowns and other men's accessories. **Dunhill** on the opposite side of the street features not only the lighters and tobaccos they are so well known for, but also handsome jewelry, leather goods, and accessories. For Meerschaum and Briar pipes **Astleys** is a must. **Geezers and Bugatti** in Kensington Church Street is a good male boutique.

TOYS

Taking children to toy shops can be a hazardous experience, especially if they are used to getting their own way. But if you want to risk it, try the following:

The **Educational Supply Association,** Shaftesbury Avenue, W.C.2, is well known for its educational toys and games.

Barnum's, 67 Hammersmith Road, W.14, and **Davenport's,** 51 Great Russell Street are both good for conjuring tricks, jokes, and disguises.

Perhaps the best-known toy shop of all is **Hamleys,** in Regent Street, which has a huge model train layout that can be relied on to fascinate any small boy. Behind Hamleys, in Great Marlborough Street, is **Galt's,** with its reputation for sensible and "intelligent" toys, in the same category is **Abbatt's** in Wimpole Street, W.1.

JEWELRY

Zales in Tottenham Court Road is a good bet. On Oxford Street you'll find **H. Samuels** and **Ciro's.** Regent Street is the home of

Herbert Woolf, Ratners, Orient Jewels and **Regent Jewelers.** In the Quadrant Arcade, off Oxford Street, see **Quadrant Pearls** and **Charles Packer Jewelry. Asprey's** on New Bond Street is one of the finest shops for all sorts of beautiful jewelry. **Cartier's** obviously needs no description—just lots of money. Con't miss **Kitchensky, Chaumet,** and **Bucheron** on either side of it. **Booty,** across the street, specializes in modern designs, **Georg Jensen** has a sparkling array, and **Piaget** and **Watches of Switzerland** hold down the timepiece department. On Old Bond Street, **Kirkby and Bunn, Ciro, Sac Frères, Andre Boggaert,** and **River** are the best-known jewelers (Baggaert also has a branch in South Molton Street). **Jean Renet** has a branch in the Burlington Arcade with a lovely display of watches and jewelry. The Arcade houses a slew of excellent jewelry shops to wander through—far too many to mention.

GIFTS

Oxford Street is a good place to stroll and you can look into **Wilson and Gill** for a lovely selection of Rosenthal china. **Wedgwood/Gered, Chinacraft,** and **Gered** are three more of London's best shops for such gifts. They also have branches in other good shopping streets. **Ireland House** on New Bond Street has a good array of Irish items. Old Bond Street is the place for lots of goodies of every description. The **Royal Copenhagen Porcelain Co.** specializes in fine china, glass, and gifts. **Burlington Arcade** is also a great place to browse for gifts. **Oxfam** in Kensington High Street is another. Brompton Road offers **Chinacraft** and **Rosenthal. Eccentrica** in Sloane Street is the perfect place to buy a gift for that person who has everything.

ANTIQUES AND BRIC-A-BRAC

Some of the most treasured souvenirs of your visit are to be had from London's many colorful street markets. You can pay the earth for a valuable antique, but you can also pick up interesting pieces for a few pence. Remember that you don't have to give the full asking price for second-hand goods; haggling is half the fun. These are some of the best haunts for bargain hunters.

CAMDEN PASSAGE ANTIQUE CENTRE AND MARKET Camden Passage, Islington, N.1 Underground: Angel Bus: 19, 38

Shopping

A mixture of antique shops and boutiques, with one or two very good restaurants. Open Monday through Saturday from 9 A.M. to 6 P.M. Forty stalls Wednesdays, 60 stalls Saturdays.

CHELSEA ANTIQUE MARKET 245 and 253 King's Road, S.W.3 Underground: Sloane Square or South Kensington Bus: 19, 22

Well over 100 stalls selling good antiques, including antique toys. Open Tuesday through Saturday from 10 A.M. to 6 P.M., Mondays from 10 A.M. to 1 P.M. Closed Sundays.

CHURCH STREET, N.W.8 Underground: Edgware Road (either station) Bus: 6, 8, 16, 176

More junk than antiques, though well worth a visit. Several small shops deal in stripped and reconditioned furniture. About 12 or 15 shops open all week, but on Saturdays there are over 100 stalls. Much of the street is due to be demolished.

LONDON SILVER VAULTS Chancery House, Chancery Lane, W.C.2 Underground: Chancery Lane Bus: 22

There is a separate entrance at Southampton Buildings. This is the largest collection of silver for sale in the world, displayed by about 50 silver merchants. Open Monday through Friday from 9:30 A.M. to 5 P.M., Saturdays from 9:30 A.M. to 12:30 P.M. Closed Saturdays preceding bank holidays.

NEW CALEDONIAN MARKET Bermondsey Square, S.E.1 Underground: London Bridge Bus: 1, 176

Much used by dealers (who get a discount). An open-air market with over 250 stalls. Open Fridays from 7 A.M. to 3 P.M., approximately.

THE OLD CURIOSITY SHOP 13-14 Portsmouth Street, Kingsway, W.C.2

Something of a cross between an antique shop and a souvenir shop, this is said to be London's oldest shop. Open daily from 9:30 A.M. to 5:30 P.M., including Sundays and bank holidays.

PETTICOAT LANE Middlesex Street, E.1 Underground: Liverpool Street, Aldgate or Aldgate East Bus: 6, 9, 22

Open Sunday mornings. Best time to go is between 9 A.M. and noon.

PORTOBELLO ROAD, W.11 Underground: Notting Hill Gate Bus: 7, 15, 52

One of the biggest and most popular street markets of all. Antique stalls Saturdays only from 8:30 A.M. to 5:30 P.M., though there are many antique shops there open all week. Vegetables, fruit, and flowers daily.

For a quieter and more genteel atmosphere in which to choose your antiques, there are hundreds of conventional antique shops in central London. Often you will find these unexpectedly on a street corner, but there are certain areas where abound:

Barrett Street, W.1 ("Antique Supermarket")
Brompton Road, S.W.3
Crawford Street, N.W.1
Cromwell Road, S.W.7
Fulham Road, S.W.10
Kensington Church Street, W.8

Marylebone High Street, W.1
Mount Street, W.1
New Bond Street, W.1
Portobello Road, W.11
Shepherd Market, Mayfair
Westbourne Grove, W.11
Wigmore Street, W.1

BOOKS AND PERIODICALS

Whatever your political or intellectual interest, Charing Cross Road is the book and magazine market par excellence. There are new, second-hand, and cut-price books for all tastes, and you can browse around with no obligation to buy. Underground: Leicester Square or Tottenham Court Road. Bus: 14, 19, 22, 29, 38, 176.

Other bookshops, especially language and specialty types, are well scattered, but you don't need to leave the West End. Most of the street markets mentioned in this chapter also deal in second-hand books.

At Farringdon Road, Clerkenwell, E.C.1, close to Farringdon underground station, there is a small market, as yet undiscovered by the majority of tourists interested in books, that deals mainly in old and rare books. Underground: Farringdon.

WESTMINSTER ABBEY BOOKSHOP Adjacent to the West Door of Westminster Abbey, S.W.1 Tel: 222-5565
This bookshop specializes in Bibles, prayer books and other literature. Its entire profits are devoted to the Abbey and its services.

REPAIR SERVICES

Handbags

W. & R. Howard 22A Lounceston Place, W.8 Tel: 937-1770

Leather

LEATHER RESTORERS 22 Brompton Arcade, Brompton Road, S.W.3 Tel: 589-1580
They do all sorts of leather and suede garments.
SUEDE CLEAN 14 Beauchamp Place, S.W.3 Tel: 584-8894; 30 Baker Street, W.1 Tel: 936-1967
Clean Suede and Sheepskin. Normal service is seven days. Repairs are also done.

Luggage

W. J. ARNOLD 25 Cromwell Place, S.W.7   Tel: 373-0323
BRANDS Notting Hill Gate
MAYFAIR TRUNK Shepherd's Market
Quick service.

Shoes and Dresses

Best to just ask the desk clerk at your hotel. Many of the little shops are rapidly going out of business due to the amount of building going on in London; the rents are just too high for the low-cost business they do. Shoe-repair services can generally be found in most department stores and some cleaners (e.g., **Collins Couture Centre,** on Brompton Road, and **Sketchleys,** located all over London) can do it for you but it does take time. There seems to be no such thing as speedy service in London.

Umbrellas

JAMES SMITH & SONS   53 New Oxford Street, W.C.1A   Tel: 836-4731

SHOPPING STREETS

Each of the main shopping streets has its own character and shopping specialties. Half the fun of shopping in London is tracking down the unexpected. There's no greater satisfaction for the shopper than finding a top-quality, inexpensive shop hidden away in a side street. The shops described on the following pages are mostly well-known, but inevitably new establishments spring up waiting for you to discover them.

The pages that follow list shopping establishments that will offer you a vast variety of choices.

Tottenham Court Road

Underground: Tottenham Court Road, Goodge Street, or Warren Street
Bus: 14, 24, 29, 73, 176 (Monday–Friday)

Tottenham Court Road's history goes back to the 12th century. Today it is a busy thoroughfare used by traffic heading north out of London, noted for its furniture shops and hi-fi and electrical equipment stores. The largest furniture shop is **Heal & Son, Ltd.** Here you'll find nearly everything needed for furnishing and equipping a house. Their furniture is well designed in the latest styles. Heal's is also a good place for gifts. **Habitat** is a very popular shop specializing in modern, functional furniture and household equipment. They have an excellent selection of kitchenware and household fabrics. **Tyman,** which specializes in office stationery and equipment, has a shop here featuring modern and office furnishings. **Maples** is just around the corner on Euston Road. The long-established store continues to carry on a tradition of fine furniture. The Road's other claim to fame is its many hi-fi and electrical equipment stores. Here you'll find anything from spare parts to the very latest in hi-fi, stereo, and quadriphonic systems. **Lind-Air** and **Lasky** are the two largest hi-fi and equipment suppliers. Each has a number of branches along Tottenham Court Road including Lind-Air's unique hi-fi department store on the corner of Store Street. **Paperchase** is a popular shop specializing in wrapping paper, posters, and other paper items. Their selection is one of the largest in London. Just down Torrington Place is **Dillons University Book Shop.** Conveniently situated across Malet Street from some of the University of London buildings, it has an excellent selection of books and is usually filled with students.

Oxford Street East

Underground: Tottenham Court Road or Oxford Circus
Bus: 1 (Monday–Saturday), 7 (Monday–Friday), 8, 25, 73

The eastern end of Oxford Street, from the underground stations of Tottenham Court Road to Oxford Circus, has really blossomed over the last few years and is now an established center for shoes and fashion, with the accent on young designs. There are some excellent clothes shops for young men, like **The Village Gate, Gary Elliott, Jr. James, Take Six,** and **The Squire Shop.** Their "off-the-peg" suits are particularly good value, and although they closely follow the latest dictates of fashion you won't be offered anything too outrageous. Sport jackets and shirts are also good buys. This is a good area for shoe shops. Fashion goes about as high as it can get at **Sacha** and **Derber,** two shops which attract trend-setting youngsters. More conservative styles can be found at **Amelio and Davide,** which also specializes in ballet slippers and theatrical shoes. **Rawhide** specializes in leather and suede goods, and although the prices are high the quality is good. Craftsmanship of a different kind can be found just outside Oxford Circus station, at **Wedgwood,** a shop selling fine pottery, porcelain, glass, and gifts.

Wedgwood pottery is world-famous, and here you can get the genuine article. If your idea of high fashion is a pair of dungarees or a saucily embossed tee shirt then the place to go is **Jean Junction**. There are three branches of this youthful boutique chain in this stretch of Oxford Street. At the other end of the sartorial scale, **Charkham** has specialized in men's tailoring for a good number of years, and although it places the emphasis on care and craftsmanship, you can get a made-to-measure suit in 24 hours. One of the most famous London stores is **Bourne and Hollingsworth**, popular with those who feel that they are perhaps a little too old for the boutiques. There's a wide variety of woman's wear, with particularly impressive racks of evening dresses. One of the most unusual shops is **Athena**, which specializes in posters and prints. Here you can buy ultramodern pop art posters or reproductions of art classics. Many of them sell for £1 ($2.50) or less.

Oxford Street West

Underground: Marble Arch and Bond Street or Oxford Circus

Bus: 1 (Monday–Friday), 6, 7 (Monday–Saturday), 8, 12, 13 (Monday–Saturday), 15, 59 (Sundays), 73, 88, 113, (Monday–Saturday), 137, 159 (Monday–Saturday), 616 express (Monday–Friday)

The busiest section of Oxford Street runs from Oxford Circus to Marble Arch. It is here that most of the major department stores are grouped, and where you'll also find chain stores like **Boots, Littlewoods, Woolworth's, British Home Stores,** and the popular shoe shops. **Selfridges** is the second largest department store in London. There are seven restaurants, a large food hall, and their kitchenware, cosmetic and trendy Miss Selfridge departments are very popular. Next door to Selfridges is the largest branch of **Marks & Spencer.** Along with Buckingham Palace and the Tower of London, Marks & Spencer is on many visitors' list of stops. They have a worldwide reputation for high quality, reasonable prices, and unmistakable value for money. They stock clothes for men, women, and children and are particularly noted for knitwear and lingerie. Other lines include housewares and food. **John Lewis** is a good shop for household equipment and fabrics. Their slogan is "never knowingly undersold" and if you buy something here and find it cheaper elsewhere in London, John Lewis will refund the difference. Both **D. H. Evans** and **Marshall & Snelgrove** are large department stores with the accent on clothes, particularly for women and children. **C & A,** specializing in inexpensive clothing for men, women, and children, has two branches in this section of Oxford Street. **Swears & Wells** also has two branches here, with fur, suede, and leather coats at reasonable prices. **Mothercare** is the place to go for baby clothes and accessories. **HMV,** on three floors, the largest record shop in London, is the place for records and tapes. **Marbles** and **Up West** are two shopping arcades designed to appeal to the young. Many of the shoe stores and men's and women's clothes shops have more than one branch in Oxford Street, so if you find just what you're looking for but the size or color is wrong, maybe their branch down the road can help.

Charing Cross Road

Underground: Leicester Square or Tottenham Court Road

Bus: 1 (Monday–Saturday), 14, 19, 22, 24, 29, 38, 176 (Monday–Friday)

Although it is right in the middle of the central shopping area, Charing Cross Road has none of the glitter and glamour that typifies its neighbors, Oxford Street and Leicester Square. Nevertheless, it is a magnet for scholars and musicians who come here to browse through books or buy musical instruments. There are dozens of bookshops; perhaps the greatest of them all is **Foyles,** with a choice of over four million books in two adjacent buildings. You can browse to your heart's content. If you have time to spare in your search for books, then rummage through the shops in Charing Cross Road, and take a detour into Cecil Court, a quiet place with some fascinating bargains. For a few pounds you can also pick up historic postage stamps or old prints (there are some good examples at **M. B. Newman**). If you want your information right up to date, foreign newspapers are on sale at **S. Solosy** shops and **Holborn Books.** For the musically minded there are several places that stock instruments, particularly guitars and amplifiers. Among them are **Macari's, Selmer** and **Scarth.** Almost the last shop on the right before the road winds down into Trafalgar Square is **Reeves,** which stocks top-quality artists' materials. Farther up on the same side of the road, and opposite Leicester Square underground station, is a small tobacconist's that sells cigars of truly prodigious lengths. And the smoker shouldn't miss **G. Smith's** snuff shop, one of the last of a fast-disappearing breed of tobacconists. It is worth visiting for the aroma alone. The off-beat thrives in Charing Cross Road. If you are searching for dance-band instruments, for instance, **Scarth** is the place. For books about Greece—and volumes in Greek—go to **Hellenic Book Service.**

Regent Street

Underground: Oxford Circus or Piccadilly Circus
Bus: 3, 6, 12, 13 (Monday–Saturday), 15, 39 (Monday–Friday), 53, 59 (Sundays), 88, 159 (Monday–Saturday)

Another of London's world-famous shopping streets is Regent Street, which was built in the early 19th century. It was designed by John Nash as part of a processional way between Carlton House, the Prince Regent's home in Pall Mall, and a proposed new place—which was never built—in "rural" Regent's Park. A fine, broad thoroughfare, with shops set well back, the street sweeps gracefully from Oxford Circus to Piccadilly Circus, and is the setting for several of London's best shops. **Liberty & Co.** is a Regent Street landmark. An unusual Renaissance-style frontage linked to a neo-Tudor building at the rear makes it one of London's most picturesque shops, noted for its fine fabrics, scarves, antiques, and fashion. **Hamley's,** one of the largest toy shops in the world, has eight floors of fun for the young and young at heart. For an impressive array of jewelry, silver, and gifts, visit **Garrard.** They're the people responsible for the care and upkeep of the Crown Jewels. The **Goldsmiths and Silversmiths Association Gift Centre, Lawleys, Gered, Rosenthal,** and **Chinacraft** are all in Regent Street. **Swan & Edgar** and **Dickins & Jones** are two department stores concentrating on fashion. **The Scotch House** specializes in Scottish fashion and gifts for men, women, and children. **Aquascutum** also stocks men's and women's fashions, and is perhaps best known for its rainwear. Another top name in rainwear fashion is **Burberry,** whose shop is in the Haymarket. **Jaeger** is famous for knitwear and fashion and its large Regent Street shop has an excellent section. A popular trend among London stores is to have a shop within a shop concentrating on young fashion. **Miss Selfridge** of Selfridges has one, and has since expanded into a chain. There are lots of men's shops here in Regent Street, among them **Austin Reed, Hector Power, Wallerby, Burton, Harry Fenton, Hepworths,** and **Village Gate.**

New Bond Street

Underground: Bond Street
Bus: 25 (Monday–Friday)

Once a muddy country lane infested with villains and highwaymen, Bond Street is today one of Europe's most fashionable shopping streets. Old Bond Street was built in 1686, New Bond Street

14 years later. Bond Street shops have always been known for finest quality goods and impeccable service. Bond Street was a fashionable rendezvous for the Regency "in set" including Beau Brummel and friends. There was even an establishment offering aspiring dandies lessons in tying cravats! Today's Bond Street is particularly noted for jewelry, antiques, fine art, and fashion. Here you'll find **Sotheby's**, one of the most famous auction houses in the world. It is a fascinating place where a nod of the head or the wave of a hand can secure an old master of the contents of a stately home. **Asprey's**, Bond Street landmark, excels as a treasure house of rare and beautiful things. The finest leather, gold, silver—much of which is made by their own craftsmen—jewelry, and antiques make this one of the finest shops in the world. **Cartier** and **Kitchinsky** are two of the fine names in jewelry, and **Booty** specializes in modern designs. The only department store in Bond Street is **Fenwicks**, which specializes in women's fashion. Two top names in fashion, **Gucci** and **Yves St. Laurent**, are also located here. **Vidal Sassoon, Elizabeth Arden,** and **Innoxa** are also here to help a woman look her best. **Savory & Moore** has one of the oldest shop fronts on Bond Street. Reputed to be the oldest chemists in London, it was often visited by the Duke of Wellington, Lord Nelson, and Lady Hamilton. Other famous Bond Street names are **W. E. Hill & Sons,** makers of string instruments, known to musicians throughout the world; **Mullins of London,** specializing in international heraldry; and **Bendicks,** famous for its fine chocolates and confectionery.

Old Bond Street

Underground: Green Park
Bus: 25 (Monday–Friday)

Old Bond Street runs from Burlington Gardens to Piccadilly. The world-famous beauty salons of **Max Factor** and **Yardley** are here. There are many fine jewelers. **Sac Frères** specializes in amber, while **Ciro's** is noted for pearls. **Kirkby & Bunn** is another famous name in jewelry, and you'll find modern styles at **Andre Boggaert** and **River. Goodes** and the **Royal Copenhagen Porcelain Company** specialize in fine china, glass, and gifts, while **Thomas Agnew & Sons** has dealt with fine art for five generations. **W. Barrett** specializes in Oriental *objets d'art*. **Charbonnel & Walker** is famous for their fine homemade chocolates. **Rayne, Delman** is a sophisticated shop for women's fashion, and Bond Street is also the home of the tobacconist **Benson & Hedges. Gieves** is a well known shop for men's fashion. It has a traditional background as outfitter to the Royal Navy; its customers have included Lord Nelson and Captain Bligh.

South Molton Street

Underground: Bond Street
Bus: As for Oxford Street West
A shopping street which has come into its own recently, just off Oxford Street, near the Bond street tube station. **Andre Boggaert** sells striking modern jewelry at reasonable prices. **The Electrum Gallery** holds exhibitions of modern designers' jewelry. Some of the newest designs and designers appear here first. **Brown's** is a fashionable shop for men's and women's clothes, while **Zero Four** supplies lovely children's clothes. **Olaf Daughters** of Sweden have great Swedish clogs for men, women, and children in a wide range of colors. Also here: **Vidal Sassoon** and **Molton Brown,** fashionable hairdressing salons; **H. R. Higgins,** coffee-maker, and a find for those who love a good cup of coffee; **Prestat's,** whose handmade chocolates are very popular.

Piccadilly

Underground: Piccadilly Circus
Bus: 9 (Monday–Saturday), 9A (Sundays), 14, 19, 22, 25 (Monday–Friday), 38
Red Arrow Bus: Single Decker: 406 (Monday–Friday)
The name Piccadilly is synonymous with the finest in London shopping. Here there is a pride in the upkeep of strict standards of quality. As such, it is a street where you examine the excellence of the merchandise first and automatically expect to pay an equivalent, but fair, price. Just across from famous Piccadilly Circus with its renowned statue of Eros is the old-established store of **Lillywhites,** supplying top-quality clothes and sportswear. This is just one of a number of first-rate stores in Piccadilly, like **Simpson's,** the tailor and outfitter, and **Swan & Edgar's,** which has grown from a small haberdashery a century and a half ago to a major London fashion shop. During the wild days of the suffragette movement, women militants smashed the store's windows; it was also here that Worth, the famous parfumier and couturier, learned his craft. The splendid-sounding **Swaine Adeney Brigg & Sons** sells equally splendid leather goods, umbrellas, riding equipment, and whips, and is an old-established and impeccably correct resident of Piccadilly. As is its near neighbor **Fortnum & Mason,** one of the great stores of the world. Fortnum's is particularly famous for its food, and among

others has provided groceries for Wellington's officers during the Napoleonic wars and the Royal family. Prices are as high as in any London shop, but offset by the atmosphere of old-world elegance and decorum. Truly a London shopping experience. **Airey and Wheeler** is renowned for its fine shirt-making and light-weight suits. **Cogswell & Harrison** is another shop for gentlemen, dealing in hunting and shooting equipment. **Tradition** is the name of a fascinating shop that sells military models, and war games and accessories. This is in no way a toy shop, but has a marvelous collection of miniatures and memorabilia for students of military history. A little farther down the road is **Jackson's of Piccadilly,** which has a mouth-watering display of gourmet foods, fine wines, and gifts. The food is so tempting that you'll feel it should only be eaten off the finest china and glassware—perhaps from nearby **Leather & Snook.** On the opposite side of the road is the **Jean Renet Galleries,** which sells magnificent jewelry, especially wristwatches.

Burlington Arcade

Underground: Piccadilly Circus or Green Park
Bus: 9 (Monday–Saturday), 9A (Sundays), 14, 19, 22, 25 (Monday–Friday), 38

For over 150 years the Burlington Arcade has been one of the most exclusive shopping centers in London. Built by Lord George Cavendish in 1819, it is one of the oldest and longest covered arcades in the world. Although the shopkeepers no longer live in tiny rooms above the shops, some are descendants of the original owners. Today the Arcade, housing jewelers, shirtmakers, antique dealers, tobacconists and other specialty shops, is known for its unique atmosphere, personal service, and high quality. Uniformed Beadles patrol the Arcade and enforce some of the original rules. Running, singing, whistling, carrying a bulky parcel, and opening an umbrella are forbidden!

Jermyn Street

Underground: Piccadilly Circus or Green Park
Bus: 9 (Monday–Saturday), 9A (Sundays), 14, 19, 22, 25 (Monday–Friday), 38
Red Arrow bus: 406 (Monday–Friday)

Parallel to fashionable Piccadilly runs an equally fashionable and, perhaps, more exclusive shopping thoroughfare. A narrow and intimate road, Jermyn Street is the haunt of those who seek only the best and know where to find it. **Turnbull and Esser** is the place to go for shirts, dressing gowns, and other gentlemen's accessories. Perfume has been blended on the premises of **Floris** since 1730. The shop is a delight to visit, filled with color and fragrance. Their potpourri, scented sachets, pomanders, and perfumes make lovely gifts. **Dunhill** is known throughout the world for its fine tobaccos and lighters. But its Jermyn Street shop also sells a beautiful array of jewelry, leather goods, and men's and women's accessories. The most unusual building in Jermyn Street belongs to **Andrew Grima**. Inside the exterior of steel and slate you'll find Grima's spectacular modern jewelry. Other shops include **Astley's**, which specializes in Meerschaum and Briar pipes, and **Paxton & Whitfield**, which has been selling traditional English cheeses for over 170 years.

Kensington High Street

Underground: High Street Kensington

Bus: 9 (Monday–Saturday), 9A (Sundays), 27, 28, 31, 33 (Monday–Saturday), 49, 52, 73

Two stores tell the tale of Kensington High Street—**John Barker's** and **Biba's**. These two great commercial concerns have been flourishing side by side, offering a fascinating contrast. Barker's, in a massive building reminiscent of an ocean liner, claims to be able to satisfy any household need, and epitomizes the quality of London's great stores. Biba, on the other hand, is the fashion boutique pioneer which blossomed with success and has been transformed into a full-scale department store. Biba's, having outgrown the smaller store across the road, is now in the building that housed stately Derry and Toms. The new Biba retains its design trademarks of mirrored walls, deep-stain woodwork, and art deco trimmings. The famous roof garden and restaurant is a special feature. Other shops on the fashion front include **Che Guevara** (very dark and mysterious), **Crocodile**, and **Feathers** for the young female trendsetter, and **Dandy** and **The Village Gate** for her boyfriend. Youngsters will also go for **Jean Machine, 62nd Precinct,** the **Suede and Leather People**, and **Jean Junction**. Beautiful clothes for the more mature can be obtained from **Rendel Dobb** (high-quality furs), **Jaeger** (especially good for knitwear), and **Austin Reed**, which makes impeccable men's suits. Like Biba and Barker, there is an interesting contrast, too, between the **Kensington Market** and the **Antique Hypermarket. Kensington Market** has 40 boutiques and 130 stalls all housed in one building, a fascinating labyrinth lined with up-to-date fashions and antiques. The Antique Hypermarket, on the other hand, and on the other side of the road, is a beautiful place to wander around in, even if you can't afford to buy an antique (most of them are top-quality collectors' items). Of particular interest are the antique dolls, and a genuine old Pullman railway carriage at the end, where you can recline gracefully and take tea. Other worthwhile spots: **Oxfam Shop** (gifts from all over the world), **Reflection** (fashion about as far out as you can get), **Cox & Co.** (beautiful china, kitchen and houseware), and **Ravel** (shoes, with some trendy lines for youngsters).

Kensington Church Street

Underground: High Street Kensington/Notting Hill Gate
Bus: 27, 28, 31, 52

Kensington Church Street is a haven for two types of shoppers—those who are looking for the up-to-the-minute fashions, which can be found at the Kensington High Street end, and the antique hunters who browse among the dozens of antique shops which line the street all the way up to Notting Hill Gate. And it's certainly an antique hunter's paradise. **Philip and Bernard Dombey** specializes in some wonderful and ornate old clocks. Dolls and doll carriages from the Victorian era and older can be bought at **Dimples and Sawdust**. Beautifully carved chess sets are a specialty of **Baum Kotter**. **Elliott and Snowdon** has an impressive range of antique arms and maps. For the fashion follower, the boutiques of Kensington Church Street are a little more exclusive and a little less frantic than their neighbors in the High Street. **Mr Freedom** has good quality avant-garde fashion for both sexes. **Geezers** and **Bugatti** offer better-than-usual boutique clothes for men, while **Tyger** and **Bus Stop** do the same for the women. And there are clothes for tots in **Martha's Nursery**. If the youngsters also happen to be crazy about chocolate, there is **Ackerman's,** one of the finest confectionery houses in London. Further up the road is the **Children's Book Centre,** with a great selection of books for 14-year-olds and under. One of the most eye-catching shops in the whole street is **Skill** selling craftsman-made leather goods and art works. There is a big range of cassettes for tape recorders at **Tape Revolution**. And finally, if you like to live your life the natural way, there are health foods and pure cosmetics at **Real Foods**.

Knightsbridge—Brompton Road—Fulham Road

Underground: For Knightsbridge and Brompton Road–Knightsbridge. For Fulham Road–South Kensington

Bus: For Knightsbridge—9, 14, 30, 52, 73, 74
For Brompton Road—14, 30, 74
For Fulham Road—14

Fashion-conscious Knightsbridge is one of London's most important shopping districts. There are a few theories as to how it derived its name but perhaps my favorite tells of two knights on their way to the Crusades who fought to the death on an ancient bridge that once existed here. The shops along the Knightsbridge Road stretch from Hyde Park Corner, skirting the park itself, to Albert Gate and the Knightsbridge underground station at Sloane Square. Here fashion shops predominate. You'll find men's shoes by Alan McAfee and three shops specializing in oriental carpets. **Harvey Nichols** is the most famous shop in this section of the road and has been since 1817. It is a luxurious department store with fashion and household goods. The stretch of road between Sloane Square and **Harrods** is filled with fashion and shoe shops. **Chenelle, St. Laurent, Maryon, Wallis, Miss Selfridge** and others cater for women's fashion. **Charles Jourdan** and **Rayne, Delman** are top names in shoes, and famous jewelers like **Kitchinsky, Mappin & Webb,** and **Ciro** are also here. The **Scotch House** concentrates on Scottish knitwear and woolens: their Tartan Room stocks hundreds of authentic tartans. There is also a range of gift items and a children's department called Hopscotch. Knightsbridge and the Brompton Road are overshadowed by the presence of **Harrods**. It is the largest department store in Europe and one of the most famous stores in the world; Harrods' telex address is "Everything, London"—and that sums it up. No trip to London is complete without an expedition to Harrods. There are over 200 departments. Whatever it is you want, Harrods will attempt to get it for you. Among the best departments are the legendary food halls, china and glass, perfumer, oriental carpets, pianos, toys, "Way In" boutique, and zoo. Services provided by Harrods include a library, funerals, piano tuning, catering, china and glass repair; the list is endless. Other Brompton Road shops are **Chinacraft** and **Rosenthal** which sell china, glass, and gifts. **Just Jane** specializes in maternity fashions. **High & Mighty** caters to chunky men who are difficult to fit. Fine furs are on sale at **Calman Links** and the **National Fur Company. Escalade** is another London's fashion arcades. You'll find clothes and accessories for men and women, a restaurant, hairdresser, and sauna. As the road bends again you'll find the **Reject Shop** specializing in seconds and discontinued housewares—good quality bargains—and **Annacat Fashion Boutique** and **Alpine Sports.** At Pelham Street and Draycott Avenue, Brompton Road runs into Fulham Road. Well known for antiques, the area is also becoming very popular for fashion. Here you'll find **Habitat,** a branch of the Tottenham Court Road shop that specializes in housewares and home furnishings. **Laura Ashley's** creations are becoming increasingly popular. She designs the fabrics as well as the clothes and all bear her individual style. Natural fibers are used and the prices are very low. Her store in Sloane Street sells clothes and dress and furnishing fabrics, while the Lower Sloane Street branch sells dress fabrics only. **Valerie Goad** is another who designs her fabrics and clothes. Her long dresses are most popular and prices are reasonable. **Piero de Monai's** elegant French and Italian clothes are created by such famous designers as Zandra Rhodes and Cerruti. There are scores of antique shops here, many specializing in furniture, and a few specializing in picture framing and restoring.

Beauchamp Place

Underground: Knightsbridge or South Kensington
Bus: 14, 30, 74

Beauchamp Place, just off Brompton Road and stone's throw from Harrods, is a delightful narrow street full of antique shops, fashion boutiques, restaurants, and specialty shops. You'll find enormous variety in a very limited space. There are plenty of antique shops, each with its own specialty, **Higgins & Horsey** stocks antique clocks while two shops, **Hart** and **Hallidays,** sell beautiful fireplaces and mantels. **Troll** specializes in antique Scandinavian country furniture, metalwork, and Scandinavian candles. **Boadicea** carries only goods made in Britain and here you'll find British craftsmanship at its best. Jewelry, pottery, and prints, some exclusive to Boadicea, make excellent gifts. This is one of the few shops in London that specializes in British goods; **Best of British** in Museum Street is another. Two Beauchamp Place shops specialize in tapestry equipment: **Tapestry Bazaar** and **Luxury Needlepoint.** Ever popular suede and leather fashions for men and women can be found at **Suedecraft** and **Cornoba. Shoosissima** sells a fine range of exclusive Italian shoes, bags and belts, **Emeline** stocks exquisite Continental jewelry, jade, ivory, and jet. **Monsoon** specializes in beautiful Indian fabrics made up into today's fashions for women. Their quilted clothes are very popular. Other women's fashion shops include **Crocodile, Adele Davis** and **Candide. Deborah & Clare** caters to both sexes, while **Millions of Shirts,** perhaps a slight exaggeration, does have scores of fashionable shirts for men.

Two shops specialize in "rejects." The goods have slight imperfections, or are of a discontinued design or color. **The Reject China Shop** sells at a discount china, pottery, and glass. Here you'll find names like Richard Ginori, Paragon, Hammersley, and Aynsley. Across the road, the **Reject Linen Shop** stocks towels, sheets, tablecloths, etc., at least 25% off the retail price.

King's Road

Underground: Sloane Square
Bus: 11, 19, 22, 49

Chelsea is traditionally the home of artists, writers, and film people. As Chelsea's main street, King's Road has long been famous for boutiques, antiques, and restaurants, and if you're looking for "swinging London," then this is it. The Road is lined with uniquely conceived and decorated boutiques, antique shops, pubs, and bistros. You'll find shops with names like **Just Looking, Stop the Shop, Gear,** and **Kweens.** The atmosphere is infectious. The shops are friendly, music pounds from most doorways. On Saturdays, when the Road is its busiest, it's like a fashion parade as London's trendies come to shop, meet friends, and be seen. Just off Sloane Square is King's Road's one department store, **Peter Jones,** one of the John Lewis group, and holding to the "never knowingly undersold" slogan of its Oxford street parent store. King's Road also has a few of the currently popular fashion arcades. The largest is **Sloane,** which sells male and female fashions and accessories and incorporates a coffeehouse, unisex hairdressing salon, and men's sauna. The latest group of shops to settle in King's Road sells blue jeans, denim trousers, jackets, and tops. Many shops sell the denim ready-faded and softened so you don't need to "break it in." Continuing on down the road just past the Town Hall, you'll find scores of antique shops including the large **Chelsea Antiques Market** filled with over 100 stalls.

Sloane Street

Underground: Sloane Square or Knightsbridge
Bus: 19, 22, 137

Sloane Street is a fabulous shopping area. The quality is high and the prices equally so. Here you can buy some of the finest antique and modern furniture, clothes, and gifts in the country. It's probably best to start at the Sloane Square end, if only because there are two banks right at the outset. Just next to one of them is the **General Trading Company,** which despite its Wild West-style name, has a wonderful collection of furniture and household goods. The merchandise is expensive, but undeniably has style. You can buy a way-out gift from **Eccentrica**. The **Jewel House** stocks a fascinating line of crystalline minerals like quartz and tourmaline, presented in their natural shapes but polished to glittering brilliance. Other lines include archeological finds, especially Roman relics. **C. P. Burge's** antique shops window offers a glance into the past. On sale are genuine and reproduction antique tea chests, sign boards, rocking horses, and other unusual items. Among the modern furniture shops which have a breathtaking range of beautiful 1970s merchandise are **Zarach**—designers include Ringo Starr—**Glahn**, with its graceful Scandinavian work, and **Archie Shine**. At the Knightsbridge end of Sloane Street are **Aquascutum** and **Harvey Nichols** department store. There's also a branch of **Susan Small**, the smart, ready-to-wear fashion house that made Princess Anne's wedding dress. Other shops likely to sidetrack you are: **Bendicks**, for handmade, elaborate confectionery; **Blanchards**, for high quality furniture; **Rocking Horse** and **Children's Bazaar** for contrasting children's fashion; **Taylor** of London for its own perfumes, **Atkinson** for good value jewelry; **Jackson's** and **Partridges** for gourmet foods; **Magli, Kurt Geiger,** and **Ferragamo** for exclusive ladies' shoes; **Sekers** for Design Council award-winning fabrics.

PART III
Outside London

15
Bath

Bath is one of Britain's most elegant and distinguished cities. It seems that almost every architect who has had a hand in the shaping of Bath, from the Roman era in A.D. 54 to the 1970s, made a vow to add a little more elegance to the city. The result is that this "Queen City of the West" fully justifies her title. Bath is the leading spa in Britain and goes way back to the days of the Romans when they, too, had need of relieving their aches and pains. The original Roman baths lay hidden from sight until rediscovered and restored in the last century. The baths are considered among the finest Roman ruins in Britain.

Queen Anne began frequenting the baths and this started a whole new life for Bath. Once she came, naturally all the fashionable people of London had to come as well. In the 18th century, Bath was rebuilt by John Wood and his son who used the yellow stone from the local hills for the buildings, still one of Bath's distinguishing features. The city today is beautiful with its Georgian townhouses, beautiful squares, quaint little shops, lovely gardens, and graceful Georgian terraces. It still functions as a spa with half a million gallons of thermal water per day gushing out of an underground spring at a constant temperature of 120° F. The water is used at the various treatment centers, and runs into the magnificent great Roman Baths through the channel built by a Roman plumber nearly 2,000 years ago. While visiting the 18th-century Pump Room you can enjoy a medicinal cocktail or coffee while being entertained by an orchestra.

THE BATH FESTIVAL
Created by violinist Yehudi Menuhin, the Bath Festival for two weeks in late May or early June includes every possible performing art: jazz,

folk singing, symphonies, recitals, drama, ballet, a film festival, etc., many featuring known artists. The performances take place all over Bath and schedules are printed for your choice. Especially interesting is the Festival Ball held at the end of the Festival, usually in a nearby castle, which changes every year. Naturally the town is full to the brim at this time of year, so if you wish to partake of the Festival you must book well in advance. Tickets are 40p ($1) to £3 ($7.50).

HOW TO GET THERE

You can get to Bath by train from London's Paddington Station. The trip takes an hour and 40 minutes. Or you may go by motor coach, from Victoria Coach Station. It takes about 4 hours.

WHERE TO STAY

THE ARUNDEL HOTEL The Circus Tel: 25523 B-C
A very small hotel with room for only 12 people, it is nevertheless a very good choice, not only because of the excellent location but because of the friendliness of the hosts themselves, who make you feel like one of the family. Rates £2 ($5) per person, including breakfast. Surprisingly enough, the bedrooms include a number of antiques, and are far more nicely furnished than some other bed-and-breakfast hotels. Each room is different and it is quite fun to take a peek at them if they are empty.

THE FRANCIS HOTEL Queen Square Tel: 24257 B-C
On a lovely little Georgian square. Single: £4 ($10); double: £7 to £8 ($17.50 to $20); including breakfast. The rooms are large, simply and traditionally furnished, and very comfortable. They also have two bars and a restaurant.

LAKES HOTEL 8 Manvers Street Tel: 25212 A-B-C
Just opposite the Manvers Street Baptist Church and near the Bath spa station, so it is extremely central. The rooms are simple, comfortable, and clean, and the price is right—£1.50 ($3.75) per person, including a good-sized English breakfast.

MANVERS HOTEL 7 Manvers Street Tel: 25979 A-B-C
Right next door to the Lakes Hotel, with the same sort of simple, comfortable, and clean rooms, but with electric heaters. Rates £2 ($5), per person, including breakfast.

REDCAR HOTEL 27 Henriette Street Tel: 60231 B-C
On a stone terrace, two row houses were combined to create this friendly little hotel. Single: £3.50 ($8.75); double: £5.50 to £8 ($13.75 to $20); including breakfast. The rooms are simple, comfortable, and quiet. In the basement there is a Brasserie for snacks.

THE ROYAL YORK HOTEL George Street Tel: 61541 B-C
Centrally located, newly renovated, Georgian-style hotel. Single: £3.75 ($9.37); double: £6.50 to £7.50 ($16.25 to $18.75); breakfast included.

Rooms are large, traditionally furnished, and very comfortable. The Queen Victoria Suite has a four-poster bed. There is also a bar and restaurant.

DINING

BRUNO'S 2 George Street   Tel: 25141
Small, with soft lights and comfortable banquettes. Bruno's features an international menu with some Italian specialties, in keeping with his home ties. Open for lunch from 12:15 to 2 P.M. and for dinner from 6:15 to 10 P.M., Saturdays until 10:30 P.M. Moderate price range.

EVANS FISH RESTAURANT   Abbey Green, near the Bath Abbey
A homey, family-type restaurant, specializing in excellent fish dinners, as the name implies. You can be sure that your fish has been freshly caught and well prepared. On the second floor there is a more modern room with large booths. The Georgian Room has a beautiful fireplace and arched windows, which is particularly nice in the evening with dimmed lights. Down below there is also a cafeteria-type arrangement for quick snacks. Open Tuesday through Saturday from 11:30 A.M. to 10 P.M. Closed Sundays and Mondays. Budget-priced.

HOLE IN THE WALL   16 George Street   Tel: 25242
A nicely done restaurant on two floors. One side of the dining room looks into the kitchen—a very brave move on the part of the owners; if they can stand such a full view of what they are doing, they must be good. An extensive menu promises you just about anything you may have a taste for. There is a bar upstairs with newspapers and magazines, should you wish just to linger for a while. Open for lunch from 12:15 to 2:15 P.M. and for dinner from 6:30 to 10:30 P.M. Closed Sundays and Mondays. Average dish about £1.80 ($4.50).

SALLY LUNN'S HOUSE   North Parade Passage
A tiny, picturesque, little Georgian-type place with gables and a bay window, Sally Lunn's House is actually a landmark, built in 1482 and supposed to be the oldest building in the city. Sally used to bake her bread and biscuits in the cellar of this building and the same homemade recipes have been carried out up until today. It is a good place for coffee and cake, or a light meal, served all day long.

SIGHTSEEING

Take the time to wander around the Royal Crescent with its wide sweep of pure grace, the Circus, Pulteney Street, and Bath Street, all of which are evidence of a bygone age of leisurely elegance. As you walk these lovely areas, you can so easily picture Beau Nash, Queen Anne, and all their fashionable followers walking there.

BATH ABBEY
Bath boasts a beautiful Abbey Church famous for its fan-vaulted roof. Originally built in 1599 on the site of a Norman cathedral, it didn't come

into prominence until Queen Elizabeth I took an interest and commanded renovation, leading to the beautiful structure that stands today, with its innumerable windows, nicknamed the "Lantern of the West." In the nave of the Abbey is the tomb of Beau Nash, a most elegant and frivolous dandy, greatly responsible for the initial popularity of Bath and Brighton. Always dressed in embroidered silks, satins, feathers, and velvets, he was the fashion pacesetter for men in his day. It was he who began the style of wearing stockings.

THE ASSEMBLY ROOMS

The 18th-century buildings you see today are a bit deceptive in that they do not really go back to that period at all. Originally built in 1769, all the buildings were destroyed during the Second World War. What you see today is a faithful reproduction and tribute to the architects. The Costume Museum is housed here and is extremely interesting. The collection, donated by Mrs. Doris Langley-Moore, is representative of the apparel worn by the English for over 400 years. The present day is represented by a dress designed by today's "mod" queen, Mary Quant. Buy the illustrated guide, partly written by Mrs. Langley-Moore herself. It is a good presentation of some of the more interesting garments on display, such as the "Little Lord Fauntleroy" suit worn by T. E. Lawrence and one of the Arab robes he learned to love when he was known as Lawrence of Arabia. In the museum, too, is the Card Room, recognizable to Dickens fans from *Pickwick Papers.* The museum is open Monday through Saturday from 9:30 A.M. to 6 P.M., Sundays from 11 A.M. to 6 P.M. During off-season open until 5 P.M. Admission 20p ($.50).

THE AMERICAN MUSEUM

Strangely enough, many Americans who see this museum out of curiosity say that they haven't seen its displays even in American museums at home. It is housed in Claverton Manor, just on the outskirts of Bath, surrounded by beautiful grounds in the Avon Valley. All of the exhibits were shipped from the United States and are authentic, such as the parlor of a New York 19th-century townhouse, a Conestoga wagon, a Rio Grande exhibit, etc. Open daily from mid-April to mid-October from 2 to 5 P.M.; closed Mondays. Admission 25p ($.62).

EXCURSIONS OUT OF BATH

BERKELEY CASTLE (32 miles)
Lived in by the same family for 800 years. It was the scene of the murder of Edward II in 1327. Visitors can see the dungeons, torture rooms, medieval kitchens, and State Apartments.

BRADFORD-ON-AVON (10 miles)
Formerly an important wool center. See the great beamed Tithe Barn, ancient bridge, and the Saxon Church of St. Lawrence.

BRISTOL (12 miles)
Rich in seafaring history, with close links with the early colonization of America. See the Cathedral, Cabot Tower, St. Mary Redcliffe Church, Avon Gorge, and the zoo. Bristol is also the birthplace of Cary Grant, who still visits the city yearly.

Bath

CASTLE COMBE (9 miles)
One of the prettiest villages in England, set beside a trout stream.

CHEDDAR GORGE (24 miles) and **WOOKEY HOLE** (20 miles)
The cave and grottoes are believed to have been inhabited thousands of years ago.

LONGLEAT HOUSE (15 miles)
The home of the sixth Marquis of Bath, who opened his beautiful home to the public 25 years ago, and was the first peer to do so. Longleat House was built by his ancestor Sir John Thynne, 1566–80, and is a superb example of Elizabethan architecture. Standing in Parkland, landscaped by the famous Capability Brown, it was altered by Sir Jeffrey Wyatville and decorated in the ornate Italian style in the last century. Famous for the finest private library in the world, and magnificent ceilings molded in the Venetian manner, it contains important 18th- and 19th-century furniture. There are paintings by Titian, Reynolds, Lawrence, Worth, Graham Sutherland. The State rooms are hung with magnificent 16th-century tapestries, Spanish leather, and Genoese velvet, and the tables in the three dining rooms are laid with the finest of silver, Sèvres porcelain, and always fresh flowers—a feature of the house. Several smaller rooms are on view, including the Victoria bathroom (one always wonders what they used in those days) and a state bedroom suite, last used by the Duke of Windsor. The family's state and garter robes and the state coach can be seen, together with many possessions of the household, including one of the waistcoats worn by Charles I at his execution. The Victorian kitchens have been completely restored and the original scene of what went on in those kitchens has been re-created with models of cooks and kitchen maids bent over ranges and massive tables—copper gleams, and the scene is set as in the old days. Beyond are the cook's pantry and sitting room. The former scullery is now a shop where kitchenware may be bought. Longleat House is similar to Woburn Abbey in its carnival atmosphere. Just outside the house itself is a doll's house museum, restaurants, cafés, souvenir kiosks, children's amusement park, donkey rides, a pets' corner, etc. To the side of the house is a huge lake with sea lions, hippos, and the like. At the top there is a chimpanzee island and there are safari boat trips to take you across the lake over to the Safari Park, Britain's first and supposedly Europe's finest. There are hundreds of wild animals roaming free in over 300 acres of woods and rolling grassland. Carnival-like as it may be, this, too, like Woburn Abbey, is very definitely worth a visit. Open daily; from Easter through October, open from 10 A.M. to 6 P.M.; the rest of the year, open from 10 A.M. to 4 P.M. Closed Christmas day. Admission Longleat House 40p ($1); Churchill collection only 25p ($.62).

Safari Park open daily from 10 A.M. to 6 P.M. Admission (if in a coach) 40p ($1); private visitors 50p ($1.25); safari boats 30p ($.75).

THE WINSTON S. CHURCHILL COLLECTION (at Longleat House)
The best of Lord Bath's private Churchill collection is displayed here. Considered to be the most comprehensive of its kind, it covers all facets, political and personal, giving the visitor a rare opportunity to learn more of this remarkable Englishman of our time. Some surprising artistic and literary efforts by Adolf Hitler(!) are also to be seen.

STONEHENGE (20 miles)

Always a subject of controversy and sometimes a disappointment, Stonehenge is still something to be seen, if only to know you stand on the spot where approximately 4,000 years ago, the Druids lived. The site itself is simply concentric circles of huge stones. When you consider the effort of initiative or ingenuity it must have taken 4,000 years ago to move these stones, which were brought from quite some distances, you begin to appreciate the importance of Stonehenge. It is sometimes claimed the huge stones actually predate the coming of the Druids. Numerous investigations have been documented in a book called *Stonehenge Decoded,* written by John B. White and Gerald S. Hawkins, who maintain that Stonehenge was probably an astronomical observatory. Whatever it was, or is today, it is worth seeing. One way to get there is by coach tour from London, combining other interesting sights as well. There is one combining Bath, Longleat, Stonehenge, and Salisbury provided by Road and Rail Tours, Ltd., for which you will have to contact the British Rail Company or British Tourist Authority. It is called Tour A and departs from Paddington Station at 8:45 A.M. every Monday and Thursday from May through October. You return to Waterloo Station at 6:14 P.M. Price £8 ($20) per person.

WELLS (20 miles)

It has a fine cathedral, built mainly in the 13th century, a moated Bishop's Palace, ancient gateways, and a museum containing prehistoric remains from the Mendip Caves.

16
Stratford-on-Avon

About 90 miles from London, this part of England is known throughout the world as the birthplace of William Shakespeare (1564–1616). Stratford attracts thousands of visitors who flock here to trace his life from his birthplace in Henley Street to his tomb in Holy Trinity Church, beside the peaceful river Avon. Opposite the Falcon Hotel in Chapel Street can be seen the foundations of New Place, the house Shakespeare bought in 1597, with a charming replica of an Elizabethan garden.

The Royal Shakespeare Theatre stands right on the Avon River but leaves much to be desired, in my mind. Somehow I simply cannot conceive of a modern Shakespearean theater here in this Elizabethan village, where one would expect the tradition of the architecture and the old Bard himself to be honored. The original memorial theater stood on this spot but it burned down in the 1920s and this modern edifice was built on the same site. I suppose the main thing is that Shakespeare's plays are still staged here and one should be more concerned about that than the building itself, so I'll say no more. The theater season begins in April and goes all the way through November. There are usually five or six Shakespearean plays in repertory at the same time. If you plan to attend any of these performances, you must make a reservation a long time in advance or you won't get a seat. If you take a tour, tickets are usually included if you specify you wish to see a performance. Tickets can be obtained more easily this way than on your own. Stall seats generally run £1 to £2.20 ($2.50 to $5.48); balcony 50p to 60p ($1.25 to $1.50).

Luckily, at least one wing of the old memorial theater survived the great fire and this has been turned into a picture gallery. Naturally the star of the show is the Bard himself and there are portraits of him all over, and paintings of some of his costume designs and of famous actors portraying Shakespearean characters. You'll recognize Sir Laurence Olivier as Macbeth. From April through November, open Monday through Saturday from 10 A.M. to 1 P.M. and from 2 to 6 P.M., Sundays from 2 to 6 P.M. From November through March, open Saturdays from 10 A.M. to 1 P.M. and from 2 to 4 P.M. Admission 15p ($.37).

HOW TO GET THERE

You can get to Stratford-on-Avon by train from London's Paddington Station. The trip takes about 2½ hours. Or you may go by motor coach, from Victoria Coach Station. It takes about 4½ hours.

TOURS

SHAKESPEARE COUNTRY: Oxford, Stratford-on-Avon, Kenilworth, Coventry Evan Evans Tour No. 15, Metropolis House, 41 Tottenham Court Road, W.1 Tel: 637-4171
Departs daily at 10 A.M., returns at 6:30 P.M. Does not operate December 25 or 26. Price £4.50 ($11.25), including all entrance fees, luncheon, and tea. Through the Buckinghamshire countryside to Oxford where a visit is made to one of the colleges, then via the Chiltern Hills and the Cotswolds to Stratford-on-Avon for luncheon and a visit to Shakespeare's birthplace and Anne Hathaway's Cottage. On to Warwick, passing the finest baronial castle in England. From Warwick to Kenilworth Castle, where, weather permitting, you stop to explore this fabulous ruin immortalized by Sir Walter Scott in *Kenilworth*. The final stop is at Coventry with a one-hour visit. You take afternoon tea and depart for London via the M1 Motorway.

SHAKESPEARE COUNTRY: Oxford, Warwick, Stratford-on-Avon Frames & Rickards Tour No. 9F from Frames, Herbrand Street
Departs Monday through Saturday at 8 A.M., returns at 7:30 P.M. Tour 9R from Rickards, 17 Woburn Place, departs Thursdays and Saturdays at 8 A.M., returns at 7:30 P.M. Price £4.70 ($11.75), including morning coffee, luncheon, tea, and all admission fees. To the city of Oxford, and a visit to one of the colleges, then through the pretty villages of the Cotswolds to Warwick, which is approached by an ancient arched gateway with a chapel above. The castle is a splendid edifice standing on the spot where King Alfred's daughter, Ethelfleda, built a fortress in A.D. 915. At Stratford-on-Avon, you'll see Anne Hathaway's Cottage, and Holy

Stratford-on-Avon

Trinity Church is passed en route. A halt is made for tea on the homeward journey via Banbury, Aylesbury, and Tring, passing Waddesdon Manor and Tring Park, home of the Rothschilds.

DINING

COBWEB RESTAURANT AND CONFECTIONERY 12 Sheep Street

A lovely old 16th-century gabled and half-timbered building so typical of its period. Even if you don't have lunch it is worth a visit for a cup of coffee just to see it. The restaurant is on the second floor spreading over three rooms, all furnished in early English traditional. You can't go wrong no matter what you order here, but they are especially good at the usual English "joint" and another house specialty, the roast chicken with bread sauce. All main dishes are accompanied by the usual potatoes and other vegetables, at about 50p ($1.25). On the main floor you will find all sorts of calorie-laden desserts which you may wish to enjoy around teatime or "elevenses." Open Monday through Saturday until 6 P.M. During the season it stays open Sunday afternoons from 3 to 6 P.M.

THE DIRTY DUCK Waterside Street on the Avon

With a garden where you can dine or just sit over coffee if you like. The Dirty Duck draws a lot of celebrities, primarily those who appear at the Royal Shakespeare Theatre such as Sir Laurence Olivier, so it is very possible you might see a familiar face quaffing a mug of ale. The grill room is open from noon to 3 P.M. and from 6 P.M. to midnight. It serves the standard grilled cutlets, fish, and steaks, accompanied by the usual chips, vegetables, and dessert. The average price of a grill is about 75p ($1.87). There is a lounge and bar in front and conversation that gets pretty gay as they fill up A lovely open fire warms your bones on chilly days and it is quite nice to sit by it with a cup of tea, or something stronger.

HALL'S CROFT FESTIVAL CLUB in the "Old Town"

This was originally the home of Shakespeare's daughter Susanna. It is actually a private club so you have to pay a token membership fee of 15p ($.37), which entitles you to one day's use of all club facilities. The restaurant is quite charming and the food very good and budget-minded. Lunch is served from 12:30 to 2:30 P.M. A good three-course lunch will cost you about 74p ($1.85). Snacks are available all afternoon. Open daily from April through November from 10:30 A.M. to 8 P.M. From November through March, open Monday through Saturday from 10:30 A.M. to 6 P.M., closed Sundays.

THE ROSE AND CROWN Sheep Street Tel: 2377

An original old Elizabethan half-timbered inn just a few steps from the Royal Theatre. The restaurant is authentic in detail and a very lovely place to spend an hour or so over a typical pub-style, moderately priced lunch.

THE SHAKESPEARE HOTEL Chapel Street Tel: 3631

A magnificent Tudor-style hotel right on the main street. The public rooms are as quaint and warm as you would imagine from looking at the building. It is a good place to stop for tea, which they serve in silver pots around the fireplace. Truly beautiful, with antiques scattered throughout, with none of the old musty, austere look about it. The antiques are combined with modern furnishings, which give the hotel an extra special comfort. You might wish to stay overnight here. The rooms all have radio, telephone, and central heating.

SIGHTSEEING

Try to allow a full day for Stratford-on-Avon so that you can fully explore the little town itself and all the surrounding area. It is great fun to walk down the cobblestone streets, have a drink at one of the half-timbered inns, poke around the quaint little antique shops, have tea at an Elizabethan tearoom, and explore the 16th-century houses with their protruding second stories. One ticket 50p ($1.25) admits you to five of the most important sights in Stratford. Buy it at the first house you visit.

Shakespeare's Birthplace is rather small and it makes you wonder about the size of people in those days. The doorways are low, the ceilings seem to come down on your head, and even the furniture seems almost child-sized. Nonetheless, this is where the Bard was born, and his cradle is still to be seen. The house has been a national shrine since 1850. There are many of Shakespeare's personal possessions around, such as books, school papers, diplomas, and toys.

One of the first stops for most romantics is **Anne Hathaway's Cottage,** just outside of Stratford in Shottery. This is where Shakespeare's wife lived before their marriage. It is a very simple cottage made of "wattle and daub," which is a rather primitive shingle-and-plaster affair. You can see the "courting" settle where Anne and the Bard often sat together prior to their marriage.

Shakespeare retired to **New Place House** in 1610. Already a celebrity and financially secure, he settled in here, to spend the rest of his life. Unfortunately, he lived here only four years since he died at the young age of 52. In the Knott Garden, you can still see a mulberry tree that Shakespeare himself is supposed to have planted. To enter the gardens, you must first pass through the home of Thomas Nash, the husband of Shakespeare's granddaughter.

The **house of Shakespeare's mother,** Mary Arden, also remains, in the village of Wilmcote, just a short distance out of Stratford. The Tudor-style house is very picturesque and in some ways far more interesting than either Shakespeare's original home or Anne Hathaway's cottage. Admission 20p ($.50).

You may wish to visit **Harvard House,** the 16th-century Elizabethan home of Katherine Rogers, mother of John Harvard, the founder of Harvard University. The furnishings are merely replicas of those used when she lived in the house, since the home was very badly run down and in disuse when it was purchased by a Chicagoan, Edward Morris, who then presented it to the American University. Open Monday through Saturday from 9 A.M. to 1 P.M. and from 2 to 6 P.M., Sundays from 2 to 6 P.M. Admission 10p ($.25).

From April through October most of these sites can be visited Monday through Saturday from 9 A.M. to 6 P.M., Sundays from 2 to 6 P.M. From November through March open Monday through Saturday from 9 A.M. to 12:45 P.M., Sundays, from 2 to 4 P.M. Shakespeare's Birthplace and the cottage of Anne Hathaway open from 2 to 4 P.M.

Just outside of Stratford you'll find the village of Bladon and at the St. Martin's Church you'll find the very simple **grave of Sir Winston Churchill** and his family. The little church is on Church Street, which is unmarked and there are no reference posts or signs anywhere, so you'll probably have to ask for it. Go through the main gate and just past the church on the right-hand side you will see the graves of the family. The government actually wanted to bury Sir Winston in Westminster Abbey but it was his wish to be buried at this tiny church of his youth with the rest of his family, including Consuelo Vanderbilt from the American side of the family. After visiting the grave site, standing in front of the church doors, look straight ahead toward the schoolyard past the trees and you will have a perfect view of Blenheim Palace, where Churchill was born.

WARWICK

Warwick is an ancient town just outside Stratford. It makes an interesting little trip, perhaps for a morning or afternoon.

You can get to Warwick from Stratford by the local bus service: Midland Red Motor Services, Red Line Bus Station, Stratford-on-Avon, Tel: 4181. They also operate tours.

WARWICK CASTLE about 8 miles from Stratford-on-Avon
The 14th-century stronghold of Richard, Earl of Warwick, stands on the center of the town, high on a ledge overlooking the Avon. Founded by William the Conqueror, the fortress was so well built that the walls and towers remain today in almost the same condition as when they were first erected. At one time the castle was a prison for Edward IV. Today the Earl of Warwick makes his home in the mansion that had been converted from the castle itself. There are many collections of armor, relics, and furnishings on view here. The castle is surrounded by beautiful gardens

202 OUTSIDE LONDON

with strutting peacocks. Be sure to visit the greenhouse and see the "Warwick Vase," a huge vase 7 feet in diameter from the 4th century, found in Rome in what was said to be Hadrian's villa. The castle is open daily from Good Friday to the middle of September from 10 A.M. to 5:30 P.M. Closed from November through February. Admission 30p ($.75), including admission to the armory, the tower, the grounds, and the garden.

LORD LEICESTER HOSPITAL

At the West Gate of Warwick is a row of quaint "Almshouses," built in the 16th century by Robert Dudley, the Earl of Leicester and one of the lovers of Queen Elizabeth I. The Earl felt a great sympathy for soldiers of that period who had nowhere to go after leaving the army, and built these houses for them. The tomb of the Earl can be seen in nearby St. Mary's Church, which also contains the tomb of Richard Beauchamp, Earl of Warwick.

Dining in Warwick

THE PORRIDGE POT Gury Street

I like to combine my dining with my sightseeing when I'm on a tight schedule and the Porridge Pot is certainly the perfect spot for this. It, too, is almost one of the sights to see. Built in the 15th century, it luckily escaped the great fire that reduced so much of the area to ashes, though just narrowly, judging by the fire-scarred beams the owners may point out to you. Sitting at the Porridge Pot makes you feel as though you are living in another century. The dining room is cozy with a well-used fireplace, brass pots and pans used as décor, a beautiful Wedgwood collection, and the usual dark wooden beams. Your hosts will be more than happy to relate the history of this building and the surrounding area if they are not too busy. The food itself is as tasty as the place is charming, featuring the traditional English recipes. Fixed-price three-course lunch 70p ($1.75).

PART IV

The Southern Coast

17
Dover

Dover may be best known from the song "The White Cliffs of Dover," which was very popular during World War II. The town's main importance today is as a ferry port to cross the Channel from England to France. With the easy-to-see and impossible-to-camouflage "white cliffs," Dover was repeatedly bombed during the war and most of it was destroyed. Miraculously, Dover Castle was not touched by the bombs and is a beautiful sight to see, all lit up at night high on a cliff above the port. Built by Henry II in the 12th century, it is one of the oldest castles in England. Since there are no great tourist reasons to go to Dover besides crossing the channel, I haven't mentioned hotels. It can also be visited directly from London.

18
Folkestone

This is a channel-crossing port and lovely holiday resort. The Leas is one of the finest seacoast promenades in England. There are excellent sporting facilities and plenty of evening entertainment: variety shows, dancing, concerts, and repertory theaters.

HOW TO GET THERE

You can get to Folkestone by train from London's Charing Cross Station. The trip takes an hour and 20 minutes.

WHERE TO STAY

BURLINGTON HOTEL Earl's Avenue Tel: 55301 A-B-C
A Victorian hotel near the famous Leas. Single: £4 ($10); double: £8 to £9 ($20 to $22.50). The rooms are quite large and very comfortable, most face the sea. In the Bay Tree Grille you can try the excellent French cuisine. Open for lunch from 1 to 2:15 P.M. and for dinner from 7 to 10 P.M., Saturdays from 7 to 10:30 P.M. Fixed-price lunch £1.50 ($3.75); fixed-price dinner £2 ($5).

CHILWORTH COURT HOTEL 39–41 Earl's Avenue Tel: 55673 A-B-C.
A small well run hotel, comprised of two converted houses. Single: £3 ($7.50); double: £6 to £7 ($15 to $17.50). The bedrooms are simple but very comfortable and clean. Public rooms, too, are comfortable and convenient.

DINING

EMILIO'S RESTAURANT PORTOFINO 124A Sandgate Road Tel: 55762

Folkestone 207

Excellent Italian food, served by Emilio himself, if you are lucky. Open for lunch from noon to 2:30 P.M., and for dinner from 6 to 11 P.M. Closed Mondays. Fixed-price lunch £1 ($2.50).

NEW METROPOLE RESTAURANT Sandgate Road, the Leas Tel. 55114

A good Italian restaurant set in an old Victorian building, it changes its locality from season to season. In the summer the restaurant is in a room overlooking the sea, and in the winter it is moved into a stone gallery room. Open for lunch from 12:30 to 2:30 P.M., and for dinner from 7 to 10:30 P.M., Saturdays until 11:30 P.M., Sundays until 10 P.M. Closed Mondays. Fixed-price lunch £1 ($2.50).

19
Rye

Rye is built on a low hill overlooking a seaside marshland. Fascinating and full of character, it was once a smuggler's haven, and today there are still secret rooms in many of the old homes. Originally an island, Rye is now part of the mainland with narrow cobblestone streets that look like pretzels, and charming little cottages, attracting tourists of every nationality. It is great fun to wander around and imagine the secret comings and goings of the smugglers of another era.

See the Ypres Tower, a 13th-century edifice housing the Rye Museum and St. Mary's Parish Church, a 15th-century church with a very unique clock.

HOW TO GET THERE

You reach Rye by train from London's Charing Cross Station. The trip takes about 1½ hours.

WHERE TO STAY

HOPE ANCHOR HOTEL Watchbell Street Tel: 2216 B-C
On a cobbled street out of the center of town, this little hotel overlooks the sea and the marsh. Single: from £3.80 ($9.50); double: £6.50 to £7 ($16.25 to $17.50). The quaint little rooms are well done and very comfortable. It also has a garden where you can sit and have your tea and coffee. They also have a typical English-type restaurant with simple but good food. Average dish £1.25 ($3.62).

THE MERMAID HOTEL Mermaid Street Tel: 3765 B-C
The Mermaid Hotel is one of the most photographed buildings in the whole of Sussex. It was visited by Queen Elizabeth I in 1573, as the royal insignia above the fireplace in the Resident's Lounge bears witness. This fine half-timbered inn, which fronts the narrow, cobbled Mermaid Street, was used for centuries by smugglers. The long narrow passages and secretive staircases add much to the unforgettable atmosphere of the hotel. Single: £3 ($7.50); Double: £8 to £9 ($20 to $22.50). The rooms are lovely, with leaded windows and beamed ceilings. Some of the rooms even have four-poster beds. The public rooms, too, offer every comfort and warmth, with fireplaces, beamed ceilings, and paneling. The Tudor-style dining room serves excellent meals. Fixed-price lunch £1.25 ($3.12); dinner £1.75 ($4.37).

MONASTERY GUEST HOUSE 6 High Street Tel: 3272 B-C
Built upon the site of the 13th-century Augustinian friary, the house is actually of the 17th century. Centrally located and with a lovely garden, this guest house is quite popular, especially since it is budget-priced. Rates £2 to £2.25 ($5 to $5.62). There are only 7 rooms, so it is wise to book in advance. All rooms are very comfortable with heating, and either double or twin beds. A good English-style breakfast is served in the lovely bay-windowed dining room.

DINING

FLETCHER'S HOUSE Lion Street
Close to St. Mary's Church. It takes its name from the Elizabethan dramatist, John Fletcher, who was born here in 1579. His father was then Vicar of Rye, and the house was then the vicarage. It is a lovely place for morning or afternoon tea or lunch. Typical English food at budget prices makes it a popular stop.

THE PLAYING CARD 68 "The Mint"
As the name suggests, the décor is that of antique playing cards. There is a huge fireplace to warm your feet by, and beamed ceilings. They specialize in typical English cuisine, such as the usual roast beef with Yorkshire pudding for 40p ($1). The desserts are out of this world! Open for lunch from noon to 3 P.M. and for tea and dinner till 9:30 P.M.

20
Hastings and St. Leonard's

Hastings is one of England's most popular South Coast resorts. The Duke of Normandy defeated King Harold here in the Norman invasion of 1066. You can still see the ruins of Hastings' Castle which was the first Norman castle built in all of England, though not much of it remains since the original fortress was destroyed in 1216. In the 14th century, it was again invaded by the French and left in rubble, upon which the present Tudor-style village was built.

Hastings is really two towns—one old and one new. In the old town you will find quaint byways, ancient timbered houses, red-tiled cottages, and tarred net lofts in which the fishermen hang their nets to dry. Modern Hastings and its partner town, St. Leonard's, provide entertainment of all kinds. Sporting enthusiasts can enjoy tennis, cricket, bowling, golf, putting, archery, sailing, and sea-angling.

The most important attraction is the Hastings Embroidery, an unbelievable piece of work that tells the story of 900 years of English history in embroidery. The historical scenes are so beautifully done that it is almost like reading a storybook. There are 81 panels illustrating such historical moments as the sailing of the *Mayflower*, the assassination of Thomas à Becket, Chaucer's pilgrims going to Canterbury, the Little Princes held in the London Tower, and the battle of Waterloo. Exhibited on the promenade at the Triodome, it is well worth a visit. Admission 10p ($.25).

Seven miles from Hastings is Battle Abbey, founded by William the Conqueror with the High Altar on the site of King Harold's death to commemorate the Battle of Hastings in 1066, the last time England was conquered. Battle Abbey has been the home of the Webster family since 1719, though at present the largest of the

Hastings and St. Leonard's 211

buildings, the Abbot House, is used as a girls' school. The sight of the battle, the ruins of the Abbey, the grounds, and the gardens are open to the public. Open April through October, Monday through Friday from 10 A.M. to 1 P.M. and November through March, Monday through Friday from 2 P.M. to 6 P.M. or dusk. Admission 15p ($.37).

HOW TO GET THERE

You can get to Hastings by train from London's Charing Cross or Victoria stations. The trip takes 1½ hours from Charing Cross, 2 hours from Victoria. Or you may go by coach, from Victoria Coach Station. The trip takes about 3 hours.

21
Eastbourne

Eastbourne is a superb seaside resort, entertainment and concert center, with beautiful gardens, strikingly clean beaches, and elegant shops. Its 8-mile-long coastline includes wide promenades and terraces, smooth lawns, and extensive flower borders that are ablaze with color most of the year. From Princes Park a narrow-gage, miniature tramway operates, the only public tramway service in the south of England. There is frequent service daily throughout the season.

You must go to nearby **Alfriston,** which is one of the most beautiful villages in all of England. As a result, unfortunately, it is always jammed full of cars and buses bearing tourists from all over the world. The houses are something right out of an old history book. Some of them still have secret rooms where smugglers hid their loot. Wander the little cobblestone streets and visit the quaint shops and marvelous old half-timbered inns.

Visit, too, **Pevensey,** a Roman fort, and a Norman Castle, and nearby **Norman's Bay** where William the Conqueror landed at Wilmington. Out in the turf of the Downs is the **Long Man of Wilmington,** a gigantic figure now believed to be of early Saxon origin. See, too, the **Benedictine Priory ruins** here, and a very interesting church. Then there is **Firle Place,** an Elizabethan mansion, **Herstmonceux Castle,** a medieval, moated castle, the home of the Royal Greenwich Observatory; and **Michelham Priory,** an Augustinian priory founded in 1229, with a magnificent moat, spanned by a stone bridge with a 14th-century gatehouse, and beautiful gardens.

HOW TO GET THERE

You can get to Eastbourne by train from London's Victoria Station. The trip takes about 1¼ hours. Or you may go by coach, from Victoria Coach Station. It takes 2½ to 3 hours.

WHERE TO STAY

CAVENDISH Grand Parade Tel: 27401 B-C
A very posh deluxe hotel and unusually crowded as a resort. Lovely rooms, some done in traditional English and some done in modern style, but all very well appointed and very comfortable. There is a new cocktail bar which is quite a contrast to the quiet, simply-furnished public rooms. Single: from £4 ($10); double: £8 to £13 ($20 to $32.50). The restaurant is also extremely posh; open for lunch from 1 to 2:15 P.M. and for dinner from 7 to 9:30 P.M., Saturdays from 7 to 10:30 P.M. Fixed-price lunch from £2 ($5); dinner from £2.50 ($6.25).

THE CUMBERLAND HOTEL Grand Parade Tel: 30242 B-C
Facing the sea, Cumberland offers very modern rooms and facilities with all comforts. Single: £4 ($10); double: £8 to £11 ($20 to $27.50). There are balconies and glassed-in lounges for sunbathing.

THE GRAND HOTEL King Edward's Parade Tel: 22611 B-C
An old favorite of vacationing royalty, the newly renovated Grand is a lovely hotel and has a beautiful garden. Single: £6 ($15); double: £12 to £22 ($30 to $55). The Victorian Dining Room serves excellent international dishes. Open for lunch from 12:45 to 2:30 P.M. and for dinner from 7 to 9:30 P.M. Fixed-price menu for lunch £2.50 ($6.25).

QUEENS HOTEL Marine Parade Tel: 26454
Near the Palace Pier on a promontory that sticks out into the sea, the Queens is a big white building straddling the entire coast. Single: from £3.75 ($9.37); double: from £6.50 to £8 ($16.25 to $20). Medium-size rooms, well-appointed with telephone and wall-to-wall carpeting. Most of them face the sea. A couple of lounges are very well done and comfortable. The restaurant in particular is very nice with a windowed alcove overlooking the sea.

DINING

THE CHANTECLER RESTAURANT 7 Bolton Road Tel: 30748
Very elegant indeed! There are two floors and fresh flowers everywhere. A gilded wrought-iron staircase is the focal point and lends its special touch of elegance. It's run by Greek proprietors and staffed by Greeks, so naturally the Greek dishes are particularly good; they also have an international menu. Open for lunch from 12:30 to 2:30 P.M. and for dinner from 6 to 10:45 P.M.; closed Sundays. Average dish £1 ($2.50).

214 THE SOUTHERN COAST

CHEZ MAURICE 118 Seaside Road Tel: 24894.
Sitting in the window alcove, you get a very good view of what is going on outside while you enjoy your lovely lunch or dinner. You sit on velvet banquettes, and the atmosphere is very warm and friendly. They specialize in French cooking. Open for lunch from 12:30 to 2:30 P.M. and for dinner from 6:30 to 9:30 P.M., Saturdays from 6:30 to 10:30 P.M.; closed Sundays and holidays. Lunch from £1.25 ($3.12).

SUMMER PALACE Park Gates Tel: 39056
Here you can have Chinese or English cuisine. A strange combination, I know, but they have built their reputation on it and this is a very popular restaurant. Extremely well prepared and generous portions. The dining room upstairs offers the usual restaurant service with linen and proper table service. In the downstairs dining room these amenities are not observed; it is more popular for snacks. Open for lunch from noon to 2:30 P.M. and for dinner from 5:30 to 11:15 P.M., Saturdays from 5:30 to 11:30 P.M., Sundays from 5:30 to 11 P.M. Fixed-price lunch 70p ($1.75); dinner 90p ($2.25).

22
Brighton

Brighton was one of the first and still remains one of the most popular seaside resorts of England. Conveniently located just 50 miles south of London on the Sussex coast, Brighton goes all the way back to the mid-1700s when it became quite fashionable to take the "sea cure." Brighton has a bracing atmosphere and many graceful terraces and squares laid out during the regency of George IV for whom the Oriental-looking Royal Pavilion was built. There are 3,000 acres of splendid parkland, like the Seafront Gardens or the romantic appeal of Preston Park Rock Gardens.

Originally just a seaside resort for those who wished to heal a few aches and pains, Brighton shot into its world-wide prominence when the Prince of Wales took notice of it and made it one of his favorite retreats. Naturally, all of his usual cortege accompanied him and it soon became "the" place to be. All the fashionable people of London migrated to Brighton like bees to honey. And it wasn't long before the small resort the Prince first knew began to spring upward and outward until it became one of the most fashionable resorts in all of Europe.

The original Victorian elegance and pomp and ceremony has long been a thing of the past and Brighton has now sprouted out into more of a "mod" resort. The beaches are as full of sweet young things in bikinis as they used to be of white-haired bankers in knee-length bathing britches. Most of the beach lovers are there for sunbathing purposes rather than swimming, because the Atlantic is cold! Only the sturdy British seem to be able to manage it. What I find quite comical is that very often on a cloudy day you will see people sitting along the promenade in raincoats or sweaters, the women knitting, the men reading their papers. All of a sudden the sun will come out and they quickly tilt their heads back, get the two or three minutes' available sun before it disappears behind a cloud, and then go back to their activity. Or you will see mothers with young children all bundled up to the ears with sweaters, scarves, and raincoats with their little beach toys and pails. The moment the sun comes out, they strip quickly, play in the sand for a full five or ten minutes before they are back into their sweaters again. Of course this does not happen all summer long, though there is no denying that Britain does not have the most beautiful climate. Perhaps that is why there are so many diversions: the two huge amusement piers, theaters, every kind of sport: sea fishing, golf, horseback riding, cricket, races, and just about anything else you can name.

The promenade (King's Road) extends along the entire seacoast region of Brighton and since this is the most favored part of the city naturally this is where you will find the very posh hotels and beautiful manor houses.

As in almost every little town or village there is always a town square with a clock tower, the meeting place of its young people. Around the square you will find all sorts of snack shops, boutiques, and newspaper and tobacco shops. North Street is particularly charming: it has a complex of little alleys leading off of it known as "The Lanes." This is where you will find all the antique shops, some of which go back to the days of Queen Victoria. Interspersed are the very up-to-date swinging, mod boutiques, à la Carnaby Street in London.

The most important sight to see in all of Brighton is, of course, The Royal Pavilion, once the seaside palace of George IV, the Prince Regent, and now open to the public. Considering the fact that the British are known for their conservatism, the Royal Palace is bound to astound you. It is a replica of an Indian Mogul's mosque that seems to have been air-lifted and set down in the middle of a park. It is truly a beautiful work of art. I have been to India and seen many of the maharajas' palaces, but the Royal Pavilion strikes an even more romantic note than many of those I saw there, perhaps because it is so completely unexpected and so out of keeping with its surroundings. Nonetheless, it is quite an experience and you certainly must not miss it.

Built in 1787 the Pavilion was not at all as elaborate as it is now but was domed and gingerbreaded until it emerged as something out of *1001 Nights*. However, King George IV loved it and spent whatever time he could there. Queen Victoria, however, did not share his love of the Royal Pavilion and, though she did spend some time there occasionally, she finally refused to ever go there again, and stripped it of all its royal fittings. In 1845 the residents of Brighton managed to purchase the Pavilion and began to restore it to its former splendor even to the point of tracking down some of the original furniture which Queen Elizabeth has been generous enough to donate.

The interior of the magnificent palace is filled with a marvelous combination of chinoiserie and Indian fittings and collections. If you are fortunate enough to be there during the time of the Regency Exhibition from July through September you will see all the Royal china, porcelain, and silver. It is quite a change from everything you may have seen in all the other manor houses and palaces throughout England. You can wander through the great kitchens and see the Duke of Wellington's personal collection of pots and pans from his own home at Hyde Park Corner in London. The State apartments themselves are something right out of a movie, all satin, dragons, serpents, lacquered furniture, and bamboo. The banqueting hall was the scene of many gay dinners in King George's time and one can almost imagine the gala feasts that took place here. Open from July through September from 10 A.M. to 8 P.M., off-season until 5 P.M. Admission from 15p to 20p ($.37 to $.50), depending on the season and what is going on at the time.

HOW TO GET THERE

You can get to Brighton by train from London's Victoria or London Bridge stations. The trip takes from 10 to 15 minutes. For train times, Tel: 928-5100. Or you may go by coach, from Victoria Coach Station. It takes about 2½ hours.

WHERE TO STAY

The city is loaded with hotels, guest houses, and rooms of every size and description. I will just give a couple of selections. I suggest that you use Brighton as your base for other sightseeing in the area, so I won't list hotels in the neighboring towns.

ASCOT HOTEL 68–77 Marine Parade Tel: 64444 A-B-C
A charming old Regency style house with good ambiance that brings out the friendliness of its guests. This is a homey place and there are all types

of people. Rooms from £3 ($7.50). Medium-sized, well furnished, and comfortable rooms with wall-to-wall carpeting and telephone, with a rear garden or balcony looking over the sea for your coffee or snacks. Bar and restaurant with very good English-style food.

BEDFORD King's Road Tel: 29744 A-B-C
Right on the promenade. The newest hotel on the South coast, with good-sized and very comfortable rooms, central heating, telephone, and wall-to-wall carpeting. Rooms from £8.80 ($22). "Dickens" Bar and International Restaurant with good service.

CHATSWORTH HOTEL 9 Salisbury Road Tel: 737360 B-C
Not in Brighton itself but just a half-mile from the clock tower and the center of Brighton. Western Road runs from the clock tower west to Hove and the hotel is on the corner of Western Road and Salisbury Road, a very short walk. Rooms are large, furnished in old, traditional style with big double beds, heavy mattresses, and thick comforters. The armchairs are deep and swallow you up as you sit in them. Many of the rooms have fireplaces. No private baths or toilets in the rooms, just a wash basin, but the baths and toilets on the floor are very clean. The high note of the day at this place seems to be breakfast, where the hosts greet you warmly and in a family-like manner. The breakfast itself is served on old-fashioned painted china, the toast is served warm in a silver service and the breakfast is the typical huge English type. Budget price for all this charm is only £2 ($5) plus service. Incidentally, it is necessary to write in advance for rooms since the hotel is small and they get the same people back every year.

HARLEYHOUSE HOTEL 11–12 Marine Parade Tel: 64928 A-B
An excellent buy for the truly budget-minded, who still want a good location. The hotel faces the Palace Pier and has a balcony completely surrounding it where you can catch the afternoon breezes while having your "high tea." The rooms are quite comfortable, especially considering the price of only £2 ($5). They are medium size, very skimpily furnished with heaters and wash basins—no private baths.

THE LANSDOWNE HOTEL King Edward's Parade Tel: 25174 B-C
An old, established, family-owned hotel facing the sea and the Western Lawn. Rates £5 to £8 ($12.50 to $20); including service. Fifty of their 140 well-furnished rooms have private bath or shower, and all have telephone and TV. All public rooms overlook the sea. A magnificent view from the cocktail bar and two restaurants.

MANSION HOTEL Grand Parade Tel: 27411 A-B-C
A Victorian-type hotel with excellent service and very comfortable rooms, newly renovated with all the necessary comforts. Single: £4 ($10); double: £7.50 ($18.75).

THE METROPOLE King's Road Tel: 775432 A-B-C
Good-sized, comfortable rooms, wall-to-wall carpeting, telephone, central heating, bar, and restaurant. Rates £5.50 to £8.80 ($13.75 to $22). Supposedly one of Brighton's most luxurious hotels, but at nonluxury rates. There is a star-lit rooftop restaurant, cameo restaurant, several bars, and a health hydro as well.

OLD SHIP HOTEL King's Road Tel: 29001 A-B-C

A well known hotel right on the seafront and near "The Lanes" antique shops. Rates £3.30 to £5.50 ($8.25 to $13.75). Most rooms have a bath, all rooms have television, telephone, central heating, and wall-to-wall carpeting. There is a bar, and the restaurant features rather an extensive menu with very good food.

QUEEN'S HOTEL Marine Parade Tel: 22822 A-B-C

A newly renovated Victorian-style hotel. They have done a surprisingly good job of blending the new décor with the original architecture. Some, but not all, of the bedrooms have been refurbished, and all are comfortable. Single: £4 ($10); double: £8 to £12 ($20 to $30). There is a terrace cocktail bar and a beef cellar.

ROYAL CRESCENT Marine Parade Tel: 66311 B-C

A Regency building with wrought-iron balconies. Rates £5.50 to £8.80 ($13.75 to $22). Very comfortable, well furnished rooms with central heating, wall-to-wall carpeting, and a telephone. There are a bar and a restaurant. The dining room and lounge are particularly lovely, done in the Regency style.

THE WISH TOWER HOTEL King Edward's Parade Tel: 22676 A-B-C

A sister to the Mansion Hotel, with equally good service. Single: £4 ($10); double: £7.50 ($18.75). Victorian and yet modern, the bedrooms have been newly renovated and are very comfortable.

DINING

Since this resort is a gathering place of all nationalities, it goes without saying that you will find restaurants of every type as well, everything from Indian to Italian to Chinese. Of course the most fun is just exploring to find your own favorite. We'll give a few suggestions here.

LA BELLE COCOTTE 41 Castle Street Tel: 28553

A very friendly informal bistro, specializing in typical French bistro-type dishes. Open for lunch from noon to 2 P.M. and for dinner from 7:30 to 10 P.M. Closed Saturdays for lunch and all day Sundays. Fixed-price lunch 65p ($1.62).

CERES HEALTH FOOD RESTAURANT 23 Market Street

For the naturalist, pure food faddist, or dieter, this is an excellent selection. The food is hearty, well proportioned, well cooked, and varied. The décor is simple, and again as natural as the food. It is a serve-yourself operation, so you can pick and choose as you go along. Open all day for snacks, for lunch from noon to 2:15 P.M., and for early dinner from 3 to 6 P.M.

CHRISTOPHER'S 24 Western Street Tel: 775048

One reason for the popularity of this French bistro-type restaurant is the fact that it is owned by a film producer, Clyde Challis, and celebrities drop by to say hello. Mr. Challis himself does the cooking and an excellent chef he is. Open for dinner only from 7 to 11 P.M.; Closed Mondays. Average dish about £1.65 ($4.12).

220 THE SOUTHERN COAST

DOLCE VITA 106 Western Road Tel: 737200
An Italian restaurant with all the charming Italian ambiance one expects in such a place. Dim lights, good service, and excellent food, open for lunch from noon to 2:30 P.M. and for dinner from 6:30 P.M. to midnight. Fixed-price lunch £1.59 ($3.99).

ENGLISH'S OYSTER BAR 29–31 East Street Tel: 27980
This is very definitely the place for excellent seafood, with four oyster bars and dining rooms. The atmosphere takes you back to the Regency period. Open for lunch from noon to 2:30 P.M. and for dinner from 6 to 10 P.M. Average dish £1.50 ($3.75).

FORTES OLD STEINE RESTAURANT 1–4 Marine Parade
Near the Palace Pier. Popular primarily because of its location and its good simple food, the cafeteria offers good tummy fillers for those on an especially tight budget. Main courses start at 25p ($.62), which is pretty hard to beat. The dining room upstairs is more comfortable and relaxed, but still inexpensive. A main-course meat dish with all the accompanying vegetables runs about 45p to 50p ($1.12 to $1.25).

THE GOLDEN EGG on North Street
Less than 150 yards from the clock tower. A modern place for light meals at budget prices. You can have salads and the English version of the American hamburger, omelets, small steaks, etc. You can also get milk shakes and a good selection of desserts. It is open all day and always crowded for morning, teatime, and on up through the dinner hour and late-night snacks.

HOWARD'S PAVILION RESTAURANT 7 Pavilion Building
Right next to the Royal Pavilion itself. For elegance this restaurant can hardly be beat. Luckily the prices don't match the décor and one can get an exceptionally good meal here without breaking the budget. The décor is turn-of-the-century, with elegant table settings, cut-velvet walls, soft lighting, and a choice of two dining rooms on two floors. The menu features typical English fare with good-sized portions. Open for lunch from noon to 2:30 P.M. and for dinner from 6 to 9:30 P.M. Fixed-price, three-course lunch 60p ($1.50); fixed-price three-course dinner 90p ($2.25).

NANKING 21 Market Street
For delicious Chinese food at low cost. Centrally located, surrounded by all the important shops, it is very popular at lunchtime. I suggest that you get in early before it starts filling up. Another reason for its popularity, besides its location, is the fact that you can have a fixed-price, three-course lunch for only 35p ($.87). There is a good à la carte menu, too.

ANN SPIELSINGER 69 Preston Street Tel: 26823
Behind King's Road. A good, homey, Jewish restaurant, with authentic recipes and very generous portions. Open from noon to 9 P.M.; closed Saturdays off-season. Average dish about 75p ($1.87).

EXCURSIONS OUT OF BRIGHTON

All around the area are beautiful historic houses, castles, manor houses, and gardens. I've listed some you'll enjoy visiting.

Brighton

GOODWOOD HOUSE near Chichester
An 18th-century house, the ancestral home of the Duke of Richmond. It has a notable collection of paintings including some by Canaletto and Van Dyck, Louis XV furniture, and Sèvres porcelain.

HAVER CASTLE 33 miles north of Brighton
The moated 14th/15th-century home of Anne Boleyn, the second wife of Henry VIII. It has a spectacular garden, a maze, and a statue-lined loggia.

PARHAM near Pulborough
An Elizabethan house with a fine collection of portraits, furniture, and needlework.

PENSHURST
A splendid battlemented building, part medieval, part Elizabethan, this was the birthplace of Renaissance poet Sir Philip Sidney, and the ancestral home of the Sidney family since 1652. The domestic great hall goes back to 1340. There is a beautiful vaulted crypt armory, fine staterooms, a picture gallery, a fascinating toy museum, Tudor gardens, orchards, a park, and a lake. Light luncheons are available with bread home-baked on the premises. Admission 30p ($.75).

PETWORTH HOUSE 29 miles north of Brighton.
A lovely old mansion containing a fine collection of paintings and examples of the work of Grinling Gibbons, 17th-century wood-carver. The old town of Ketworth clusters at the gate of this lovely home, and nearby is a Roman villa at Bignor.

ST. MARY'S in Bramber
A perfect 15th-century timber-backed house.

Arundel

21 miles northwest of Brighton, a lovely old town and a good center for exploring the South Down.

Its main claim to fame is: **Arundel Castle,** an imposing fortress associated with Alfred the Great, William the Conqueror, and King Henry III, stands on the banks of the river Arun, beside Swanbourne Lake, which is mentioned in the Domesday book. Now the seat of the Duke of Norfolk, who has preserved its historical quality. What you see today is not at all what the castle was when it was built 500 years ago as it has gone through many restorations, primarily in the 18th century.

The castle is open to the public and gives one a chance to view its excellent collections of paintings, tapestries, and antiques. Open Monday through Friday, from late June to the end of September, from noon to 4:30 P.M. and from mid-April through mid-June from 1 to 4:30 P.M. Admission 25p ($.62).

Hove

Virtually a suburb of Brighton, it is really a continuation of all that Brighton has to offer, though it is a bit more residential and perhaps more quiet since all the activity centers on the promenade in Brighton.

Tunbridge Wells

Thirty-two miles north of Brighton, and certainly worth a visit. Tunbridge was a very fashionable spa in the 18th century. It was frequented by much of the royalty of England following the discovery in 1606 by Lord North of the famous Chalybeate Springs, said to cure everything from headaches to gout.

No longer the mecca of royalty nor even of the more fashionable people of England, Tunbridge is still, nevertheless, a charming little village known particularly for its **Bantiles,** a colonnaded arcade for shopping or browsing. You can also sample the famous mineral water here. The gracious Georgian and Victorian houses that still remain are very interesting sights to see, and all in all, this does make for a good few hours' excursion.

23
The Isle of Wight

The Isle of Wight has two special distinctions. First, it is said to have more sunny days than anywhere else in England. Second, it is quite a yachtsman's paradise. Connected to Southampton by ferry, hydrofoil, and hovercraft, the town of Cowes on the north coast is one of the world's best known sailing centers. Its frontage is a fascinating array of wooden buildings and quaint warehouses. It has excellent views of the harbor. Newport, the capital of the island, is where King Charles I was imprisoned at Terracebrook Castle. It also has some marvelous old coaching inns. A nature trail along the river Medina starts from Newport Quay.

Sandown and Shanklin are twin resorts on beautiful Sandown Bay, one of Britain's sunniest spots. From here you can visit Godshill, perhaps the island's prettiest little village.

Ventnor is a popular resort that has towering cliffs and shady woodland, hillside houses and glorious displays of colorful flowers basking in the mild climate. It boasts good beaches, safe bathing, and plentiful evening entertainment.

HOW TO GET THERE

You can reach the Isle of Wight by train from Waterloo Station to Portsmouth, where you connect with the ferry to Ryde, on the Isle. The train trip takes about two hours, and the ferry about an hour. The train ticket includes the ferry fare.

You can also take either a ferry or a hydrofoil from Southampton to Cowes. The ferry crosses six times a day. This trip takes 1 hour and 10 minutes; the fare is 70p ($1.75) one way. A roundtrip ticket costs £1 ($2.50) for use the same day, or £1.40 ($3.50) if you stay on the Isle more than 24 hours. The hydrofoil runs every hour and takes about 15 minutes. The rate is £1.20 ($2) one way or £2 ($5) roundtrip.

On the Isle transport is by the local bus or taxi.

Index

Abbatt Toys, 171
ABC Sauna, 163
Ackerman (chocolates), 184
Violet Adair at Galataea (sauna, massage), 163
Adelphi (theater), 93
Admiralty Arch, 125
Thomas Agnew & Sons (art), 180
Airey and Wheeler (men's clothes), 171, 182
Albert Hall, 124
Albert Memorial, 124
Aldeburgh Festival, 42
Alexe (hairdresser, wigs), 153, 164
Alfriston, 212
Allan (hairdresser), 153
Allan Clinic (beauty clinic), 158
Alpine Sports, 185
Alvaro Pizza e Pasta (restaurant), 77
Ambassadors (theater), 93
Ambulance, 38
Amelio and Davide (shoes), 176
American Express, 3, 40
American Museum (Bath), 194
Anchor (pub), 106
Andora (hotel), 51
Andrea's Continental Restaurant, 77
Angel (restaurant), 87
Annacat Fashion Boutique, 185
Antique Hypermarket, 183–184
Aquascutum (clothes, men and women), 171, 179, 188

Archie Shine (furniture), 188
Micheline Archier (aromatherapy), 160
Micheline Arcier (beauty clinic), 158
Elizabeth Arden (beauty salon), 153, 157, 158, 180
Army and Navy Stores, 90
W. J. Arnold (luggage repair), 175
Arts Restaurant (Cambridge), 141
Arundel, 221
Arundel Castle, 221
Arundel Hotel (Bath), 192
Ascot Hotel (Brighton), 217–218
Ascot Race Course, 137–138
Laura Ashley (clothes, fabrics), 186
Asprey (jewelry), 172, 180
Assembly Rooms (Bath), 194
Astleys (pipes), 171, 183
Athena (prints), 177
Atkinson (jewelry), 188
Australian Ballet, 90
Marion Ayres Salon (aromatherapy), 160, 163
A–Z (book), 109

Bag O'Neils (discotheque), 101
Baker and Oven (restaurant), 77
Bally (shoes), 170
Bands (luggage repair), 175
Bantiles (Tunbridge Wells), 222
John Barker (household goods), 183
Barkers (hairdresser), 153

226 Index

John Barnes (department store), 168
Baroum (toys), 171
Barque & Bite (restaurant), 77, 87
W. Barrett (Oriental *objets d'art*), 180
Barrie Grill (restaurant), 63
Basil Hotel, 48–49
Bath, 191–194
Bath Abbey, 193–194
Bath Festival, 41–42, 191–192
Battersea Park (jazz), 103
Battle Abbey, 210–211
Baumkotter (chess sets), 184
Beachcomber Nightclub and Restaurant, 61
Bear Gardens Museum, 121
Olive Beauchamp (beauty clinic), 158
Beauchamp Place, 186–187
Beauty Clinic, 153, 158
Beauty without Cruelty (cosmetics), 161
Beckwell House (hotel), 57
Bedford (hotel, Brighton), 218
Beefeater Restaurant, 55
Beefeater's Grill Room (restaurant), 48
Belgravia (restaurant), 77
Belgravia Royal (hotel), 46
La Belle Cocotte (restaurant, Brighton), 219
Bendicks (confectioner), 180, 188
Benedictine Priory (ruins, Eastbourne), 212
Benson & Hedges (tobacconist), 180
Berkeley Castle, 194
Berkeley Hotel (swimming), 152
Andre Bernard (hairdresser), 153
Best of British (gifts), 186
John Bewl & Croyden (all-night pharmacy), 39
Bib and Tucker Restaurant, 57
Biba Boutiques, 170, 183
Le Bistingo (restaurant), 77–78
Blaise's (discotheque), 101
Blanchards (furniture), 188
Blenheim Palace (Woodstock), 144, 201
Bliss Chemist (all-night pharmacy), 39
Blue Angel (cabaret), 97

Lilo Blum's Riding Establishment, 151
Boadicea (gifts), 186
Boat Tours, 112–113
Andre Boggaert (jewelry), 172, 180, 181
Bond Street, 123–124, 170, 179–181
Boots (all-night pharmacy), 39, 177
Booty (jewelry), 172, 180
Bourne and Hollingsworth (department store), 177
Bourne and Hollingsworth (hairdresser), 153
Bradford-on-Avon, 194
Brighton, 215–220
Brighton Festival, 42
Bristol, 194
Bristol Hotel, 60
British Airways, 18, 40
British Broadcasting Co. (BBC), 91
British Home Stores (chain store), 177
British Museum, 127, 128
British Overseas Airways Co. (BOAC), 18
British Rail Travel Center, 39
British Railway, 18–19, 37
British Theatre Museum, 128
British Tourist Authority, 40, 108, 133
British Travel Association, 89
British Travel Centre, 18
Brompton Grill (restaurant), 66
Brompton Road, 184–186
Brown (clothes, men and women), 181
Molton Brown (hairdresser), 181
Brown's Hotel, 52
Bruno and John (hairdresser), 153, 156
Bruno's (restaurant, Bath), 193
Bucheron (jewelry), 172
Buckingham Palace, 114, 125, 126
Bucks Hotel, 50
Budapest (restaurant), 78
Bugatti (men's clothes), 184
Burberry (clothes, men and women), 171, 179
C. P. Burge (antiques), 188
Burlington Arcade, 172, 182
Burlington Hotel (Folkestone), 206
Burton (men's clothes), 171, 179

Bus Stop (boutique), 184
Joy Byrne (beauty clinic), 158–159

C & A (department store), 177–178
Cadogan Hotel, 49
Caledonian Suite (restaurant), 66–67
Calman Links (furs), 185
Cambridge, 139–140
Cambridge University, 139–141
Camden Passage Antique Centre and Market, 172–173
Candide (women's clothes), 186
Canterbury, 145–146
La Cantina di Capri (restaurant, Oxford), 143
Capital Hotel, 46
Caprice (restaurant), 67
Captain's Bar, 55
Carlton Tower (hotel), 45–46
Carnaby Street, 124, 127, 170
Carriers (restaurant), 67
Le Carrosse (restaurant), 67
Cartier (jewelry), 172, 180
Carvery (restaurant), 54, 73
Casa Pepe (restaurant), 73–74
Casse Croute (restaurant), 74
Casserole (restaurant), 78
Castle Combe, 195
Cathay (restaurant), 78
Cavalry Room Restaurant, 47
Cavendish (hotel, Eastbourne), 213
Cavendish Hotel, 60
Celebrity (cabaret), 98
Ceres Health Food Restaurant (Brighton), 219
Chalet Suisse (discotheque), 101–102
Champneys Nature Cure Resort (health hydro), 165
Changing of the Guard, 113–114
Chanticleer (cabaret), 99
Chanticler Restaurant (Eastbourne), 213
Charbonnel & Walker (chocolates), 180
Charing Cross Road, 174, 178
Charing Cross Station, 40
Charkham (men's clothes), 177
Chateaubriand (restaurant), 61
Chatsworth Hotel (Brighton), 218
Chaumet (jewelry), 172

Chavila (leather), 170
Che Guevara (boutique), 183
Cheddar Gorge, 195
Chelsea Antique Market, 173, 187
Chelsea Flower Show, 42
Chelsea Foot Clinic, 162
Chelsea Lounge, 46
Chenelle (women's clothes), 185
Cheshire Cheese (pub), 78, 127
Chester Festival and Mystery Plays (Chester), 42
Cheveux (hairdresser), 154, 163
Chez Maurice (restaurant, Eastbourne), 214
Chez Solange (restaurant), 74
Chichester Festival Theatre Season (Chichester), 43
Chicken Inn (restaurant), 85
Children's Bazaar, 188
Children's Book Centre, 184
Chilworth Court Hotel (Folkestone), 206
Chinacraft, 172, 179, 185
Mr. Chow (restaurant), 81
Mr. Chow's Mont Pelier Grill (restaurant), 75–76
Christophe (restaurant), 74
Christopher's (restaurant, Brighton), 219
Church Street (antiques), 173
Winston S. Churchill Collection, 195
Churchill Hotel, 53
Churchills (cabaret), 98
Sir Winston Churchill's Grave (Bladen), 201
Ciro (jewelry), 171, 172, 180, 185
City Barge (restaurant), 87
Clarence House, 126
Clarendon Court Hotel (sauna), 163
Claridge's (hotel), 52
Cleopatra's Needle, 126
Clifton-Ford (hotel), 55–56
Cloverly House (hotel), 50
Coach tours, 37, 106, 109–113, 133–135, 198–199
Coal Hole (pub), 106
Cobweb Restaurant and Confectionery (Stratford-on-Avon), 199
Cockney Pride (restaurant), 78

228 Index

Cogswell & Harrison (hunting clothes, men's), 182
Collins Couture Centre, 175
Commonwealth Institute, 128
Concord Hotel, 51
Connaught Hotel, 52
Connaught Restaurant, 67
Contact Lens Clinic, 162
Coombe Hill Stables (Kingston-upon-Thames), 151
Copacabana (cabaret), 99
Le Coq d'Or (restaurant), 68
Cordon Bleu Cooking School, 109
Cordon Bleu Restaurant, 79
Cornoba (leather), 171, 186
Cosmetics à la Carte, Ltd., 161
Courtauld Institute Galleries, 129
Covent Garden, 124
Cox & Co. (china), 184
Crank's Salad Bowl (restaurant), 79
Crimpers (hairdresser), 154
Criterion (theater), 93
Crocodile (boutique), 183, 186
Cruft's Dog Show, 41
Countess Csaky (beauty clinic), 159
Cumberland Hotel, 53–54
Cumberland Hotel (Eastbourne), 213
Mme. Angela Curtin (hand and nail care), 162
Cut 'n' Dry (hairdresser), 154
Cyclax (beauty salon), 157

Dandy (men's clothes), 183
Danish Food Center (restaurant), 79
Davenport's (toys), 171
Adele Davis (boutique), 186
Deborah & Clare (boutique, men and women), 186
Delman (shoes), 170, 180, 185
Dental Emergency Service, 38
Derber (shoes), 176
Derby and the Oaks, The (Epsom), 42
Derry and Toms (hairdresser), 154, 183
Design Centre, 168
Dickens's House, 121
Dickens Inn (restaurant), 79
Dickins & Jones (department store), 179

Dillons University Book Shop, 176
Dimples and Sawdust (antiques), 184
Diplomat (hotel), 50
Dirty Dicks (pub), 106
Dirty Duck (restaurant, Stratford-on-Avon), 199
H.M.S. *Discovery*, 123, 127
Dizzy Diner, 74
Dolce Vita (restaurant, Brighton), 220
Dolcis (shoes), 170
Dolphin Square (swimming), 152
Philip and Bernard Dombey (antiques), 184
Dorchester (hotel), 58
Dorchester Grill and Terrace Restaurant, 68
Dover, 205
Dover Castle, 205
Downing Street, 121
Drury Lane (Theatre Royal), 89, 93
Duet, Dehems Pub (club), 89–90
Duke of Cumberland (pub), 106
Duke's Hotel, 60
Dulwich Riding School Common, 151
Dumpling Inn (restaurant), 79–80
Alfred Dunhill (tobacconist), 171, 183

Eastbourne, 212–214
Eccentrica (gifts), 172, 188
A l'Ecu de France (restaurant), 66
Educational Supply Association (toys), 171
Edwards & Edwards, 90
18th-century London Tower (restaurant), 59
Electrum Gallery (jewelry), 181
Queen Elizabeth Hall, 91, 125
Elliott and Snowdon (antique arms and maps), 184
Gary Elliot (men's clothes), 171, 176
Emeline (jewelry), 186
Emergency Medical Service, 38
Emilio's Restaurant Portofino (Folkestone), 206–207
English Opera Group, 91
English Oyster Bar (restaurant, Brighton), 220

Enton Hall (health hydro), 165
L'Epee d'Or (restaurant), 54
Eros Hotel, 62
Escalade (hairdresser), 154, 163
L'Escargot Bienvenu (restaurant), 75
Estate (pub), 106
Estelle Riding Stables, 151
Eton College, 137
Euston Station, 40
D. H. Evans (department store), 177
D. H. Evans (hairdresser), 154
Evans Fish Restaurant (Bath), 193
Evan Evans Tours, Ltd., 109
Evansky (hairdresser), 154
Eve (cabaret), 98
Evening News, 168
Evening Standard, 168
Express Coach Guide, 20
Eye Care Information Bureau, 39, 162
Eyelure "Let's Face It" (beauty salon), 157

Face Place (beauty salon), 157
Max Factor (beauty salon), 157, 180
Father Thames (restaurant), 87
Feathers (boutique), 183
Fenchurch Street Station, 39
Harry Fenton (men's clothes), 179
Fenwick (department store), 180
Fenwick (hairdresser), 154
Ferragamo (shoes), 170, 188
Festival Gardens (restaurant), 87
Robert Fielding (hairdresser), 154
1520 A.D. (restaurant), 86
Fina de Paris (beauty clinic), 159
Fiori's (restaurant), 80
Fire, 38
Firle Place (Eastbourne), 212
Firth Manor School (Finchley), 151
Elizabeth Flair (beauty clinic), 159
Flanagans (restaurant), 74–75
Die Fledermaus (discotheque), 102
Fletcher's House (restaurant, Rye), 209
Floris (perfume), 163, 183
Mr. Fogg (restaurant), 81
Folkestone, 206–207
La Fontaine Restaurant, 58
Forest Mere (health hydro), 164, 165

Fortes Old Steine Restaurant (Brighton), 220
Fortnum and Mason (department store), 80, 125, 168, 169, 181–182
Fortune (theater), 93
Four Seasons Restaurant, 56, 59
Foyles (books), 178
Frames & Rickards, 109
Francis Hotel (Bath), 192
Mr. Freedom (boutique, men and women), 184
Frigate (restaurant), 80
Fulham Road, 184–186

Gala of London (beauty salon), 157
Galatea (hairdresser), 154
Galeries Lafayette (perfume), 163
Gallipoli Restaurant (cabaret), 99–100
Galt (toys), 171
Garden (restaurant), 68
Gardening Centre (Syon House), 147–148
Garrard (jewelry), 179
Garry's Coffee Shop, 62
Le Gavroche (restaurant), 68
Gay Hussar (restaurant), 68
Gear (boutique, men and women), 187
Geezers and Bugatti (men's clothes), 171, 184
Kurt Geiger (shoes), 188
General Trading Company (furniture), 187–188
Gennaro's (restaurant), 68–69
Geological Museum, 125
George Inn (pub), 106
Gered (china), 172, 179
Gieves (men's clothes), 171, 180–181
Gigi (beauty clinic), 154, 159
Gilles (sauna and massage), 163
Ginger Group (hairdresser), 154, 156
Glahn (furniture), 188
Glyndebourne Festival Opera, 42
Valerie Goad (women's clothes, fabrics), 186
Golden City (restaurant, Oxford), 143

Goldsmiths and Silversmiths Association Gift Centre, 179
Goodes (gifts), 180
Goodwood House, 221
Barbara Gould (beauty salon), 157
Marc Goutier (hairdresser), 154
Grand Hotel (Eastbourne), 213
Grand National (Aintree), 41
Grange (restaurant), 69
Dorothy Gray Hair and Beauty Salon, 55, 157, 163
Gray's Inn, 122
Grayshott Hall Health Centre (health hydro), 164, 166
Great American Disaster (restaurant), 80
Great Smith Street Baths (swimming), 152
Greenline Coach, 20, 37, 133
Green Park, 132
Grey Room (restaurant), 55
Grill Room (restaurant), 58
Andrew Grima (jewelry), 183
Grosvenor Guide Service, 39
Grosvenor House Hotel (swimming), 58, 152
Gucci (leather), 170, 180
Guildhall, 121–122
Guildhall Museum, 129

Habitat (home furnishings), 176, 186
Julie Hacker (beauty clinic), 159
Hairline (hairdresser), 154
Seymour Hall (swimming), 152
Hall's Croft Festival Club (restaurant, Stratford-on-Avon), 199
Hallidays (antiques), 186
Hamleys (toys), 171, 179
Hampton Court, 138–139
HMV (records), 178
Hand and Nail Culture Institute, 162
Harley Muse (hairdresser), 154
Harleyhouse Hotel (Brighton), 218
Harrods (department store), 90, 169, 185
Harrods Hair and Beauty Salon, 154, 162, 163
Hart (antiques), 186
Harvard House (Stratford-on-Avon), 200–201

Hastings, 210–211
Hatchetts (music hall), 95
Hatfield House, 146–147
Anne Hathaway's Cottage (Stratford-on-Avon), 200
Haver Castle, 221
Haymarket Theatre, 125
Hayward Gallery, 126
Headfort Place Hotel, 50
Heal & Son, Ltd. (home furnishings), 168, 175–176
Health and Beauty (sauna and massage), 163
Heath and Heather (restaurant, Oxford), 143
Hellenic Book Service, 178
Henley Royal Regatta (Henley-on-Thames), 43
Henlow Grange (beauty farm), 164, 165
Prince Henry's Rooms, 127
Hepworths (men's clothes), 179
Her Majesty's (theater), 89, 94
Herstmonceux Castle (Eastbourne), 212
H. R. Higgins (coffee), 181
Higgins & Horsey (antiques), 186
High & Mighty (large men's clothes), 185
Hilcote Riding Stables (Wimbledon), 152
W. E. Hill & Sons (musical instruments), 180
L'Hirondelle (cabaret), 98
His and Hers (beauty salon), 54
Holborn Books (foreign newspapers), 178
Hole in the Wall (restaurant, Bath), 193
Holiday Inn, 54
Sherlock Holmes (restaurant), 83–84
Hoop and Grapes (pub), 106
Hope Anchor Hotel (Rye), 208
Hornes (men's clothes), 171
Maria Hornes (beauty clinic), 159
Horse of the Year Show (Wembley), 41
Hotels, classification of, 44–45
Household Cavalry, 114
W. & R. Howard (handbag repair), 174

Index

Howard's Pavilion Restaurant, (Brighton), 220
Hove, 221–222
Hungry Horse (restaurant), 75
Hyde Park, 131
Hyde Park Hotel, 46–47

L'Ile de France (restaurant), 59
Imperial College, 124
Indigo Jones (restaurant), 69
Inn on the Park (hotel), 58
Innoxa (beauty salon), 157, 180
International Boat Show, 41
International Motor Show, 41
International Restaurant, 59
Ireland House (gifts), 172
Isle of Wight, 223–224
Ivy (restaurant), 75

Jackson's of Piccadilly (gourmet foods), 182, 188
Jaeger (knitwear), 179, 183
Au Jardin des Gourmets (restaurant), 66
Jean Junction (boutique), 177, 183
Jean Machine (boutique), 183
Jean Shop (men's clothes), 171
Georg Jensen (jewelry), 172
Jermyn Street, 182–183
Jewel House, 188
Jewish Museum, 129
Jingles (hairdresser), 154
Michael John (hairdresser), 155
John, Marc and Paul (hairdresser), 155
Johnson's House, 127
Jolyon (restaurant), 85
Maggie Jones's (restaurant), 75
Peter Jones (department store), 168, 187
Peter Jones (hairdresser), 155
Joseph Salon (hairdresser), 155, 164
Charles Jourdan (shoes), 170, 185
Jr. James (men's clothes), 171, 176
Just Jane (maternity fashions), 185
Just Looking (boutique), 187

Kardomah (restaurant), 83, 85
Keats (restaurant), 69
Kensington Church Street, 184
Kensington Court Hotel, 52
Kensington Gardens, 132
Kensington High Street, 183–184
Kensington Hilton, 62
Kensington Market, 183
Kensington Palace, 119–120
Kensington Palace Hotel, 62–63
Kent Theatre Tickets, 90
King's College, 127
King's College Hospital (dental health), 38
King's Cross Station, 40
King's Head and Eight Bells (restaurant), 87
King's Road, 124, 170, 187
Kirby & Bunn (jewelry), 172, 180
Kitchensky (jewelry), 172, 180, 185
Knightsbridge, 124, 184–186
Knightsbridge Hotel, 50
Blanche Kramer, Helena Harnik and Agnes Balint (beauty clinic), 159
Kweens (boutique), 187

Lakes Hotel (Bath), 192
Lancaster House, 120–121
Lancome (beauty salon), 158
Lily Langtry Lounge and Restaurant, 49
Lansdowne Hotel (Brighton), 218
Lanvin Perfumes, 163
Lasky (hi-fi), 176
Latin Quarter (cabaret), 100
Lawley (china), 179
Leadenhall Market, 126
Leather People (boutique), 183
Leather Restorers, 174
Leather & Snook (china), 182
Lord Leicester Hospital (Warwick), 202
Leiths (restaurant), 69
Lentheric (perfume), 163
Leonard (hair problems), 156
Leonard and Twiggy (hairdresser), 155
Mme. Leoni (beauty clinic), 159
John Lewis (department store), 168, 177
John Lewis (hairdresser), 155
Liberty & Co. (department store), 179
Lillywhites (women's clothes), 181
Lincoln's Inn, 122–123
Lind-Air (hi-fi), 176

Index

Littlewoods (chain store), 177
Liverpool Street Station, 40
Locks (hairdresser), 155
John London (wigs), 164
London Bridge Station, 40
London-to-Brighton Veteran Car Run, 41
London Country Bus Service, Ltd., 20
"London From a Bus Top," 109
London Health and Fitness Centre (sauna and massage), 164
London Hilton (hotel), 59
London Museum, 119–120
London Philharmonic Orchestra, 91
London Silver Vaults, 173
London Steak House (restaurant), 80–81
London Symphony, 91
London Theatre Guide, 89
London Tourist Board, 39
London Tourist Board Student Center, 39
London Transport Company, 37–38, 39, 108–109
Londonderry (hotel), 59
Londoner (hotel), 56
Long Man of Wilmington (Eastbourne), 212
Longleat House, 195
Peter Lord (shoes), 170
Lorelei (discotheque), 102
Lowndes Hotel, 47
Mme. Lubatti (beauty clinic), 159
Sally Lunn's House (restaurant, Bath), 193
Luxury Needlepoint, 186
Lyons (restaurant), 85

Macari's (musical instruments), 178
Maggie and Stump (pub), 106
Magli (shoes), 188
Maison Lyons (restaurant), 54
Mall, 125, 126
Mandeville (hotel), 56
Mansion Hotel (Brighton), 218
Mansion House, 126
Manvers Hotel (Bath), 192
Maples (furniture), 176
Mappin & Webb (jewelry), 185
Marbella Restaurant (cabaret), 100

Marble Arch, 124
Marbles (shopping arcade), 178
Mario and Franco's King Bomba (restaurant), 81
Mario and Franco's Trattoo (restaurant), 70
Markham Arms (pub), 107
Marks and Spencer (department store), 169, 177
Marquee (discotheque), 101
Marshall & Snelgrove (department store), 177
Martha's Nursery (children's clothes), 184
Maryou (boutique), 185
Mavala International Manicure School, 162
May Fair Hotel, 61
Mayfair, 124
Mayfair Trunk (luggage repair), 175
Mayflower (restaurant), 87–88
Mediaeval Feestes (restaurant), 86
Mermaid (theater), 94
Mermaid Hotel (Rye), 209
Metropole (hotel, Brighton), 218
Metropole Health Hydro, 166
Hotel Meurice, 61
Michelam Priory (Eastbourne), 212
Middlesex Hospital (emergency), 38
Millions of Shirts (for men), 186
Milo and Franco's Tiberio (restaurant), 70
Mirabelle (restaurant), 70
Piero de Monai (boutique), 186
Monastery Guest House (Rye), 209
Monsoon (Indian fabrics), 186
Montague Arms (pub), 107
Montcalm (hotel), 52
Moorfield Eye Hospital (emergency), 38
Moss Brothers (men's clothes), 168
Mostyn Hotel, 56
Mothercare (baby clothes), 178
Mount Royal Hotel, 56
Mudra (ballet), 91
Mullins of London (heraldry), 180
Mumtaz (restaurant), 81–82
Museum Tavern, 127

Nag's Head (pub), 107
Nanking (restaurant, Brighton), 220
National Bus Company, 20

Index 233

National Film Theatre, 91, 125, 126
National Fur Company, 185
National Gallery, 125, 129
National Portrait Gallery, 129
National Theatre Company (Old Vic), 89, 92, 93
Natural History Museum, 124–125
Needle Woman Shop, 168
New Caledonian Market (antiques), 173
New London (theater), 94
New Metropole Restaurant (Folkestone), 207
New Place House (Stratford-on-Avon), 200
New Victoria (theater), 94
M. B. Newman (stamps), 178
Harvey Nichols (department store), 169, 185, 188
Harvey Nichols (hairdresser), 155
Nick's Diner, 76
Nodumky (hairdresser), 155
Norman's Bay, 212

Oasis (swimming), 152
Olaf Daughters (clogs), 181
Old Bailey, 121, 126
Old Caledonia (restaurant), 88
Old Curiosity Shop (antiques), 173
Old Kentucky (restaurant), 82
Old Ship Hotel (Brighton), 218–219
Old Swan (restaurant), 88
Old Vic (National Theatre Company), 89, 92, 93
Mrs. O'Mahoney (ear-piercing), 161–162
100 Club (jazz), 104
L'Opera (restaurant), 70
Orient Jewels, 172
Orlando (sauna and massage), 164
Oxfam Shop (gifts), 172, 184
Oxford, 141–143
Oxford and Cambridge Boat Race, 41
Oxford Street, 170, 176–178
Oxford University, 141–143

Charles Packer (jewelry), 172
Paddington Station, 40
La Paesana (restaurant), 82
Palace (theater), 89

Palladium (theater), 89, 94, 95
Palm Court Lounge and Tea Room, 60
Paperchase (paper items), 176
Park House Hotel, 52
Park Restaurant, 70
Parkham, 221
Parkwood (hotel), 57
Houses of Parliament, 117–118, 126
Parrot Club (lounge), 49
Partridges (gourmet food), 188
Pasticceria Amalfi (restaurant), 82
Patio (lounge), 59
Paxton & Whitfield (cheese), 183
Dr. Payot's Salon (beauty clinic), 159
Penhurst, 221
Penta Hotel, 47–48
Penta Hotel (hairdresser), 155
Pentworth House, 221
Samuel Pepys at Brooke Wharf (restaurant), 88
Pettycoat Lane (antiques), 173
Pevensey, 212
Phoenix (theater), 95
Piaget (watches), 172
La Piazza Restaurant, 58
Piccadilly, 123, 181–182
Piccadilly (theater), 95
Piccadilly Circus, 125
Piccadilly Hotel, 61
Pied Bull (pub), 107
Pindar of Wakefield (music hall), Place (restaurant), 82
Players Theatre (music hall), 96
Playing Card (restaurant, Rye), 209
Police, 38
Porridge Pot (restaurant, Warwick), 202
Portman Hotel, 54–55
Portobello Road (antiques), 173
Hector Power (men's clothes), 179
Prestat (chocolates), 181
Preston Park Rock Gardens (Brighton), 215
Princes Room (restaurant), 88
Prince of Wales Theatre, 95, 104
Prospect of Whitby (pub), 107
Keith Prowse Group (theater tickets), 90
Maison Prunier (restaurant), 69
Pub Information Center, 105–106

Public Records Office, 130
Purcell Room, 91

Quadrant Pearls, 172
Quaglino's (restaurant), 61, 71
Quality Inn (restaurant), 86
Queen's (theater), 95
Queen's Hotel (Brighton), 219
Queens Hotel (Eastbourne), 213
Queen's Restaurant, 56

Ragdale Hall (health hydro), 166
Ratners (jewelry), 172
Ravel (shoes), 170, 184
Raw Deal (restaurant), 82
Rawhide (leather), 170, 176
H. M. Rayne, Ltd. (shoes), 170, 180, 185
Real Foods (health food), 184
Rebelle (hairdresser), 155
Redcar Hotel (Bath), 192
Austin Reed (men's clothes), 171, 179, 183
Reeves (artists' materials), 178
Reflection (boutique), 184
Regency Beauty Centre (beauty clinic), 159
Regent Grill (restaurant), 62
Regent Jewelers, 172
Regent Palace (hotel), 62
Regent Palace Hotel (hairdresser), 155
Regent Street, 123, 170, 179
Regent's Park, 132
Reject China Shop, 187
Reject Linen Shop, 187
Reject Shop (bargain housewares), 185
Le Relais (restaurant), 71
Rendel Dobb (furs), 183
Jean Renet Galleries (jewelry), 172, 182
Rib Room (restaurant), 46
Riche (hairdresser), 155, 157
Richmond Court, 52
Riddlesdale Room (restaurant), 60, 71
Ritz Hotel, 59–60
River (jewelry), 172, 180
Riverside (restaurant), 88
Mr. Robert Hairdressing and Sauna, 155, 164

Rocking Horse (children's clothes), 188
Rolley's (restaurant), 82–83
Roof Restaurant, 59
Rose and Crown (restaurant, Stratford-on-Avon), 199
Rosenthal (china), 172, 185
Rotisserie Normande (restaurant), 55
Round House, (theater), 89
Round Table (pub), 107
Royal Academy, 125
Royal Albert Hall, 91–92
Royal Ascot (Ascot), 42
Royal Ballet, 91
Royal Ballet New Group, 91
Royal College of Music, 124
Royal College of Surgeons, 127
Royal Copenhagen Porcelain Co., 172, 180
Royal Court (theater), 89, 94
Royal Crescent (hotel, Brighton), 219
Royal Exchange, 126
Royal Festival Hall, 91, 125, 126
Royal Festival Hall (restaurant), 88
Royal Greenwich Observatory (Eastbourne), 212
Royal Opera House, 91
Royal Pavilion (Brighton), 215, 216–217
Royal Philharmonic, 91
Royal Shakespeare Company, 89, 94
Royal Trafalgar Hotel, 57
Royal York Hotel (Bath), 192–193
Helena Rubenstein (beauty salon), 155, 158
Annie Russell (hairdresser), 155
David Russell (leather), 170
Rye, 208–209
Daniele Ryman (beauty salon), 159, 160

Sac Frères (jewelry), 172, 180
Sacha (shoes), 170, 176
Saddle Room Club (discotheque), 102
Sadler's Wells Opera, 91
St. George Bar, 59
St. George's Hospital (dental), 38
St. James's Park, 126, 132

Index

Yves St. Laurent (couturier), 180, 185
St. Leonard's 210–211
San Lorenzo (restaurant), 83
St. Martin-in-the-Fields, 125
St. Mary's (Bramber), 221
St. Michael (wigs), 164
St. Paul's Cathedral, 120, 126
Salisbury (leather), 170
Salisbury (restaurant), 83
H. Samuels (jewelry), 171
Romano Santi (restaurant), 83
Vidal Sassoon Beauty Salon, 58, 155–156, 180, 181
Savoy (hotel), 57
Savoy Hotel Restaurant, 57, 71, 88
Savoy Grille (restaurant), 57
Savoy & Moore (chemists), 180
Scandinavian Sandwich Shop, 59
Scarth (musical instruments), 178
Schmidt's (restaurant), 83
Dr. Scholl Foot Care, 162
Science Museum, 124
Scotch House (gifts), 171, 179, 185
Ronnie Scott's (jazz), 103–104
Seafront Gardens (Brighton), 215
Sekers (fabrics), 188
Miss Selfridge (boutique), 179, 185
Selfridge Hotel, 55
Selfridges Department Store, 156, 170, 177
Selmer (musical instruments), 178
Serpentine, 124
Shaftesbury Avenue, 124
Shakespeare Hotel (Stratford-on-Avon), 199
Shakespeare Season (Stratford-on-Avon), 41
Shakespeare's birthplace (Stratford-on-Avon), 200
Shakespeare's mother's house (Stratford-on-Avon), 200
J. Sheekey, Ltd. (restaurant), 83
Shenley Lodge Health Resort, 165
Shezan (restaurant), 84
Shoosissima (shoes), 170, 186
Showboat (cabaret), 100
Shrubland Hall Health Clinic (hydro), 166
Simpson, Ltd. (sportswear), 90, 181
Simpson's-in-the-Strand (restaurant), 76
Sissors (hairdresser), 156
Six Bells (discotheque), 102
Sixty-Nine Hotel, 51
62nd Precinct (boutique), 183
Sketchleys (shoe repair), 175
Skill (leather), 184
Skyline Park Tower (hotel), 48
Sloane (arcade), 187
Sloane Hall Hotel, 51
Sloane Street, 187–188
Sloop John D. (restaurant), 88
Susan Small (couturier), 188
G. Smith (snuff shop), 178
James Smith & Sons (umbrellas), 175
Soane Museum, 127
Soho, 65, 124, 127, 170
S. Solosy (foreign newspapers), 178
Son et Lumière:
  Bristol Cathedral
  Royal Greenwich Observatory, 43
  St. Paul's Cathedral, 42
Sorbonne Hotel, 52
Sotheby's (auctions), 180
South Molton Street, 181
Spaniards Inn (pub), 107
Ann Spillsinger (restaurant, Brighton), 220
Squire Shop (men's clothes), 171, 176
Stable (restaurant), 71
Stafford Hotel, 61–62
Stars and Garters (cabaret), 98–99
Steak Room Restaurant, 57
Steiner (hairdresser), 156, 157
Dr. Peter Stephen (cell therapy), 161
Stetson Bar, 62
Stock Exchange, 126
Stonehenge, 196
Stop the Shop (boutique), 187
Strand Corner House (restaurant), 84
Strand Palace Hotel, 58
Stratford-on-Avon, 197
Stratford Court (hotel), 57
Jack Straw's Castle (pub), 106
Subrosa Bar, 60
Suede (boutique), 183
Suede Clean, 174
Suede and Leather People, 170–171

236 Index

Suedecraft, 171, 186
Sulgrave Manor, 144–145
Summer Palace (restaurant, Eastbourne), 214
Summit Restaurant, 72
Susan (leather), 170
Swaine Adeney Brigg & Sons (leather), 170, 181
Swan & Edgar (clothes, men and women), 179, 181
Swears & Wells (furs), 178
Sweeny's (hairdresser), 156
Syon House, 147

Tackley Hotel (restaurant, Oxford), 143
Take Six (men's clothes), 171, 176
Talk of the Town (revue), 89, 99
Tao Clinic (beauty clinic), 159
Tape Revolution (cassettes), 184
Tapestry Bazaar, 186
Tate Gallery, 130
Taylor (perfumes), 188
Teeda (wigs), 164
Templars Grill (restaurant), 72
Temple, 123
Temple Gardens, 127
Thirlmere Health Hydro, 166
37th Antique Fair, 41
This Month in London, 89
Tiffany's (discotheque), 102–103
Tiger Cavern (pub), 107
Top-of-the-Park Cocktail Lounge, 48
Top of the Tower (restaurant), 72
Torrington Music (jazz), 104
Tottenham Court Road, 175–176
Tourist offices, 18, 108
Tours:
 boat, 112–113
 coach, 109–113, 133–135
 London, 37, 106, 109–113
 Shakespeare country, 198–199
Tower of London, 114–116
Town and Country Health Salon (beauty clinic), 160
Trader Vic's (restaurant), 59, 72
Tradition (military miniatures), 182

Trafalgar (discotheque), 103
Trafalgar Square, 122, 125
Trafalgar Square Post Office (all night), 39
Trat West (restaurant), 76
Triodome (Hastings), 210
Troll (antiques), 186
Trooping the Colour, 43
Troubadour Coffee House (jazz), 104
"Tube" (underground), 37
Turk's Head Grille (restaurant, Cambridge), 141
Tunbridge Wells, 222
Turnbull and Esser (men's clothes), 171, 183
Madame Tussaud's, 118–119
Tyger (boutique), 184
Tyman (office supplies), 176
Tyringham Naturopathic Clinic, 166

Underground, 37
Union Tavern, 105
Up West (shopping arcade), 178

Vanilla (hairdresser), 156
Vassery (restaurant), 55
Vecchia Riccione (restaurant), 76–77
Joel Vella (hairdresser), 156, 157
Venus Kabob House (restaurant), 84
Victoria (pub), 107
Victoria and Albert Museum, 125, 131
Victoria Coach Station, 20, 40
Victoria Palace (theater), 89
Victoria Station, 40
Victoria Taverns (restaurant), 84
Village Gate (men's clothes), 171, 176, 179, 183
Vintage Room (restaurant), 59

Waddesdon Manor, 148
Waldorf Restaurant, 72–73
Wallace Collection, 130
Wallerby (men's clothes), 179
Wallis (boutique), 185
Warwick, 201–202
Warwick Castle, 201–202

Index

Watches of Switzerland, 172
Waterloo Bridge, 125, 127
Waterloo Station, 40
Webster & Girling, 90
Wedgwood/Gered (china), 172, 176–177
Wellington Museum, 130–131
Wells, 196
Westbury Hotel, 55
Westminster Abbey, 116–117, 126
Westminster Abbey Bookshop, 174
Westminster Bridge, 125, 126
Whiskey a Go-Go (discotheque), 103
White Tower Restaurant, 73
Whitehall, 120
Whiteleys (hairdresser), 156
Wiggery, 164
Wigmore Hall, 92
Cyril Wilkinson (ear-piercing), 162
Willett Hotel, 51
Wilson and Gill (china), 172
Wilton's (restaurant), 73

Wimbledon Lawn Tennis Championships (Wimbledon), 43
Windsor, 136–138
Windsor Castle, 136–137
Wish Tower Hotel (Brighton), 219
Woburn Abbey, 148–150
Wookey Hole, 195
Herbert Woolf (jewelry), 172
Woolworth (chain store), 177

Xavier (hairdresser), 156

Yardley (beauty salon), 158, 180
Ye Olde Cheshire Cheese (pub), 107
Ye Olde Cock Tavern (pub), 107
York Mystery Plays and Festival of the Arts (York), 43

Zales (jewelry), 171
Zarach (furniture), 188
Zero Four (children's clothes), 181
Zodiac Cocktail Lounge, 48